Andrew Percy
Dorota Iwaniec

Teenage Drinking

Andrew Percy
Dorota Iwaniec

Teenage Drinking

Causes and Consequences

LAP LAMBERT Academic Publishing

Impressum/Imprint (nur für Deutschland/ only for Germany)

Bibliografische Information der Deutschen Nationalbibliothek: Die Deutsche Nationalbibliothek verzeichnet diese Publikation in der Deutschen Nationalbibliografie; detaillierte bibliografische Daten sind im Internet über http://dnb.d-nb.de abrufbar.

Alle in diesem Buch genannten Marken und Produktnamen unterliegen warenzeichen-, marken- oder patentrechtlichem Schutz bzw. sind Warenzeichen oder eingetragene Warenzeichen der jeweiligen Inhaber. Die Wiedergabe von Marken, Produktnamen, Gebrauchsnamen, Handelsnamen, Warenbezeichnungen u.s.w. in diesem Werk berechtigt auch ohne besondere Kennzeichnung nicht zu der Annahme, dass solche Namen im Sinne der Warenzeichen- und Markenschutzgesetzgebung als frei zu betrachten wären und daher von jedermann benutzt werden dürften.

Coverbild: www.ingimage.com

Verlag: LAP LAMBERT Academic Publishing GmbH & Co. KG
Dudweiler Landstr. 99, 66123 Saarbrücken, Deutschland
Telefon +49 681 3720-310, Telefax +49 681 3720-3109
Email: info@lap-publishing.com

Herstellung in Deutschland:
Schaltungsdienst Lange o.H.G., Berlin
Books on Demand GmbH, Norderstedt
Reha GmbH, Saarbrücken
Amazon Distribution GmbH, Leipzig
ISBN: 978-3-8383-4716-5

Imprint (only for USA, GB)

Bibliographic information published by the Deutsche Nationalbibliothek: The Deutsche Nationalbibliothek lists this publication in the Deutsche Nationalbibliografie; detailed bibliographic data are available in the Internet at http://dnb.d-nb.de.

Any brand names and product names mentioned in this book are subject to trademark, brand or patent protection and are trademarks or registered trademarks of their respective holders. The use of brand names, product names, common names, trade names, product descriptions etc. even without a particular marking in this works is in no way to be construed to mean that such names may be regarded as unrestricted in respect of trademark and brand protection legislation and could thus be used by anyone.

Cover image: www.ingimage.com

Publisher: LAP LAMBERT Academic Publishing GmbH & Co. KG
Dudweiler Landstr. 99, 66123 Saarbrücken, Germany
Phone +49 681 3720-310, Fax +49 681 3720-3109
Email: info@lap-publishing.com

Printed in the U.S.A.
Printed in the U.K. by (see last page)
ISBN: 978-3-8383-4716-5

TABLE OF CONTENTS

1. INTRODUCTION   1

   ALCOHOL AND SOCIETY   1
   DEVELOPMENTAL PSYCHOPATHOLOGY: AN INTEGRATIVE CONCEPTUAL
   FRAMEWORK FOR THE STUDY OF ALCOHOL PROBLEMS   3
   POLICY AND PRACTICE IMPLICATIONS: PRIMARY PREVENTION   5
   AIMS OF THE STUDY   8

2. TRENDS IN UK ALCOHOL CONSUMPTION   12

   PER CAPITA CONSUMPTION LEVELS   12
   SOCIAL SURVEYS OF DRINKING BY YOUNG ADULTS   21
   TRENDS IN ALCOHOL RELATED PROBLEMS   27
   POLICY PRIORITIES   34
   SUMMARY   36

3. A DEVELOPMENTAL PERSPECTIVE ON TEENAGE ALCOHOL CONSUMPTION   38

   ADOLESCENT PROBLEM DRINKING: A DEVELOPMENTAL DISORDER   39
   IMPLICATION FOR RESEARCH DESIGN   45
   SUMMARY   56

4. BCS70: BACKGROUND, DESIGN AND METHODOLOGY   58

   THE 1970 BRITISH COHORT STUDY   58
   METHODOLOGICAL AND PRACTICAL ASPECTS OF SECONDARY ANALYSIS 68
   AGE, PERIOD AND COHORT EFFECTS   69
   ATTRITION AND SAMPLE REPRESENTATIVENESS   71
   STRATEGIES TO ADDRESS MISSING DATA   75
   SUMMARY   77

5. THE IDENTIFICATION OF HAZARDOUS DRINKING PATTERNS AT 16: A LATENT
   CLASS ANALYSIS   79

   METHODOLOGICAL ISSUES   79
   METHOD   85
   RESULTS   93
   DISCUSSION   113
   SUMMARY   117

Contents

6. CORRELATES OF HAZARDOUS DRINKING AT AGE 16   **119**

CONCURRENT ASSOCIATIONS WITH OTHER ADOLESCENT PROBLEMS   120

METHOD   128

RESULTS   133

DISCUSSION   147

SUMMARY   150

7. ANTECEDENTS OF HAZARDOUS DRINKING   **152**

A CAUSAL MODEL OF ADOLESCENT PROBLEM DRINKING.   152

METHODS   166

RESULTS   172

DISCUSSION   183

SUMMARY   189

8. LIFE COURSE OUTCOMES OF HAZARDOUS DRINKING IN ADOLESCENCE   **192**

CONSEQUENCES OF TEENAGE DRINKING   192

METHODS   200

RESULTS   204

DISCUSSION   211

SUMMARY   222

9. CONCLUSIONS   **224**

KEY FINDINGS   225

OVERARCHING POLICY AND PRACTICE IMPLICATIONS   234

STRENGTHS AND LIMITATIONS OF THE STUDY   239

FUTURE WORK   244

SUMMARY   246

REFERENCES   **351**

APPENDIX: SUPPLEMENTARY ANALYSIS   **397**

1 INTRODUCTION

ALCOHOL AND SOCIETY

Alcohol is a drug enjoyed by millions within the UK (Department of Health, 1999; 2000). It plays a central role in many aspects of western culture, and has done so for a considerable number of years (Walton, 2001). We drink alcohol to celebrate, and also to commiserate, when we are socialising with friends, and when we are relaxing on our own. Most social activities, from playing and watching sport to eating in restaurants or going to the theatre, are accompanied by the consumption of alcohol.

Indeed, it would be hard to overestimate the role alcohol plays in modern society. It is a drug that is used by over 95% of adult men and 90% of adult females (Department of Health, 1999; 2000). We consume on average around 10 litres of 100% (pure) alcohol per year (British Licensed Retailers Association, 2000). For most people, drinking alcohol is a pleasant social activity. In 1999, the Health Survey for England estimated that the mean weekly consumption of alcohol was 17 units for men and 7 units for women (Department of Health, 2000). Over half of the population drank less than 10 units per week. However, a small number of people drank excessively. Over 14% of men and 2% of women consumed more than 35 units of alcohol per week.

In comparison with the rest of Europe, the UK ranks around 20th (out of 40 corresponding countries) in terms of per capita consumption levels (Harkin, Anderson, & Goos, 1997). However, such broad ranking masks considerable cross-national differences in alcohol consumption (Hupkens, Knibbe & Drop, 1993). Southern Europe (e.g. Italy, France, and Spain) has an alcohol culture based mainly on the high frequency and low volume consumption of wine with food. In northern Europe, beer is the most popular drink, which is usually consumed in the absence of food and in lower frequency but higher volume. In recent years, the general trend in consumption across Europe has been towards a greater harmonisation of drinking patterns (Silbereisen, Robins, & Rutter, 1995; Walsh, 1997). In particular, there has been a sizeable increased consumption of moderate wine consumption within northern European countries. Even

1

with this general harmonisation, differences in the "weekly rhythm" of alcohol consumption (consumption spread relatively evenly across the week versus consumption concentrated in one or two days per week) and in the social situations in which drinking is undertaken (at meal times with family versus in evening with friends) do still persist (Simpura & Karlsson, 2001).

Since the 1950s there has been a doubling of the per capita consumption of alcohol within the UK (Academy of Medical Sciences, 2004). While increases in beer and spirit consumption have contributed to this trend, the main factor underlying this change has been the growth in wine drinking (Brewers and Licensed Retailers Association, 2000). In 1999 UK consumer expenditure on alcohol consumption reached £32 billion, generating some £11.5 billion in taxation for the exchequer, which was equivalent to 4.4% of the total tax revenue (British Licensed Retailers Association, 2000). At the individual level, the Family Expenditure Survey estimated that the average household spends over £13, or 4% of the total weekly household expenditure, on alcohol (Department of Health, 1999).

Behind the USA and Germany, the UK is the third largest importer of alcohol, accounting for some 12% of all world imports of alcohol (Walsh, 1997). The UK is also, as documented by Walsh (1997), a major exporter of alcohol - second only to France - controlling almost 20% of the world export trade. This is equivalent to the combined alcohol beverage exports of Germany, Italy and Spain.

For most adults within the UK alcohol forms a normal part of social life.[1.1] For them the adverse consequences of alcohol consumption amounts to little more than a hangover or mild sickness and the morning spent in bed following the occasional over indulgence. But for others, their drinking develops into what Orford (1984) termed an 'excessive appetite' for alcohol. This pattern of drinking is characterised by the regular excessive consumption of alcohol and can lead to family problems, damage to physical and mental health, employment difficulties, and even premature death (Edwards et al., 1994). It is the continued consumption in the face of mounting social and health concerns that characterises the problem drinker. Evidence of this includes the 72,000 hospital admissions, 300,000 road traffic accidents, 50,000 prosecutions for

---

[1.1] While most adults do consume alcohol there are noticeable exceptions such as Muslims, other religious groups, reformed drinkers and abstainers.

drunkenness, and 1.9 million violence offences that are linked to alcohol each year (Department of Health, 1999; Home Office, 1994; Mirrlees-Black, Mayhew, & Percy, 1996). Recent Office of National Statistics figures recorded an almost doubling of alcohol related deaths between 1991 and 2004 from 7 per 100,000 to 13 per 100,000 (Office of National Statistics, 2006).

The global burden of alcohol related disease and illness is considerable. Alcohol accounts for around 9% of the total disease burden in Europe (Rehn, Room, & Edwards, 2001). The overall harm associated with alcohol consumption is generated by three main processes, a) the physical toxicity of alcohol and its long term impact on the body, b) acute effects of alcohol intoxication including accidents and violence, and c) the social and health consequences of alcohol dependence (Babor et al., 2003). Chapter 2 provides a more detailed analysis of the historical trends in alcohol consumption within the UK and its associated health and social costs.

DEVELOPMENTAL PSYCHOPATHOLOGY: AN INTEGRATIVE CONCEPTUAL FRAMEWORK FOR THE STUDY OF ALCOHOL PROBLEMS

Problem drinking arises from the interaction of numerous genetic, cognitive, behavioural and social factors operating across the lifespan (Hawkins, Catalano, & Miller, 1992; Rutter, 1995; Rutter & Smith, 1995). This is reflected in the range of genetic, psychological and sociological theories that attempt to explain the development of behavioural problems such as problem drinking, including general strain theory, social learning theory, social control theory, social ecology model and the social stress model (Agnew, 1985; Akers, 1985; Hirschi, 1969; Kumpfer & Turner, 1991; Rhodes & Turner, 1990). In a major review, Kaplan (1995) argued that these so called 'competing' theories of problem behaviour might not in fact be in competition. Rather, they may focus on different aspects of behaviour or subsets of explanatory factors and may not necessarily rule out other explanatory models. Instead of testing competing models, Kaplan suggested an integrative approach to theoretical development might be more useful.

Achenbach (1990) proposed *'developmental psychopathology'* as an overarching conceptual framework, or macro paradigm, which could be used to integrate what he termed 'micro paradigms' (for example, biomedical, sociological and cognitive

3

perspectives) as well as the individual theories grounded within each paradigm. Developmental psychopathology contrasts sharply with earlier conceptualisations of adolescent behavioural, social or mental health problems. Rather than seeing problem drinking as the progression of a particular disease – as in adult psychopathology - its focus is on individual differences in the developmental pathways and trajectories from childhood to adulthood, and the bio-psychosocial factors that contribute to adaptive or maladaptive outcomes (Compas, Hinden, & Gerhart, 1995; Cicchetti, 1989).

Risk and protective factors

Developmental psychopathology is inextricably linked to notions of risk and protective factors. At a basic level a *risk factor* can be defined as characteristics, experiences or events that if exposed to can increase the probability of a particular outcome (that is, using alcohol at hazardous levels) over that recorded for people not exposed to the risk factor (Compas et al., 1995; Kazdin, Kraemer, Kessler, Kupfer, & Offord, 1997).

Spencer et al., (2006) further refined this conceptualisation by defining a risk factor as an exacerbation or exaggeration of the normal developmental challenges or tasks faced by adolescents, for example the successful transition to secondary school (Masten & Coatsworth, 1998; Masten et al., 1995). It is through the successful negotiation and resolution of these challenges that adaptation and growth is achieved (Cicchetti & Rogosh, 2002). Protective factors are therefore defined as individual, social and material resources that help individuals to cope with these exacerbated normative challenges, and individual vulnerability is the net effect of risk and protective factors experienced (Spencer et al., 2006). The source of risk and protective factors can be both internal characteristics (for example, psychological systems shaped by the successful or unsuccessful completion of previous stage tasks) and environmental processes. Here, the term environment is used in its widest sense, referring to influences external to the individual including the physical environment, life events and the social and cultural world in which the live.

Cicchetti (2006) suggested that individual or environmental process must fulfil two essential criteria before being considered a risk (or protective) factor. Firstly the potential risk must procedure the behavioural outcome, permitting a greater accuracy in

4

the prediction of the outcome. Secondly, the association between potential risk and outcome must be causal, in that when altered its results in a change in the outcome under consideration (Hinshaw, 2002). Testing these criteria requires the application of research designs that can determine the temporal relationship between potential risk and outcome and can differentiate between correlation and causation (Rutter, 1994a; Rutter, 2000)

Risk and protective factors must not be seen as static, unchanging markers, rather they are dynamic, and interacting. They can be either bipolar, where risk and protection are the opposite ends of the same continuum; unipolar, as in a protective buffer mitigating the effects of a particular risk factor; or a risk mulitplier increasing the action of another risk factor. The interaction of risk and protective factors is often nonlinear, bi-directional, or reciprocal, and dependent on context (for example, timing, duration, level, etc.) (Kazdin et al., 1997).

Resilience

In recent years there has been an upsurge of interest in resilience, stemming primarily from an increased understanding of the role individual temperament plays in explaining individual differences in coping with stress (Rutter, 1990). Rather than examining the pathways and mechanisms involved in negative outcome, the study of resilience has focused on how children in adversity have managed to achieve good developmental outcomes. Resilience is not conceptualised as simply successful developmental adaptation. Rather, resilience is competency in the face of serious risk conditions (Rutter, 1999b; Spencer et al, 2006). Masten and Coatsworth (1998) identify a number of important factors underpinning childhood competency, ranging from the child's cognitive/motivational system (self-esteem, self-efficacy and expectancies) and individual self-control and self-regulation, through to parental care giving and attachment, positive peer relations and academic achievements. Chapter 3 of the thesis provides a detailed overview of developmental psychology and the implications for research design and analysis.

POLICY AND PRACTICE IMPLICATIONS: PRIMARY PREVENTION

As mentioned above, research into psychosocial risk processes has had a major impact on clinical practice with children and adolescents with emotional and behavioural problems (Rutter, 1998). Risk factor research has also had considerable influence on the design and development of primary prevention programmes. Increasingly, primary prevention is being seen as a long term, cost-effective method of reducing behavioural and social problems in children and adolescents. However, there is little evidence that any single prevention strategy or approach produces any lasting impact on adolescent problem behaviour (Dorn & Murji, 1992; Goldblatt, Nutall, & Lewis, 1998). Even those approaches that have been identified as the most promising, such as life skills training or peer education, have only been able to produce modest 'effect sizes' in controlled trials (Durlak & Wells, 1997; Moskowitz, 1989; Tobler, 1986; 1992). A recent Cochran meta-analysis concluded that there was limited evidence of the effectiveness of primary prevention education and information campaigns in either reducing the onset of alcohol use or alcohol misuse. (Foxcroft, Ireland, Lister-Sharp, Lowe, & Breen, 2003).

One explanation for the lack of single intervention 'success' is that any one primary prevention intervention is likely to impact on only a few of the range of intrapersonal, interpersonal and situational risk factors that contribute to individual behavioural and social problems. This leaves many risk and protective factors unaddressed. In recognition of this, researchers have argued that prevention interventions, if they are to be effective, need to be delivered on a large-scale, comprehensive and co-ordinated basis, via a number of different channels, for example, schools, community development mass media, with each channel aimed at mitigating the effect of different potential risk factors while promoting other factors which appear to protect against the development of adolescent problems (Coie et al., 1993; Durlak & Wells, 1997; Hawkins, Catalano, & Miller, 1992). Likewise gaps in the current knowledge base regarding the causal processes (potential risk and protective mechanisms) may hamper the design and development of next generation programmes.

Lerner, Ostrom and Freel (1997) identified a number of key guiding principles for the design of successful programmes aimed at preventing and reducing health-compromising behaviours amongst young people.

There is no single solution to adolescent problems: Adolescents are influenced by multiple layers of social context, be it their friends, families, schools or neighbourhoods (see Boyce et al., 1989; Cook, 2003). Risk factors for social problems such as alcohol misuse can and do arise from these multiple layers (Gilvarry, 2000; Oetting & Donnermeyer, 1998). Therefore, effective interventions should recognise these multiple layers, and the multiple risk factors that exist across these contexts (Hawkins & Catalano, 1992). A better understanding of the multiple risks and how they impact on adolescent drinking behaviours should provide insights into the design and development of effective prevention interventions.

High-risk behaviours are inter-related: High-risk behaviours are not evenly distributed but tend to cluster within particular individuals (Fergusson, Horwod, & Lynskey 1994). In particular heavy alcohol consumption is associated with increased levels of psychiatric morbidity (Armstrong & Costello, 2002, Clark & Bukstein 1998; Clark et al., 1997), delinquency (Fergusson, Lynskey, & Horwood, 1996; Fergusson, Swain-Campbell, & Horwood, 2002; Rutter, Giller, & Hagel, 1998), smoking (Dawson, 2000; Sher, Gotham, Erickson, & Wood, 1996) and illicit drug use (Lynskey, Fergusson, & Horwood, 1998; Ramsay & Percy, 1996). Understanding the complex relationship between alcohol and other comorbid conditions has considerable implications for the provision of effective preventions and treatment programmes (Angold, Costello, & Erkanli, 1997; Crawford, Crome, & Clancy, 2003). However, as Armstrong and Costello (2002) noted, the current research knowledge base on the associations between alcohol problems and psychiatric disorders is limited.

A package of services is needed within each community and such services must be fully integrated: Given the first two points it stands to reason that a policy and practice response to alcohol related harms must address the multiple and interconnected facets of the problem. Coie and colleagues (1993) proposed an approach in which the individual components of the overall prevention service package were grounded in epidemiological research that identified specific risk factors associated with the distribution of need. Here, the services developed are required either to mitigate the effects of a known risk agent or to promote the development or consolidation of a known protective agent. Hawkins, Catalano and Arthur (2002) outlined a model of comprehensive community prevention systems (*Communities That Care*) designed to activate local communities to identify local risk and protective factors, and to plan and implement effective interventions to address them. However, risk and protective factors are not static entities and may vary over time and may vary across social contexts (for example, UK versus US). In a further extension of this general prevention science framework, Ialongo and colleagues (Ialongo et al., 2006) emphasised that the development of effective prevention interventions requires access to the findings from high quality basic developmental research into problem behaviours. Such research is essential in advancing our understanding of the development of problem behaviour and the social forces that shape this development.

The timing of the intervention is crucial: Prevention, by its very name should occur before the development of serious harm. In general, effective prevention tends to be less expensive that treatment interventions, particularly when directed towards high-risk youth (Bukoski & Evans, 1998). Noting earlier points, consideration must also be given to the timing of risk exposure. If prevention services are aimed at mitigating the effects of risk, particular risks may require formal intervention before or at least at a similar time to the risk exposure. Other risks may be amenable to amelioration after exposure, however this may require a greater expenditure of resources than if applied earlier.

AIMS OF THE STUDY

In light of the above discussion, the proposed study is a developmental analysis of alcohol misuse from adolescence to adulthood among a representative sample of individuals born in 1970. The study will utilise an existing longitudinal cohort data set, the 1970 British Cohort Study (BCS70). There are a number of key assumptions underlying this analysis, which have been touched upon above and are outlined in more depth in later chapters. The first assumption is that there has been a change in the drinking behaviour of young people over the last few decades or so that warrants research and policy attention, in particular, the increase in average consumption amongst young people. The second assumption is that the efficacy of current interventions to prevention or reduce problem drinking amongst adolescents are limited by gaps in the current evidence base regarding key modifiable risk and protective factors. Interventions can only be effective if they prevent or modify exposure to known causal risk processes

8

or promote the development of protective factors that may lessen the impact of risk exposure. Thirdly, longitudinal research methods provide the most appropriate method for examining risk and protective factors. There are a number of technical requirements that must be fulfilled by studies attempting to identify risk and protective factors and longitudinal cohort address many of these requirements.

Such data sets such as the BCS70 provide a powerful resource for addressing many research questions surrounding teenage alcohol use, particularly those concerned with identifying the causal processes associated with increased vulnerability to alcohol problems found amongst some young people. However, certain legitimate research questions, for example those concerning cross-national or regional variations in alcohol consumption or those looking at changes in drinking between different generations or periods, are not within the range of existing large-scale cohort studies such as the BCS70. The technical issues involved in this study are outlined in chapter 4 and further elaborated within the various analysis chapters (5-8). The study has four key aims:

1. To establish a typology of adolescent drinking patterns: At present there is no agreed definition of adolescent problem dinking. However, recent development in statistical methodology, in particular the development of individual clustering methods for categorical data (latent class analysis – Hagenaars & McCutcheon, 2002), have offered new opportunities in the development of behavioural classification. It will be argued here that latent class analysis addresses many of the existing weaknesses in more traditional data reduction/classification approaches. In light of this, the study aims to construct a new empirically based typology of adolescent drinking patterns drawing on multiple behavioural indicators.

2. To examine the correlates of adolescent drinking: This element of the study will examine whether drinking patterns at age 16 are associated with other health, social or educational problems at age 16. For example, is heavy drinking associated with poor school performance, self-esteem, or substance use? A key aspect of this analysis will be the extent to which alcohol misuse is a comorbid condition of other homotypic adolescent problem behaviours, such as smoking and delinquency, and heterotypic conditions such as depression or anxiety disorders. Another perspective on the correlates of adolescent drinking is to search for the existence of problem clustering. Can groups of individuals be identified who experience multiple problems such as alcohol misuse, delinquency and mental health problems? High-risk sub-groups of adolescents are of importance to social and public health policy. Given the likely lifetime use of public services amongst such groups, the potential saving would be considerable if such multiple problems could be prevented before occurring (Catalano, Haggerty, Gainey, Hoppe, & Brewer, 1998). This analysis of the covariates of drinking at age 16 can also be exploited to provide a check on the validity of the typology constructed.

3. To examine antecedents of adolescent drinking that may explain individual variations in drinking behaviours at age 16: This is essentially the attempt to identify environmental processes that shape early drinking behaviour. While alcohol consumption in the teenage years is widely accepted as a normal part of adolescent development within the UK (Plant & Plant, 1992; Parker, Aldridge, & Measham, 1997), the question remains as to why some young people stray into alcohol misuse while others do not? Do particular life experiences, family circumstances or specific characteristics increase an individual's vulnerability to developing maladaptive alcohol consumption patterns in late adolescence?

4. To examine the adult consequences (at age 26) of alcohol consumption (at age 16): This aspect of the study will address two main objectives. The first is a comparison of drinking patterns at age 16 and at age 26 to assess the degree to which adolescent patterns of drinking are continued into adulthood. This will require an examination of the long-term stability of adolescent onset alcohol misuse. The second objective will be to examine non-alcohol outcomes at age 26. Does heavy drinking at age 16 increase the likelihood of suffering health, social or economic problems at age 26? Not only may developmental pathways link adolescent drinking patterns with adult drinking patterns, but pathways may also link adolescent drinking behaviour with other social competencies. This is an assessment of multifinality – similar developmental pathways may lead to multiple outcomes (Cicchetti & Rogosh, 1996).

This monograph is presented in two main sections. Section one provides a general scene setting overview of alcohol consumption within the UK, the theoretical and conceptual framework employed in this study, and the background design and methodology of the British Cohort Study 1970. Section two presents the empirical analysis of the cohort data utilised in this study. This section is broken down into four analysis chapters each relating to one of the specific aims outlined above. The final chapter is a summary and discusses the policy and practice implications of the work.

2 TRENDS IN UK ALCOHOL CONSUMPTION

This chapter provides a historical review of selected indicators of alcohol consumption within the UK. It presents a broad overview of the extent and nature of alcohol consumption within the UK and how this has changed over time, against which the drinking behaviours of a specific group of young people (all born within a single week in 1970) can be examined and interpreted.

It begins by examining official indicators of population consumption levels, including revenue excise statistics on per capita consumption levels (these provide the longest trend data) and official statistics on alcohol related social and health costs. While these provide valuable information on changes in the extent of drinking over time, they rarely provide information disaggregated by age. As a result, such statistics reflect adult drinking patterns more than those of teenagers and young adults. To address this weakness, the chapter reviews social survey findings on the actual drinking behaviours of teenagers. It also examines the range and magnitude of problems associated with hazardous and problematic alcohol consumption, and considers changes within the alcohol industry and how they have altered young people opportunities to consume alcohol. The focus of the review is on the period of 1970 to 1996, as this is the period covered by the survey sweeps analysed here. However, during the 1970s and 1980s social surveys of alcohol use were in their methodological infancy, which somewhat limits the available research. More recent survey data has also been included to provide information on how alcohol trends amongst teenagers have continued into the new millennium. Finally, the chapter examines current policy responses to teenage drinking.

PER CAPITA CONSUMPTION LEVELS
Pre-war drinking patterns

Alcohol production and consumption have always been subject to influence from public policy, and wider social and economic trends. For example, during the mid 19th century, changes in spirit duty[2.1], population migration[2.2], and increases in the number of public houses[2.3] resulted in a major switch away from drinking unlicensed home produced alcohol to purchasing alcohol from licensed brewers and distillers, who were able to compete for the first time with illicit production in terms of both quality and price (Wilson, 1940).

Notwithstanding the weaknesses in the available data[2.4], historical consumption estimates clearly show that beer has always been the United Kingdom's favourite

---

[2.1] In 1823, duty on spirits was reduced in Scotland and Ireland by almost two thirds. In England spirit duty was reduced by about one third in 1825 (Wilson, 1940).

[2.2] The shift in population from agricultural land into manufacturing towns that began in 1750s may be responsible for the general decline in private brewing of beer (Spring & Buss, 1977).

[2.3] The Beer House Act of 1830 saw the opening of 40,000 new public houses within 5 years (Spring and Buss, 1977). In addition, beer duty was repealed in 1830 (Wilson, 1940).

[2.4] In government statistics terms, consumption refers to the quantity of alcohol that is released for sale on which duty has been charged. By analysing duty returns it becomes possible to estimate the amount of alcohol sold to the general public. Such consumption figures are usually presented on a per capita or per drinker (population aged 15 or more) basis. When considering consumption statistics three points should be borne in mind. First, not all alcohol produced or consumed passes through Customs and Excise. Alcohol may be illegally produced within the UK, may be smuggled across international borders, or imported across European borders without UK tax being paid. Regardless of the method, such alcohol would not be included in the consumption estimates. This undercounting is not just a recent phenomenon. Historically, the unlicensed distilling of both whiskey and gin by illicit and licit producers has been a sizeable problem. Wilson (1940) estimated that in 1822 over 2 gallons of illicit whiskey were produced for every legitimate gallon of Irish whiskey distilled. More recently the trade in smuggled alcohol from Europe may be responsible for a considerable under estimation of the alcohol consumption within the UK. Interestingly, the popularity of illicit cheap alcohol, both in the 17th century and today, corresponds with periods of high duty and little opportunity costs (Allen, Andrew, Southworth, & Webb, 1998; Wilson 1940). Second, official statistics are subject to changes in the recording procedure or the counting rules. In relation to alcohol consumption statistics, changes in the way alcohol duty has been levied has affected the consumption trends. For example, up to 1933, taxation on beer was on the hypothetical 'standard barrel' (36 gallons at a specific gravity of 1,055⁰ assessed prior to fermentation) produced from 'standard materials'. However, if beer with a lower specific gravity was brewed it was possible to produce a greater quantity of alcohol from the same standard materials, resulting in the need to count the hypothetical 'bulk barrels'. Subsequent changes in the way duty has been levelled on higher and lower gravity beers have affected the volume estimates. Finally, over recording of consumption may also occur, that is alcohol may pass Customs and Excise

alcoholic beverage. In the mid seventeenth century (when duty records were first recorded) it was estimated that the UK population drank around 340 litres[2.5] of beer per person. However, by the mid nineteenth century beer consumption had steadily declined to around 90 litres per person (Spring & Buss, 1977). In 1880, Gladstone instigated major changes in beer production with repeal of malt duty[2.6] (see Wilson (1940) for a full discussion of the Gladstone Budget Speech). The resultant reduction in price, coupled with a period of economic prosperity, saw a short-lived beer consumption increase to around 145 litres per head. There then followed a substantial period of stability in beer consumption. Spring and Buss (1977) suggested that consumption trends during this period corresponded to periods of economic prosperity, stability and depression. What they proposed is that in periods of economic boom, alcohol consumption rises, only to decline again in periods of economic bust.

Today there is a vast array of spirit based beverages. However, in the late 19th and early 20th century there were only four types of spirit available to the public, gin and

---

within a particular period but not actually be consumed by the public within that interval. In addition to spills and wastage at both production and sale, a proportion of annual production may be placed in stock or storage. Usually alcohol is placed in stock for maturing. This is particularly important with wine and to a smaller degree with certain conditioned beers. Both producers and purchasers may place alcohol in stock. In addition, with the advent of tinned beer with a long shelf life, retailers may also hold increasing stocks of beer. Few academic studies of early alcohol consumption exist. Only one statistical text of UK alcohol consumption pre 1940 could be located, that produced by Wilson (1940). Later publications such as that produced by Spring and Buss (1977), extend Wilson's consumption analysis until 1975. Today consumption figures are compiled and published annually by the Brewers and Licensed Retailers Association (see for example, Brewers and Licensed Retailers Association, 2000). As such this initial section draws heavily on these key source texts. At present, there is limited consumption data available that covers the 2nd World war and immediate post-war period. Spring and Buss (1977) do not provide detailed tables of annual consumption, and the more recent figures from the British Licensed retailers Association only extend back as far as 1959.

[2.5] Per capita rates originally presented by Spring and Buss (1977) were in gallons and converted using a 1gallon = 4.54609lt multiplier.

[2.6] Between 1830 and 1880 duty was not charged on beer directly but on the principal constituents of the brewing process, malt and hops. In his budget speech in 1880, Gladstone repealed the malt duty and replaced it with a direct tax on beer. He also instigated the free mash tun system, giving brewers greater flexibility in both materials and methods. Hop duty was repealed in 1863 (see Wilson 1940).

14

whiskey, both of which were distilled within the UK, and rum and brandy, both of which were imported. Between the 1870s and 1940s, the main trend in spirit consumption was similar to that observed for beer drinking. That is to say, two major peaks in 1875 and 1899, with per capita consumption reaching around 3½ litres of 100% alcohol, [2.7] followed by a long and sustained decline in spirit consumption (Wilson, 1940).

In contrast to beer, imported spirits have been subject to developments in international trade. For example, Wilson (1940) commented that between 1881 and 1888, a phyllorxera outbreak in brandy producing regions in France severely curtailed annual production resulting in considerable price increases within the UK. This undoubtedly depressed brandy consumption.

In the 1870s, wine consumption within the UK was just over 68 million litres (2.2 litres per capita), peaking in 1876 at 81 million litres (2.5 litres per capita) (Wilson, 1940). Spring and Buss (1977) suggested that the subsequent decline in wine consumption - it fell to just over 59 million gallons (1.6 litres per capita) by 1885 - was largely due to the late Victorian economic depression, although they also suggested that the increasing fashion of after dinner smoking may also have affected the drinking of fortified wines. Apart from a small peak at the turn of the century (around 75 million litres in 1899) - also corresponding with peaks in both beer and spirit consumption - wine drinking went into a steady decline until after the First World War.

This pre-war period also saw the emergence of various Temperance movements aimed at restricting the consumption of alcohol and the level of drunkenness (Berridge, 2005). While the common perception is that the Temperance movement was a rather ineffectual female-lead prohibitionist campaign, historical analysis by Berridge concluded that the movement was much more varied in the methods it employed. These included local licensing reforms, public media campaigns, liaison with the drinks industry and political lobbying to achieve progressive modification of alcohol consumption habits. While the early temperance reformers wanted to remove the "public house", late Victorian policy makers initiated moves to modify the design and function of pubs as a method for altering drinking habits (Greenway, 1998). Many policy debates

---

[2.7] Source: 1870-1935 Wilson (1940); 1960-1996 BLRA (2000). Proof gallons of spirit presented in Wilson were converted to litres of 100% alcohol using the following conversion; 1 gallon proof spirit = 2.60427litres of 100% alcohol.

from this time mirror contemporary discussions surrounding the nature of alcohol consumption and the methods needed to "civilise" it (Berridge, 2005).

The war years (1914 to 1945)

The turn of the century marked a major shift in drinking trends. Following a substantial period of decline, the 30 years prior to 1900 saw relatively little change in beer consumption. However, between 1900 and 1930 the downward trend in beer drinking was resumed, punctuated only by the post First World War celebrations. With the outbreak of the First World War in 1914, beer duty was increased to 23 shillings per barrel (36 gallons of ordinary strength beer). Over the next six years duty was increased 5 times reaching 100 shillings in 1920 (see Wilson, 1940). As well as heavy increases in duty, 1914 saw the introduction of the Defence of the Realm Act, further restricting public house opening hours. In addition, the war lead to a substantial reduction in beer production, together with a decrease in original gravity (strength), as cereal crops, formerly used in the brewing process, were redirected towards food production. Even through beer consumption increased dramatically following the end of the First World War, the general downward trend soon reasserted itself between 1921 and 1932. In contrast, the Second World War years saw a slight increase in alcohol consumption followed by a slight slump again to existing 1930s levels.

The onset of the First World War saw a marked increase in spirit consumption reversing the steady downward trend from the turn of the century. Some of this increase was due to large purchases of rum made by the Army, primarily for its troops in the trenches (Wilson, 1940). As Wilson noted, this was seen as a medicinal intervention instigated by the Army Medical Authorities rather than a recreational diversion. However, the transfer of grain from the distilling industry to food production saw a rapid decline in spirit consumption over the next few years (Spring & Buss, 1977). Post-war celebrations contributed to a sharp increase in consumption recorded in 1919, but even this was somewhat lower than the indexed increase recorded for beer consumption. Once the revelry was over however, a downward trend continued until the early 1960s, seeing consumption fall lower than even that recorded during the First World War. Following a relatively stable period during the 1960s, spirit consumption rose to a peak in 1979 (beer consumption also peaked in this year). But unlike beer, which saw an almost substantial recovery in its market, this peak represents less than eighty percent of the amount of spirits consumed in 1886 - 1.9 litres in 1979 compared to 2.4 litres in 1886. The next 20 years saw only modest variations in spirit consumption.

Given the fact that wine is almost exclusively imported, it is not surprising that wine consumption collapsed during the First World War, to around 31 million litres. The decline was mainly amongst French and Spanish sectors. Portuguese imports remained fairly stable during the conflict. As with other beverages, wine drinking increased sharply after the war. However, in percentage terms, the increase in wine exceeded those recorded for either beer or spirits. Also, once the post-war alcohol boom stabilised, wine consumption continued its upward trends, whereas beer and spirit drinking fell away again. Soon after the end of the Second World War, wine consumption began to increase again. While other beverages have undergone peaks and troughs in consumption, wine has increased in popularity at a considerable rate. In 1940, Wilson noted that 'wine is an exotic drink in this country... is in no sense a national beverage and with the exception of the commoner qualities is admittedly outside the financial reach of the general community' (pg. 30). In 1935, wine consumption averaged about 63.6 million litres compared to 3.8 billion litres of beer.

Modern era

The 1960s marked the beginning of an increase in beer drinking within the UK. This upward trend continued until the early 1980s (over 123 litres per head) (Brewers and Licensed Retailers Association, 2000). This was over 90% of the consumption recorded in 1886. Over the next 20 years there was only modest fluctuation in beer consumption levels; however, these figures belie significant changes in drinking culture during this period. In 1971 the most popular beer was bitter followed by mild. Lager accounted for a small proportion of beer consumed in Great Britain at this time. By 1979 however, excluding larger, the market shares of all other beers (bitter, mild stout and premium bitter) had declined. This period also saw the market breakthrough of continental/imported premium lagers. By the mid 1980s lager was the dominant beer type commanding the largest market share. This trend has continued.

Not only do the 1980s mark the rise of lager as the most popular alcoholic drink in Great Britain but they also mark a decline in overall pub sales. In 1971 less than 10%

17

of beer was purchased in off-licences for home consumption. The pub was the place where alcohol was consumed. By 1986, however, off-licence sales had risen to 17% of all beer sales. This rise continued over the next decade, reaching 28% in 1996 (Brewers and Licensed Retailers Association, 2000). What is interesting here is that while the market share of draught beer has declined over this 26-year period, the number of public houses has increased by over 10 thousand; in addition, almost 20 thousand new off-licences have appeared.[2.8] One implication of an increase in the density of alcohol retail outlets, particularly off licences, is an increase in the availability to alcohol to underage drinkers (Babor et al., 2003; Gruenewald, Ponicki & Holder, 1993). This increase in the number of points of access to alcohol (both on and off licence) has also been accompanied by a liberalisation of alcohol retail opening hours, to an extent where in most urban areas alcohol is available at any time (Raistick, Hodgson & Ritson, 1999).

Recent years have also seen the relaunch of many established spirits in new formats – premixed blends of spirits, soft drinks, fruit juices and other flavouring. Examples of this include Smirnoff Ice and Bacardi Breezer, which are vodka and white rum based drinks respectfully. These brand extensions of traditional established spirits are targeted primarily towards the young drinker market and have been accompanied by extensive media campaigns (Jackson et al., 2000). To an extent, such repackaging has successfully revitalised the market for spirits amongst a new generation of drinkers. By way of evidence, the spirit market share of whiskey, which has not seen similar brand extensions, has declined from 47% in 1986 to 39% in 1996, whereas other spirits (including vodka and white rum) have increased their share of the spirit market from 53% to 61% (BLRA, 2000). Whiskey still has the image of an "old person's" drink while the new flavoured spirit based drinks have a much younger appeal.

Since the 1950s wine consumption has increased 100-fold and post-war wine sales have continued to boom. Kortteinen (1984) estimated an annual growth in wine production of around 1% per annum during the period of 1960 to around 1980. While the economic recession that occurred in the early seventies may have slowed the upward trend slightly it soon regained momentum once the economy began to pick up again.

[2.8] Figures for England and Wales only. The number of public house licenses increased from 64,000 in 1970 to 75,000 in 1995. Off-licences increased from 27,000 in 1971 to 46,000 in 1995 (Source: BLRA, 2000).

While beer still remains the number one drink within the UK, in terms of the quantities drunk, the most dramatic change in drinking behaviours has been the rapid growth in wine consumption (Academy of Medical Sciences, 2004).

One of the main factors to have contributed to this change in drinking habits was undoubtedly the advent of relatively cheap travel to France, Spain and other Mediterranean countries (Simpura, Karlsson, & Leppanen, 2002). From the seventies onwards, British tourists have been introduced to a southern European drinking culture that is predominantly wine based. Here, drinking is undertaken in conjunction with eating and not as a separate social activity. The introduction of a more Mediterranean pattern of alcohol consumption is not something limited to the UK. Other Northern European countries with a predominant beer and spirit drinking culture, such as Belgium, Netherlands, Germany and the Nordic countries, on the whole have seen increased wine consumption and falling beer consumption (Norstrom, 2002). In contrast, Southern European wine producing countries such as France, Portugal, Italy, and Spain are seeing declining wine consumption and increasing beer and spirit consumption (Edwards et al., 1994).

Not only is there a convergence of beverage preference but also of the amount of alcohol consumed per capita. In countries that have traditional high alcohol consumption, drinking levels are in general falling, while in countries with a traditionally low per capita level of alcohol consumption, drinking seems to be on the increase (Norstrom, 2002). However, it must be remembered that per capita rates may mask major differences within sub-populations of drinkers within each country, even those with similar rates. For example, the proportion of the drinking population that are problem drinkers may vary from country to country. Silbereisen, Robins and Rutter (1995) referred to this general trend as a homogenisation and modernisation of drinking behaviour, where cross-cultural differences in drinking behaviour are reducing. In a study of alcohol consumption in southern Europe, Gual and Colom (1997) reached a similar conclusion. However, evidence from the European Comparative Alcohol Study indicated that while convergence is occurring, national drinking patterns change relatively slowly and considerable cross-national differences still remain (Norstrom, 2002).

Similarly, homogenisation and modernisation have also occurred within the drinks industry itself. The international brewing industry is increasingly under the control of a small number of international companies, such as AB InBev, Heineken, and SABMiller, representing over one per cent of the value of all world trade (Walsh, 1997). Central to the approach of transnational alcohol companies has been the production and promotion of certain key international brands in all their major national outlets. The marketing of these brands also occurs on a transnational basis, where advertising campaigns are handled by local affiliates of international advertising companies (Jernigan, 2000). As Jernigan (2000) suggested, changes in alcohol consumption are the product of the interaction of the global alcohol supply network (including globalised marketing), state alcohol control policies and local drinking cultures. Edwards and Holder (2000) remind us that we can no longer consider changes in drinking behaviour within any nation as simply the product of changing demand amongst drinkers, as global suppliers of alcohol have an active role in shaping future alcohol demand to maintain their market share. These international brewers and distillers, have had considerable marketing success against the small local producers, for example the wine producers in southern Europe and the traditional independent 'real ale and stout' producers within the UK. The UK, without its wine tradition, has seen the beverage marketed less in terms of individual small producers, but rather in terms of specific grape varieties (for example, Riesling, Chardonnay). The main producers to market single grape brands have been large-scale 'new world' producers from Australia or the USA (for example, Gallo).

This international trend towards fewer national differences in drinking behaviour is likely to continue for the foreseeable future. The globalisation of the alcohol industry is protected by numerous international free trade agreements (Grieshaber-Otto, Sinclair, & Schacter, 2000). Also, as global alcohol suppliers are a major economic force in the countries in which they operate, they are now in the position to influence alcohol policy at a national and regional level (Giesbrecht, 2000).

While per capita alcohol consumption rate in the 1980s and 1990s may be somewhat lower than in previous historical periods, there has been a dramatic increase in alcohol consumption since the 1950s. This increase has been driven predominantly by the increase in wine consumption and the emergence of spirit-based ready to drink brand extensions. While beer, cider and spirit use has increased since the 1950s, consumption of these drinks peaked in the early 1980s and have reminded relatively static, when assessed by per capita litres of pure alcohol. This has been coupled with a similar increase in the levels of alcohol related health and social problems, and a similar decrease in the price of alcohol relative to income (Academy of Medical Sciences, 2004).

Changes in per capita consumption highlight the need for policy attention on alcohol and alcohol related problems, which have also increased in recent years (see below). They also highlight a number of potential new avenues of research, particularly in explaining cross-national differences in drinking behaviour, how these differences are themselves changing over time, and the role of the alcohol industry plays in driving this homogenisation of alcohol consumption across Europe. Unfortunately these questions are not within the scope of this study. In contrast, this work is attempting to examine the internal characteristics and environmental factors that shape individual drinking behaviours within a single cultural context. At present, most of the work in this area has been undertaken in either the US or New Zealand (see chapter 4, 5 and 6). This study is an attempt test the extent to which risk factors identified in existing longitudinal analysis also apply to the development of drinking problems within the UK. With an emerging tradition of longitudinal studies within mainland Europe, particularly in Scandinavian countries, future research may compare the findings from this work with evidence of other European cohort studies.

SOCIAL SURVEYS OF DRINKING BY YOUNG ADULTS

While production and consumption figures provide a useful insight into changes in national drinking behaviour over time, they fail to provide details of how the overall change in consumption is distributed across the population. For example, a decline in consumption may be the result of an increase in the proportion of abstainers or a reduction in the consumption of heavy drinkers. To examine changes in drinking behaviour or changes in the pattern of drinking within particular sub-populations, social surveys of drinking behaviour are required.

As surveys are based on individual rather than aggregate level data, as is the case with consumption statistics, they can be used to explore the relationship between drinking behaviour and age, gender, and other individual level explanatory variables, such as age and gender. Surveys can also be used to collect information on the nature and patterns of drinking behaviours, such as the age of first use, drinking locations, frequency of drinking, and the amount consumed. Surveys of drinking are a rather recent phenomenon. Few can be found before 1970. Of those that have been conducted with young adults, most are single cross-sectional surveys (for example, Marsh, Dodds & White 1986; O'Connor 1978; Hawker, 1978; Plant, Peck, & Samuel 1985; Plant, Bagnall, Foster, & Sales, 1990). While they provide a useful point in time perspective on drinking behaviour, comparisons across surveys and across time are complex due to methodological differences.

Plant and Plant (1992) suggested that between the late 1970s and late 1980s available survey data showed little change in the level of drinking amongst young people. Published research gives a broad consensus on drinking patterns during this period (Parker, Aldridge & Measham, 1998; Wight, 1999). Most young people have their first drink around the time of transition from primary school to secondary school, between ages 10 and 13 (Plant, Peck & Samuel, 1985, Swadi, 1988). In many cases this first introduction is in a controlled setting, usually at home, with parents allowing children to taste alcoholic drinks (Plant & Plant, 1992).

In 1979/80 Plant and colleagues found that by age 15-16 few young people had not tried alcohol – about 2% (Plant, Peck & Samuel 1985). While few were regular drinkers, half had consumed alcohol in the previous two weeks and over a third reported being drunk in the previous week – some two years before they reached the legal age for purchasing alcohol. Amongst younger adolescents (age 13) the overall prevalence rate of contact with alcohol was also high (96%). However, the rate of drunkenness was substantially lower with only 20% reporting experiencing a hangover (Bagnall, 1998).

The Office of Populations, Censuses and Surveys conducted the first English survey of adolescent alcohol use in 1986 (Marsh, Dodds, & White, 1986). While the study confirmed the findings of earlier local studies, the survey did identify considerable regional variations, not only in the prevalence of drinking but also in the types of drinks consumed. Swadi (1988), in a survey of young people living in London, found that 45% of 11-year-olds had used alcohol. This rose to 80% amongst 16 year olds. Not only were the prevalence rates lower in the London sample compared with other local rates, but the frequency of consumption was less, with only 12% of 11 to 16-year-olds drinking alcohol more than once a week. In a later national study, Plant and colleagues (1990) found that around 96% of young people in England aged 14-16 had drunk alcohol. While drinking amongst this age group can be relatively frequent, the amounts consumed were in general not excessive - less than 30% had drank more than 4 units (or 2 pints) in the previous week, and less than 7% had drank 11 units (5½ pints) or more.

As demonstrated above, alcohol consumption increases with age. Also the location of consumption changes with drinking more likely to occur away from parental supervision, in pubs, in parks, or on the street (for example, O'Connor 1970; Hawker 1978; Plant, Peck & Samuel 1985, Plant et al., 1990). O'Connor (1970), in one of the first cross-national studies of young adult (aged 18-21) alcohol consumption, found differences across countries and cultures. Of the three groups compared, abstinence rates were highest amongst young people living in Dublin (18%). This was considerably higher than the abstinence rates for young people living in London, both of English and Irish descent, which was 3% in each group. Very heavy drinking (defined here as over about 35 units or 18 pints per week) was more prevalent amongst the Anglo-Irish and English respondents (34% and 26% respectfully) compared with 19% amongst Irish young people.

While alcohol consumption by young people was relatively stable throughout the 1970s and 1980s, changes in drinking patterns and behaviour amongst young people can be detected during the 1990s, coinciding with wider changes in young culture (Brain, 2000; Parker, et al., 2000; Parker, Aldridge, & Measham, 1997). Parker and colleagues argued that the 1990s saw a large growth in dance clubs and other recreational facilities for young people, coupled with the introduction of new alcoholic beverages including high strength white ciders, fruit wines and the spirit brand extensions previously discussed. Many of these shifts are associated with periods of social and economic change. From the 1980s onwards young people, growing up have been exposed to an alcohol market place that is dominated by a small number of global alcohol producers/distributors, an increasing range of high-strength brand extensions, ready-to-drink spirit mixers and 'shooters', licensing regulation which is moving towards '24-hour' drinking, a culture where extreme drunkenness is largely tolerated, and increased opportunities for engaging in "hedonistic consumerism" (Measham & Brain, 2005).

Jackson et al., (2000) suggested that extensive media campaigns, targeted at the young-adult drinker, backed many of these new ready to drink drinks. In recent years, white ciders have been found to be popular with young people under 15, alongside traditional and premium larger (Hughes et al., 1997; McKeganey, Forsyth, Barnard, & Hay 1996). The appeal of these so called 'starter drinks' is that they are cheap, strong and sweet tasting and readily available in small shops and off-licences (Hughes et al., 1997; Jackson et al., 2000). In contrast, premium priced brand extensions such as Bacardi Breezer, have less appeal to this age group and are targeted more at the 18-24 year old (Jackson et al., 2000). Similar changes in brand preference amongst young drinkers have also been noted in other European countries (Romanus, 2000).

The Survey of Smoking, Drinking and Drug Use amongst Young People in the UK showed that during the 1990s there was little change in the proportion of 11-15 year olds who drank in the last seven days (stable at around 25% for boys and 22% for girls). However, over the same period the mean number of units of alcohol consumed per week by 11-15 year olds doubled from 5 (boys – 6; girls – 4) to over 10 (boys – 11; girls – 10) (Westlake & Yar, 2006). Likewise, the Health Survey for England, which has interviewed about 1,000 young people aged 16-24 annually since 1993, has found that young people are drinking more (Erens & Hedges, 1998). Amongst 16 and 17-year-olds the mean weekly units consumed has increased from 9 in 1993 to 14 in 1997. Similarly, for 18-19 year olds weekly consumption has increased from 18 units in 1993 to 23 units in 1997.

However, not all surveys have shown recent increases in alcohol use amongst young people. The General Household Survey, the main measure of adult drinking since 1984, failed to show an upward trend, during the 1990s, in the proportion of young adults (here defined as 18-24 year olds) drinking above the sensible drinking levels (21 units per week for males and 14 units per week for females) (Wright, 1999). While it did show considerable variations on the annual proportion of young people drinking above the sensible levels – from 35% to 41% of 18-24 year olds – no definitive trend could be detected. In a national study of 15-16 year olds conducted in 1995, Miller and Plant (1996) found 6% of the sample had never drunk alcohol, while 21% of girls and 23% of boys had never been drunk. Although not directly comparable to earlier studies undertaken by Plant and colleagues, no real change in the abstinence rate was observed.

While certain changes in drinking culture amongst young people may have occurred in the 1990s many aspects of drinking remain the same. Social drinking in pubs with friends continues to form a major part of the social lives of young people. In 1970 drinking with friends was one of the most common social activities for young people aged 18-21, with about 80% of males and 50% of females drinking with friends at least once a week (O'Connor, 1970). For around a quarter it was their usual recreational activity. In the 1990s this is still the case (Parker, Aldridge, & Measham, 1998). The relationship between alcohol consumption and age also remains in the 1990s. The Health Survey for England showed that at age 16-17, average weekly consumption for males is around 10 units and for females it is around 6 units. Amongst males, this rises to 25 units by age 20-21, and for females it rises to 12 units (Erens & Hedges, 1998). By this age, young people, while still less frequent drinkers than older consumers, are more likely to be heavy drinkers and to drink more at a single session than any other age group (Wright, 1999). Heavy single session drinking is particularly prevalent amongst the undergraduate student population (Gill, 2002). Wright (1999) reminded us of the role that 'round' drinking (i.e. drinking in social groups in pubs) plays in fostering the consumption of large amounts of alcohol at a single session, where the 'round' acts as an informal drinks counter and places pressure on individuals to keep up with the group. Drinking in large social group where drinks are purchased in rounds increases alcohol consumption (Aitken, 1985). In adulthood, the frequency of consumption may increase but the amount consumed at a single session decreases.

While the primary focus of this section has been on alcohol consumption trends from 1970 till the mid 1990s, the expansion of health related social surveys does permit the examination of the trends beyond this period. Findings from the Health Survey for England Study have indicated that binge drinking, defined as double the recommended daily intake (8 units for men and 6 units for females) amongst young adults (16-24) has steadily increased for both males and females from the late 1990s (NatCen, 2003). Results from the General Household Survey also confirmed this general increase in the average weekly units consumed since 1998 (when the figures were first recorded) (Department of Health, 2004). Drinking amongst teenagers also showed a similar increase (average weekly units). The English School Survey on Smoking, alcohol and Drug Use has revealed that between 1988 and 2006, a relatively stable proportion of 11 to 15 year olds had drunk alcohol in the week previous to the survey interview, around 20%. In contrast, the average volume of alcohol consumed by teenagers had almost doubled to over 11 units per week, during the corresponding period (Department of Health, 2004; NatCen/NFER, 2007; Westlake & Yar, 2006).

Although the figures are not directly comparable, due to methodological differences, surveys of teenage drinking in other UK jurisdictions also report an increase in consumption. Analysis of the Northern Ireland Health and Well-being Survey showed an increase in the proportion of 16-24 year olds dinking above the recommended sensible drinking levels between 1997 and 2001 (Miller, Devine, & Schubotz, 2003). For men the increase was around 4 percentage points (up to 36% in 2001), while from females the increase was around 10 percentage points (up to 30% in 2001). The authors suggested that the rapid increase amongst women may in part be due to the increased availability of brand extension style drinks, as women were three times more likely to consume them. Using data from the 1995 and 1997 European Schools Project on Alcohol and Drugs surveys (ESPAD), Miller and Plant (2001) found that while there was no real change in the proportion of school children drinking alcohol, the proportion who had drank five or more drinks in a row during the last 30 days had increased for both boys (53% in 1995 to 60% in 1997) and girls (40% to 46%). The 1995 and 1998 Scottish Health Surveys confirmed an increase in average weekly alcohol consumption amongst young people aged 16-24 (Scottish Executive, 2002b). While the proportion of Scottish teenagers drinking alcohol actually declined slightly between 2004 and 2006, as recorded by the Scottish School Adolescent Lifestyle and Substance Use Survey, (it had reached a ten year peak in 2002), the average number of units consumed in the last week had increased over the two-year period (Maxwell, Kinver, & Phelps, 2006). This increase in volume occurred over a period when the frequency of teenage consumption remained stable and the proportion of complete abstainers at age 15 actually increased to 16%, the highest level since 1998 (14%). The increase in the proportion of abstainers at age 13 was also greater (32% in 2004 to 43% in 2006).

Overall, recent years have seen a clear increase in the level of alcohol consumption amongst teenagers and young adults. This is due mainly to increases in the quantity consumed rather than the frequency of consumption. This increase in alcohol consumption also coincides with certain changes in the social context of drinking amongst young adults. Firstly, there appears to be more of a consumerist attitude amongst young people to the consumption of both licit and illicit drugs. Sociologist such as Parker, Measham and Brain, have suggested that there now exists a new consumerist culture of intoxication amongst young people (Measham & Brain, 2005; Parker et al., 2000). Structural changes within the alcohol industry have also occurred during this period. This has included an increase in the access to and availability of alcohol to young people (increased number of retail outlets and increased opening hours) and the development and marketing of new spirit-based ready to drink drinks. As the market for beer and spirits has remained relatively flat (in contrast to the wine market which has seen considerable growth), it is unsurprising that the alcohol industry has attempted to stimulate new growth in these areas. The strategy employed for this (increased opening hours and new product lines) may have a particular impact on the young emerging drinker. And finally, young people who grew up in the 1980s and 1990s have experienced a considerable increase in social fragmentation and health inequalities under the premiership of Margaret Thatcher (Shaw, Dorling, & Brimblecombe, 1998).

This study is an attempt to explore how young people have responded and adapted to these social challenges. It will focus on individual experiences and behaviours, in particular, the emergence and development of alcohol consumption amongst a cohort of young people exposed to alcohol for the first time. It will not, however, examine how the experiences and behaviours of this cohort differ relative to earlier generations of drinkers who experienced different social conditions (more limited access, lower social inequality and different social norms regarding alcohol use). Such analysis requires comparisons of multiple longitudinal cohorts. While this is possible (see Centre for Longitudinal Studies, 2007), a logical starting point is the examination of the development of alcohol behaviours within a single cohort, in this case the 1970 cohort.

TRENDS IN ALCOHOL RELATED PROBLEMS
Alcohol related mortality and morbidity

Health outcomes associated with drinking alcohol can be both positive and negative. Existing research has suggested a modest link between light drinking (one to two units per day) and a reduced risk of coronary heart disease compared with abstention (see Edwards et al., 1994), although further work is needed to explore the

27

positive impact that different drinking patterns may have on population mortality and morbidity (Single, Ashley, Bonby, Rankin, & Rehm, 1999). On the other side of the coin, heavy drinking is associated with an increased risk of malignancies (mouth, pharynx, larynx, oesophagus and liver) high blood pressure and strokes, cardiac conditions other than coronary heart disease and liver cirrhosis (see Academy of Medical Sciences, 2004; Babor et al., 2003; Edwards et al., 1994; for major reviews). In their review, Edwards and colleagues concluded that for cancer the relationship between an individual drinking behaviour and their risk of mortality is linear, with curvature at the higher levels of drinking. For drinking and liver cirrhosis the relationship is exponential. For the other pathologies the risk curves are less understood.

Depending on the calculation method used, estimates of the number of alcohol related deaths range from 5,000 to 40,000 per annum (Department of Health 1999). In 1996, the main causes of alcohol related death were chronic liver disease and cirrhosis (3,800 deaths), fatal road accidents (580), alcohol dependence syndrome (150), toxic effects of alcohol consumption (150), non-dependant abuse of alcohol (140), and alcoholic cardiomyopathy (140). The decade between 1986 and 1996 has seen substantial increases in deaths attributable to liver disease, toxic effects and cardiomyopathy. While deaths due to alcohol dependence and non-dependence abuse have remained fairly constant, alcohol related traffic deaths have fallen sharply over the ten-year period, from 990 in 1986 to 580 in 1996 (Department of Health, 1999).

In addition to these mortality rates, over 174,000 British hospital admissions were recorded where there was a primary or secondary diagnosis of an alcohol related disease. The most common diagnosis categories for admission were mental and behavioural disorders due to alcohol (72,500 admissions), dependency syndrome (31,300) acute intoxication (22,100) alcoholic liver disease (14,400) and toxic effects of alcohol (13,600) (Department of Health, 1999). World Health Organisation research estimated that alcohol contributed to about 4% of the total global burden of disease (WHO, 2002). This burden is equivalent to that resulting from smoking (4.1%) or high blood pressure (4.4%) (Ezzati et al., 2002; Room, Babor, & Rehm, 2005). In developed countries, such as in Western Europe, this disease burden increases to nearly 7% (WHO, 2002).

The trend in recent years has been a steady increase in alcohol related mortality and morbidity within the UK (Academy of Medical Sciences, 2004). Since 1995, hospital admissions due to alcohol significantly increased (The Information Centre, 2006). Alcohol related mental health admissions increased from around 32,000 in 1995/6 to over 35,000 in 2004/5. Likewise, admissions due to alcohol liver disease increased from 7,000 to nearly 13,000. In England and Wales the number of alcohol related deaths increased by over 1,000 from 1999 to 2004 (The Information Centre, 2006). In Scotland, both hospital admission and alcohol related deaths increased (Information Service Division, 2007). Over the five-year period, 2000-2005 alcohol related deaths increased by 15%. In Northern Ireland there has be a modest increase in alcohol related deaths from around 210 to 260 between 2001 and 2004 (Register General, 2005).

Alcohol related crime

Alcohol is related to offending behaviour in a number of ways. First, the offending behaviour can be the direct result of alcohol consumption, as in the case of drinking and driving. Here, drinking over a set limit of alcohol together with driving a car is considered an offence. Second, alcohol can precipitate an offence. For example, alcohol increases aggression, impairs decision-making and reduces inhibitions, increasing the likelihood of violence particularly between young men. Third, the desire for alcohol may contribute to certain offences being committed. Individuals may be tempted to steal alcohol or commit other income generating crimes to pay for alcohol. Fourth, alcohol may be consumed to provide the offender with 'Dutch Courage' to commit an offence. Not only does alcohol increase the risk of certain offences occurring, if consumed in excess, it may also increase the chances of detection and arrest.

Estimating trends in alcohol related offending, however, is problematic. Not all alcohol related offences that are committed are made known to the police or result in either an arrest or a prosecution. As a result they do not appear in official police statistics. This undercounting is known as the 'dark figure'. Also, for those offences that are not directly alcohol-related, it is difficult to estimate the proportions that are associated with the consumption of alcohol by the perpetrator. The police do not routinely collect this information for offences such as burglary. Even for offences where the relationship with alcohol is implicit, such as drunkenness and drinking and driving, police statistics may not be an unbiased measure. The Police may not record all offences made known to them. An officer confronted by a drunk and disorderly individual may decide to take no action depending on the specific situation or to avoid the associated paper work. Changes in police policy and procedures may impact on criminal statistics. For example, if a police force decides to concentrate activity and resources on drink driving offences, this will be associated with an increase in recorded offences data irrespective of the base rate of actual offending.

Trends in police statistics are also subject to changes in the recording procedures or counting rules. In a similar way, new legislation or amendments to existing legislation, for example, decreases in the permitted level of blood-alcohol when driving a car, would affect the numbers of people prosecuted. And finally, most alcohol-related crime statistics are not disaggregated by age in their published form. This limits their application to teenage drinkers. Notwithstanding the weaknesses above, it is possible to calculate trends in key alcohol related offences.

In 1970, over 79,000 people were found guilty or cautioned for an offence of drunkenness.[2.9] Between 1970 and 1980, there was a steady increase in the number of people convicted, from 79,000 to 110,000. This equates to a 40% increase in drunkenness offences. The rate of increase in drunkenness convictions closely matches increases in the consumption of alcohol over the same period. It also increased by 40% between 1970 and 1980, rising from 5.4 litres of 100% alcohol per person per year to 7.4 litres per person per year (British Licensed Retailers Association (2000).

In 1981, however, we see the start of a downward trend in the numbers of people found guilty or cautioned for offences of drunkenness. In 1986 fewer than 68,000 drunkenness offences were prosecuted. This equates to 163 per 100,000 of the population aged 14 or over. As in previous years the majority are males (93%). The ratio of people cautioned to those found guilty is almost equal (1:1.3). While the numbers of people convicted of drunkenness offence declined between 1980 and 1986, the level of alcohol consumption has remained stable at around 7.5 litres per person per year.

While the numbers of drunkenness offences increased slightly in 1987 and again in 1988, they began to fall again in 1989. This downward trend continues until 1995, where 43,000 people were either found guilty or cautioned for drunkenness. This is a decline of 45% in the number of offences since 1970. In 1996 there was a slight increase

---

[2.9] Source: British Licensed Retailers Association (2000).

again in the number of drunkenness offences to 50,000. Arrests for drunkenness are largely made against adults. In 2004, there were 2,200 magistrates' proceedings for cases of simple drunkenness and 23,000 for cases of aggravated drunkenness. Of these 25,000 or so cases around 2,400 were against individuals aged under 18 (Home Office, 2005).

It is difficult to identify possible causes for this decline in drunkenness offences. It is not a decline in alcohol consumption by the general public or by young men in particular – the group most likely to be prosecuted for drunkenness. As Figure 2.6 shows, alcohol consumption in general continued to rise during this period. Also, survey data presented above, confirms no diminution of young male drinking.

It is more likely that the decline in drunkenness offences is an artefact of changes in police practice or other situational factors than a reduction in the number of people being drunk in public places. New public order legislation was introduced in 1985[2.10]. As a result there may be a degree of substitution of Section 5 Public Order Offences for Drunkenness Offences (Brown & Ellis 1994). As Brown and Ellis (1994) noted, in over 40 per cent of section five offences alcohol was consumed beforehand by the perpetrator. Technically, these incidents could have been prosecuted under both Section 25 of the Criminal Justice Act 1967 (drunk and disorderly) and Section 5 Public Order Act 1986. However, Brown and Ellis (1994) found that police officers preferred Section 5 in many cases as it meant that the offender was more likely to be placed before the court, the courts took the offence more seriously and there was no need to prove drunkenness. This may also explain the increased use of cautioning in drunkenness cases. Given the cited benefits of the public order legislation, Section 5 may be used for more serious cases where a court case is deemed appropriate by the police, and drunk and disorderly used for more minor cases where a caution is deemed appropriate. Taking this into account, it is unlikely that the incidents of drunk and disorderly behaviour have declined as much as offender statistics indicate.

The other main offence that has a direct relationship with alcohol consumption is drinking and driving. Under current legislation it is an offence to drive motor vehicles with a blood-alcohol concentration exceeding 80mg%. As alcohol affects decision-making, reaction times, risk assessment and task functioning, drinking can impair

---

[2.10] Public Order Act 1985.

driving ability increasing the risk of an accident. Breath tests, as a measure of blood alcohol concentration, were introduced in 1968, under the Road Traffic Act (1967). From the first available figures in 1969, the number of positive breath tests increased rapidly from just over 4,000 in England and Wales to almost 12,000 in 1974, a growth of about 300% (see figure 2.6). A similar trend in the number of offences of drinking and driving also occurred during this period. Between 1974 and 1977, both the number of breath tests made and the number of drink driving convictions declined. Since 1977, there has been a substantial increase in the number of breath tests conducted by the police. Between 1977 and 1985 this increase in breath testing was paralleled by an increase in the number of drunk driving convictions. Since 1985, however the number of convictions has been less dramatic than the increase in the number of test conducted. The number of drink-driving convictions peaked in 1988 at 105,000. Between 1985 and 1994 there has been a decline in the annual number of convictions to 78,000, but this has increased again in 1995 and 1996 (81,000 and 85,000 respectfully).

The British Crime Survey (BCS) asks a probability sample of the residents of England and Wales about the crimes in the past year, where they or a household member had been a victim, irrespective of whether it had been reported to the police. For violent crimes, the victims are asked whether or not they thought the offender had consumed alcohol. As such it can be used to provide an indicator of the prevalence of alcohol related crime not subject to the same biases as police recorded crime. In 1988, the BCS estimated that in 44% of violent crime committed that year – around 1 million offences - were perpetrated by a drunken offender (Mayhew, Aye Maung, & Mirrlees-Black, 1993). As expected, violence in and around licensed premises frequently involved a drunken assailant (86%). However, alcohol was also involved in a sizeable proportion of violence within the home, against both male victims (57%) and female victims (39%). In 1996, the number of alcohol related crime estimated by the BCS had increased to over 1.9 million offences (41% of all contact crime) (Mirrless-Black, Mayhew, & Percy, 1996). Alcohol was most prevalent in violent crimes committed against strangers (53%), with a third of these committed in and around licensed premises. Another third were committed close to public transport. Alcohol was also a common contributory factor in incidents of violence where the offender was known to the victim (but not domestic violence). In 45% of these incidents the offender was under the influence of alcohol. Muggings were least likely to involve alcohol; here in only 17% of incidents did the offenders appear to be drunk. Drinking by the offender was a part of a third of domestic violence incidents against both male and female victims.

Age is strongly related to the risk of alcohol related assault, with young people aged 16-19 at greatest risk (Budd, 2003). The BCS does not collect detailed information on the age of perpetrators; it only uses very broad age categories. However, the survey would suggest that alcohol related stranger assaults were more likely to be perpetrated by young people aged 16-24, while alcohol related acquaintance assaults were more commonly perpetrated by older adults (25+) (Budd, 2003). The annual survey of arrestees established a clear link between offending and alcohol problems (Boreham, Fuller, Hills and Purdey, 2006). Around 57% of offenders scored above the clinical cut-off on the Fast Alcohol Screening Test (FAST) scale. While gender differences were observed (51% amongst females compared with 58% of males) no age variations were found, with offenders age 17-24 having similar rates of problem alcohol use as older offenders.

Other social costs

Alcohol has also be implicated in a range of other social and economic problems including family problems, social functioning, child maltreatment, accidents, lost productivity, unemployment and unwanted pregnancies (Clark, 2004; Edwards et al., 1994; Rehn, Room, & Edwards, 2001). Klingemann (2001) estimated that the direct (impacts on the drinker) and indirect (impacts on others) social costs amounted to around 3% of the gross domestic product of developed countries. Experiences of direct alcohol related social harm have been shown to be associated with heavy episodic drinking (Rehm & Gmel, 1999).

Rossow and Hague (2004) estimated that the experience of minor indirect harm (for example, being kept awake at night by drunk people) was relatively common; reported by over 20% of adults in a general population survey. More serious harm was less frequently reported (5% reported having property damaged). The statistics above clearly demonstrate the impact that alcohol misuse has on society. It is wide ranging including effects on individuals' health, social order, and public safety. It also affects families, friends and employers.

The economic and social costs associated with alcohol are considerable. This study will specifically examine the association between drinking and problem behaviours (smoking, illicit drug use and crime) in adolescence at the individual level. It is will also attempt to assess the impact that teenage drinking has on social and health problems in early adulthood (up to age 26), again at the individual level. This provides a robust test of the causal relationship between alcohol consumption and the corresponding risk of serious health or social problems. Examination of net changes in alcohol consumption and relevant problem outcomes over time provides a less satisfactory test of the relationship between consumption and outcome.

POLICY PRIORITIES

The basic facts and figures presented above give some indication of the overall health and social harm that result from the consumption of alcohol. In a major review, Sewel (2002) identified a number of recent emerging trends in international alcohol reduction policies. These included a move away from state level initiatives (i.e. increased alcohol taxation of reduced access), as recommended by the Academy of Medical Sciences (2004) to more focused prevention strategies at the individual/community level, be it universal prevention (for example, schools based alcohol education), selective prevention targeting particular vulnerable and high-risk groups; or indicative prevention that aims to address the harm associated with drinking amongst problem drinkers rather than alcohol consumption per se.

Current Northern Ireland alcohol policy strives to reduce the "level, breadth and depth of alcohol [and drug] related harm to users, their families and/or their carers and the wider community" (Department of Health, Social Services and Public Safety, 2006, pg, 17). Specifically, in relation to adolescent alcohol use, the regional strategy places considerable emphasis on the development and implementation of alcohol education and prevention programmes (priority 4), targeting "vulnerable and at-risk" young people (priority 5), addressing underage drinking (priority 6), tackling alcohol related antisocial behaviour (priority 8), and addressing binge drinking (priority 10) (Department of Health, Social Service and Public Safety, 2006).

The English strategy also echoes these general priorities. Its stated overall aim is to "reduce the harm caused by alcohol misuse" (Strategy Unit, 2004, pg 16). While the

English model contains separate alcohol and drug strategies, the remits of the National Treatment Agency and the local Drug Action Teams were extended to cover alcohol as well as illicit drug use. The English Strategy also places considerable emphasis on communication and education against binge drinking, the promotion of social responsibility within the drinks industry, and the development of new criminal justice deterrents and enforcement powers to clamp down on alcohol related offending.

Likewise, the overall purpose of the Scottish Alcohol Plan (Scottish Executive, 2002a) is to reduce alcohol related harm, with key priorities of reducing binge drinking and dinking by children and young people. Interestingly, the Scottish plan specifies that its aims are to reduce consumption within specific population sub-groups, reduce harmful patterns of drinking and reduce public nuisance. While highlighting the standard tripartite approach to alcohol (education, treatment and legal control), the Scottish plan places considerable emphasis on achieving direct and indirect cultural change in relation to Scotland's relationship with alcohol. While accepting that multiple drinking cultures do exist within the nation, the plan does define the general cultural milieu as one focused on intoxication (pg. 31). Three key tools have been identified through which this cultural change could be achieved. The first is a national communication strategy to distribute agreed messages about drinking behaviour. The second is a change in the drinking environment, in particular the introduction of smoke-free family-friendly licensed premises. And finally, the strategy strives to achieve change within work, sport and leisure organisations in relation to their attitudes and behaviour towards alcohol.

While there is much to welcome in the new UK alcohol strategies some commentators have criticised identified limitations. Drummond (2004) was highly critical of the unwillingness of the UK government (or the regional assemblies) to impose any restrictions on the availability of alcohol, either through licensing or taxation. Given the strong associations between alcohol consumption and economic conditions shown above, and the empirical evidence of the positive relationship between consumption and affordability amassed over the last decade and more (see Babor et al., 2003; Edwards et al., 1994) he argued that this was a major public health opportunity missed. Room (2004) suggested that the reluctance of the government to invest in effective high impact public health measures, that is strategies aimed at increasing price

35

or reducing availability, was due to their perceived political unpopularity amongst the general public, and the undue influence and lobbying of the alcohol industry.

SUMMARY

The analysis of per capita consumption figures demonstrates that major changes in drinking behaviour, drinking culture and 'brand' preferences have occurred. The last century and a half has seen periods of both increasing and falling levels of alcohol consumption. In many cases such trends have been precipitated by specific events, such as wars, crop disease or failure, international trade agreements, changes in licensing laws or changes in alcohol duty and price. Drinking levels have also been influenced by background social and economic trends. There is an accepted, although modest, relationship between individual consumption patterns and the national economic cycles (Silbereisen, Robins & Rutter, 1995; Spring & Buss, 1977; Wilson, 1940). Also, social changes, such as the movement of population from the country to towns and cities, increasing consumerism and globalisation of the alcohol industry, have all been shown to influence the secular alcohol trends.

Traditional brands such as bitter and stout have declined in popularity, while new products have emerged. Lager is now the most dominant alcoholic drink, with new spirit based drinks also increasing in popularity. Similarly, more alcohol is consumed within the home than in previous years. This may be somewhat explained by the rise in canned larger sales but also by the considerable growth in wine drinking within Great Britain. While wine bars have emerged, it is still a beverage that is more readily consumed within the home than on a licensed premise.

The resultant economic costs of our current drinking culture are considerable. While problem drinkers pay a heavy price in terms of health costs, so too do their immediate social contacts such as partners, families and friends. The costs to the wider society are also substantial. A better understanding of the natural history of alcohol problems in young people that can be gained through the analysis presented here, should provide insights into the design and development of effective programmes aimed at preventing and reducing alcohol related harm. Developmental research in this area should be able to provide new knowledge on the individual and social problems that promote the development of problem drinking. Improvements in the efficacy and effectiveness of appropriate policy and practice response to alcohol related health, legal and social harm are irrefutably intertwined with the advancement of knowledge on the development of such problems amongst individuals and local communities.

3 A DEVELOPMENTAL PERSPECTIVE ON TEENAGE ALCOHOL CONSUMPTION

This chapter outlines the broad theoretical and conceptual framework in which this study is grounded. It will argue that adolescent problem drinking is a behavioural "disorder"[3.1] that is best understood from a developmental perspective, which, if ignored, restricts our understanding of why some young people drink alcohol at levels that are potentially harmful to themselves and their families.

The chapter will introduce *developmental psychopathology*, a general high-level theoretical approach to the study of adolescent developmental disorders, and its core components, including the study of developmental pathways, the transition between "normal" and "abnormal" behaviour and the comorbid relationships than can exist between different developmental disorders. The chapter will finish by assessing the implications of adopting a developmental psychopathology perspective for research design, and in particular the importance of longitudinal research in addressing outstanding gaps in our understanding of developmental problems in adolescents. It will also consider some of the methodological issues and challenges facing researchers and theoreticians working in this area.

[3.1] It is recognised that the use of terms such as 'disorder', 'abnormal' and 'pathological', are somewhat contested (see for example, Horwitz, 2003). Rather than ignoring the complexity of the debates surrounding these terms, developmental psychopathology has attempted to embrace them (see Jensen, Hoagwood & Zitner, 2006). It recognises that the distinction between normal and abnormal behaviour is grounded in the social and cultural context in which it is made, and that this boundary is not a fixed entity (Cicchetti, 2006). It accepts the duality of behaviours, in that they can be represented by both continuous dimensions and by discrete categories (see Pickles & Angold, 2003). However, it also acknowledges that there are benefits to the categorisation of individual behaviour and the identification of individual in need of intervention, which is to say giving a 'diagnosis' (Jensen et al., 2006).

ADOLESCENT PROBLEM DRINKING: A DEVELOPMENTAL DISORDER
Interindividual and intraindividual variations in drinking behaviour

Alcohol consumption, by its very nature, is not a static phenomenon but is dynamic. Not only do alcohol consumption patterns vary from one person to the next (interindividual variation), but within each individual drinking patterns also vary from one month to the next or from one year to the next (intraindividual variation). Changes in drinking patterns can be observed across the life span and its various developmental stages. Individuals tend to drink more at certain periods in their life and less at others, and these ebbs and flows are important in understanding the development of excessive alcohol consumption.

Cross-sectional survey research has consistently shown that drinking behaviour varies with age (Plant & Plant, 1992; Wright, 1999). Little alcohol consumption is recorded amongst children under the ages of 10. Between age 10 and 18 the prevalence of alcohol consumption increases with each increasing age band. For most people, their first unsupervised use of alcohol usually occurs in their early teens (many children will have been introduced to alcohol by their parents at an earlier age). Initiation into unsupervised drinking tends to be followed by a rapid increase in both the frequency and amount of alcohol consumed that peaks in early adulthood. After this, alcohol consumption usually declines to more moderate levels with increasing age. However, at the individual level this age related drinking pattern does not hold for all people, and wide variations in drinking behaviour do exist. Within each age group a proportion does not drink alcohol at all, while others may drink to excess. While population-level per capita alcohol consumption may vary year to year, that is there may be more drinkers in the population from one year to the next, or they may be drinking less, this basic distribution remains stable. Drinking increases in early adolescence, peaks in late adolescence/early adulthood then begins to tail off. To explain why some people drink excessively, while others do not, it becomes necessary to explain temporal and interpersonal variations in alcohol consumption.

Following from this, it can also be argued that similar interindividual and intraindividual variations also exist in individual vulnerability to excessive drinking. Alcohol misuse can occur at any age from early adolescence onwards (Anthony, Warner, & Kessler, 1994), and arises from the interplay of genetic and environmentally mediated processes (Tarter & Vanyukov, 1994; Tarter et al., 1999). Cox and Klinger (1988) suggested that an individual's alcohol consumption is a function of their past experiences of drinking – including attitudes and behaviours learned in teenage years – and their genetically determined biochemical reactivity to alcohol. These combine with the individual's personality characteristics – which may also have genetic and experiential components – and the current positive and negative incentives to drink produced by the social context in which they are situated.

In recent years there has been increasing recognition of the role that social context plays in adolescent development including alcohol use (Boyce, et al., 1998). Social context can be both broad interpersonal contexts (such as family relationships) and specific situational contexts (such as a family party in which young people are permitted to try alcohol) both of which can influence adolescent behaviour in complex reciprocal ways (Duncan, Duncan, Biglan, & Ary, 1998; Foley, Altman, Durant, & Wolfson, 2004; Henrich, 2006). Context is also important in deciding if adolescent behaviour is appropriate and acceptable or if it is inappropriate and problematic (Cicchetti & Aber, 1998).

The extent and nature of exposure to the environmental processes (arising from different social contexts) that influence individual vulnerability to alcohol problems do vary at the interindividual and intraindividual level. If we assume that there is a genetic component to alcohol misuse, we must also acknowledge that there is individual variation in that genetic risk, and in particular, within the gene-environment interactions that translate the genetic vulnerabilities into actual drinking behaviour (Dawes et al., 2000; Tarter & Vanyukov, 1994; Tarter et al., 1999). Key risk processes may be age indexed, that is to say, they may only operate at certain ages. For example, parental supervision may limit drinking in early adolescence but may have little influence on the drinking behaviour of young adults. Likewise, certain processes may have a differential effect at different ages. For example, leaving home may increase the risk of problem drinking for young teenagers but may be a protective factor for young adults as they set up home and take on adult responsibilities (Ramsay & Percy, 1996).

Individual vulnerability is dependent on the extent, nature and timing of risk exposures (Schoon et al., 2002). Adopting a developmental perspective provides a suitable conceptual framework for linking the various genetic, personality, experiential (including early life experiences) and situational factors that influence the course of adolescent drug use (Cicchetti & Rogosch, 2002; Glantz & Leshner, 2000; Tarter & Vanyukov, 1994, Tarter, et al., 1999)

There is evidence that problem alcohol use varies across the life span, and that important causal processes that may shape drinking behaviours are also development (or age) indexed. It is argued therefore that a comprehensive understanding of the natural history of alcohol problems requires a developmental analysis. This call for the re-analysis of a behavioural disorder from a developmental perspective is not new. Similar reappraisals have occurred in other areas of psychopathology, such as depression and schizophrenia, and in crime and delinquency (Rutter, 1999a; Rutter et al., 1998; Rutter & Sroufe, 2000; Tonry, Ohlin, & Farrington, 1991). Such work falls under the general label of developmental psychopathology (see Cicchetti, 1984; Cicchetti, 1989).

Developmental Psychopathology

Developmental psychopathology contrasts with alternative conceptualisations of adolescent behavioural, social or mental health problems. Rather than seeing depression, delinquency or drug use, for example, as the progression of a particular disease that exists outside of ongoing development – as in adult psychopathology - its focus is on individual differences in the developmental pathways and trajectories from childhood to adulthood, and the bio-psychosocial factors that contribute to adaptive or maladaptive outcomes (Cicchetti, 1989; Compas, Hinden, & Gerhart, 1995; Ebata, Petersen, & Conger, 1990; Glantz & Leshner, 2000). Developmental psychopathology is concerned with both normal and abnormal development, the interface between normal and abnormal, and the patterns of behavioural adaptation and maladaptation that emerge over time (Ciccetti & Sroufe, 2000; Sroufe, 1989).

It also differs from traditional theories of child development (for example, psychodynamic theory, or Piaget's theory). Development is not conceptualised as a linear progression through a single series of discrete stages where abnormal development is regarded as a failure of progression to the next age-appropriate stage. Rather than viewing a disorder as resulting from a developmental delay, within developmental psychopathology a disorder (for example problematic alcohol

41

consumption) is conceptualised as a "developmental deviation" from a normative developmental path (Sroufe, 1989; pg 13). Cicchetti & Rogosch (2002) conceived adolescent development as a number of age related tasks, and that successful adaptation emerges as a result of the resolution of these stage salient tasks. These developmental tasks are defined as accepted social or cultural standard for behaviour and achievement within a particular society (Masten, 2006). Successful resolution is, in itself, a function of the nature of the specific task, the resources or competencies (derived from past stage-salient tasks) brought to the task by the individual adolescent, and the support or challenges they receive from the social context(s) in which they live. The competence and adaptiveness attained, or in fact not attained, at any particular milestone, has predictive implications for later functioning. As a result, developmental divergence can occur depending on the nature of the skills and competencies obtained by adolescents in response to the developmental tasks faced. It is also possible that once having deviated from a normative developmental path, individuals can and do resume normal development (Sroufe, 1989).

Within this perspective individual agency is fully acknowledged (Masten, 2006). Individual adolescent choices, to an extent, can determine their experiences, behaviours and the context in which they spend their free time. As such, these choices contribute to their overall vulnerability to problem behaviour such as excessive alcohol consumption and their deviation from and resumption of normal development.

While differences exist between developmental psychopathology and earlier models of adolescent psychopathology, Costello and Angold (2006) noted that both developmental psychopathology and psychodynamic approaches to childhood disorders place development centre stage, in sharp contrast to prevalent phenomenological approaches to child disorders. Here the emphasis has been on the search for "diseases that have a standard etiology, and set of manifestations" (pg. 55).

A key issue for researchers adopting a developmental perspective is the boundary between the normal and abnormal. In general, this interface is assumed to lie somewhere along a continuum of developmental patterns. Research interest is not however, only focused on the extreme ends of the spectrum but also in the mean position and in slight deviations from this average pattern (Cicchetti, 2006). Understanding these subtle deviations from the usual that may reveal insights into the early origins of the more extreme behaviour patterns.

Normal and abnormal adolescent drinking

Adolescent alcohol consumption provides an interesting example for the discussion of the interface between normal and abnormal behaviour. As cultural studies have constantly confirmed the extensive use of alcohol, cannabis and other substances across all periods of human history (Blackman 2004; Walton, 2001) it is hard to define adult substance use, per se, as culturally pathological.

A legal definition, in contrast, would apply a relatively arbitrary age restriction (age 18 within the UK) to the definition of appropriate or inappropriate alcohol use. Young people under the age cut-off cannot purchase alcohol, although the consumption of alcohol under this age can be permitted under special circumstances. However, such a position fails to acknowledge individual variations in adolescent drinking, the possibility that adolescent alcohol consumption may play an important role in the development of individual self-regulation skills required to maintain control over drinking patterns in adulthood, and that abstinence in adolescence may be a poor indicator of positive outcomes in adulthood.

An alternative framework would be based on the assessment of individual drinking patterns, where the controlled ingestion of psychoactive substances with minimal individual or social harm within certain social contexts could be considered "normal" or "acceptable" behaviour. It may be appropriate, therefore, to restrict a definition of "abnormal" or "pathological" alcohol use to the uncontrolled use of substances or the continued use of substances in the face of harm to the individual, friends or family. Gmel and Rehm (2003) provided a detailed overview of the harm that uncontrolled drinking could cause for both the drinkers and those around them. These can include reduced and lost earnings and productivity, accidental injuries, alcohol related violence, debt, child neglect and abuse, and other marital and family conflicts. These harms are somewhat reflected in the Diagnostic and Statistical Manual of Mental Health Disorders (Fourth Edition – Text Revision) definition of alcohol abuse (American Psychiatric Association, 2000). DSM-IV-TR defines abuse as alcohol consumption that results in a failure to fulfil major obligations, occurs in situations of physical harm, results in recurring legal problems or results in recurring interpersonal problems. Alcohol dependence, as distinct from abuse, is defined within the DSM in relation to specific aspects of particular impaired control, tolerance, withdrawal symptoms and blackouts. The assumption underlying this distinction is that abuse is a distinct milder precursor stage of later dependency.

As the DSM criteria were developed specifically for alcohol problems amongst adults they may not necessarily translate well to teenage drinkers (Clark, 2004). In particular, tolerance and impaired control are rare amongst adolescents due to their very short drinking careers. Even amongst those young people who qualify for a DSM diagnosis of alcohol abuse or dependency, considerable variation in drinking behaviour and associated problems exists (Tarter, Kirisci, & Mezzich 1997). Using alternative methods for classifying drinking problems amongst young people in treatment, in this case latent class analysis (LCA), Chung and Martin (2001) found only a modest level of agreement between DSM and the alternative typology. In particular, they identified cases that failed to meet the DSM criteria for alcohol abuse but had similar levels of alcohol problem severity (as assessed by patterns of drinking and problems experienced) to those who did. Pollock and Martin (1999) termed such cases 'diagnostic orphans', in that they would have similar patterns of use to DSM cases, would exhibit elements of alcohol dependency and abuse, but failed to meet the criteria for either. At present, no agreed definition of adolescent problem drinking exists. Chung and Martin (2001) argued that the latent class models provided much better coverage of adolescent symptoms and a better indicator of the relative severity of adolescent drinking problems than DSM. However, very few latent class models of teenage drinking exist within the research literature.

Alcohol and the development of other problem behaviours

In a major review, Angold, Costello and Erkanli (1997) identified the main functional variants of comorbid relationships between behavioural disorders. Keeping a developmental perspective, comorbid disorders can be both *homotypic* and *heterotypic* continuations of the original behaviour pattern. Homotypic refers to the continuation of a single phenomenon, for example the fact that adolescent problem drinking may give rise to higher rates of adult problem drinking. Heterotypic also refers to a single underlying continuous process, which rather than giving rise to a single disorder, such as problem drinking, generates different behavioural manifestations over time, for example adolescent problem drinking and adult depression. Angold and colleagues (1997) also draw the distinction between *concurrent* and *successive* comorbid conditions. This reflects the various temporal relationships that can exist between comorbid disorders. In the first, the disorders occur at the same time within the individual, while in the second there is no temporal overlap between the two. It is also possible to distinguish between *primary* and *secondary* comorbid conditions. Here, two distinct processes exist in which the secondary condition is caused by the primary disorder. However, although Angold et al., (1997) recognised the existence of such primary-secondary comorbid disorders within clinical medicine they were unable to identify similar relationships between existing distinct behaviour disorders. Finally, there was a need to recognise that comorbidity not only occurs at the *individual* level but also at the *family* level. The fact that much of the research on adolescent problem drinkers has focused on the offspring of adult alcoholics (as a convenient high-risk population in which to study the development of alcohol misuse problems: for example, Sher, 1991; Sher et al., 1996; Vanyukov et al., 2003) provides supporting evidence of the widely recognised phenomenon of familial comorbidity.

Early theories on the development of problem behaviour in adolescents recognised the extent to which alcohol, drug use and delinquency tended to cluster in individuals (Jessor & Jessor, 1977). Fergusson, Horwood and Lynskey (1994) estimated that around 3% of adolescents displayed multiple and complex problem behaviours. The co-occurrence of multiple disorders is associated with increased levels of severity and functional impairment, raising numerous challenges for their successful management and treatment (Newman, Moffitt, Caspi, & Silva, 1998).

IMPLICATION FOR RESEARCH DESIGN
The need for longitudinal studies
Central to developmental psychopathology has been the application of prospective longitudinal methods to the study of behavioural disorders (Magnusson & Caesar, 1993; Rutter, 1988). Longitudinal research has permitted advances in both the mapping of the natural histories of disorders and the causal processes underlying them. Longitudinal

research is essentially the study of change over time, and in particular the study of intraindividual change, and interindividual differences in intraindividual change (Bates, Resse, & Nesselroade, 1977; Farrington, 1988; Loeber & Farrington, 1994). Longitudinal research is distinct from other studies with repeated measurement in that it identifies and links reports form the same individuals over time. Cohort studies which track a single age cohort of young people, are able to examine how each cohort member changes and develops over time (intraindividual change) and the extent to which individual development is similar or different to other cohort members (interindividual differences in intraindividual change). When non-longitudinal repeated measures studies examine change they are limited to the estimation of *net* change (the eve of change at the population level only) rather than *gross* change (change at the individual level).

Much longitudinal research has been descriptive, focused mainly on mapping the developmental pattern of disorders. An example of this is the pioneering work of Denise Kandel in relation to the patterns of initiation, persistence and cessation of substance use (Chen & Kandel, 1995; Kandel & Logan, 1984; Kandel, Yamaguchi & Chen, 1992). This research established the stage-sequential pattern of drug use, where young people first started with licit drugs (alcohol and tobacco) before progressing to cannabis and then on to harder drugs such as amphetamine and cocaine.

Here, the concept of the developmental pathway has proved useful. A pathway represents a group of individuals experiencing a similar identified temporal sequencing of a behavioural progression from less serious to more serious forms of the disorder distinct from other groups (Kelley, Loeber, Keenan, & DeLamatre, 1997). Developmental psychopathology differs considerably from traditional theories of development that have assumed an age-dependant universal pathway, with a single outcome, along which all individuals progress (Rutter & Sroufe 2000; Rutter 1993). First, it does not assume a single developmental progression for all individuals; rather multiple pathways can exist (Compas, Hinden & Gerhart 1995, Kelley et al., 1997). Second, not only do multiple pathways occur but multiple outcomes also exist ranging from the normal to the disordered (Cicchetti & Rogosh 1996; Rutter 1993; Rutter 1999b). Finally, individuals can change pathways. Life events or prevention intervention can alter an individual's developmental pathway. What is important, here, is the identification of factors that influence the origins and course of particular pathways.

Two key concepts in understanding the complexity of such developmental systems are *equifinality* and *multifinality* (Cicchetti & Rogosh, 1996). Equifinality refers to the processes by which different pathways from childhood to adulthood, involving the interactions of different risk and protective factors, may lead to a similar developmental outcome. Multifinality is the reverse of this. In other words, individuals with a shared starting point may progress towards different developmental endpoints. Particular risk exposure may not have the same effect on different individuals or at different points in time. In fact, one factor, that may increase risk at one developmental stage, may promote protection if it occurs at some other time.

Developmental studies, such as this one, therefore need to consider the possibilities that problem behaviours have multiple causes, have multiple starting points, and have multiple potential outcomes. In the study of adolescent problems drinking, this is requires recognition that there is not a single pathway to problem drinking (see chapter 6 for further discussion of this). Also there is a need to recognise that problem drinking in adolescent may lead onto multiple adult pathways some of which are associated with positive outcomes and some with more negative outcomes. This study in response examines adult outcomes and childhood antecedents and multiple across a range of domains (social, employment, education, and heath) and informants (child, parent, teacher, health professional).

Identification of causal mechanisms underlying development disorders

Not only does a longitudinal design permit the description and mapping of a developmental disorder such as problem drinking, it also facilitates the examination of the causal processes underlying its onset, course and termination. The identification of such mechanisms underlying alcohol misuse would have a considerable impact on the prevention and treatment services. Coie et al., (1993) argued that the prevention of public health problems requires services to be targeted at the fundamental causal processes underlying the problem, including those associated with increased risk and those with increased resilience. Services that mitigate the effects of risk processes whilst promoting protective factors may prevent the development of drinking problems in individuals. This notion lies at the centre of the emerging discipline of *prevention science*, which brings together developmental and etiological theory with epidemiological-based intervention trials (Hawkins, Catalano, & Arthur, 2002).

Michael Sobel (1994) suggested that two main notions of causation can be found in social sciences. The first is defined in relation to *predictability,* and is commonly found within econometric research. In this case, a causal relationship can be inferred between X and Y, if X occurs before Y and X and Y co-vary, that is X predicts Y, and ideally all other sources of spuriousness are taken into account. The second notion of causation is based on the *counterfactual*. This is a statement that outlines a situation that is opposite (counter) to the proposed causal relationship (fact). At the centre of a counterfactual notion of causation is the idea of manipulating one variable and observing its effect on another variable. The most common example of this is experimental research, where the counterfactual (or null hypothesis) is clearly defined.

Non-experimental research, such as BCS70, sits somewhere between these two notions of causality. While, at an intuitive level, a longitudinal study of drug use fits well with a predictive view of causation, many of the statistical tests commonly used (for example, regression analysis) assume a counterfactual approach to causal testing. What is common across both notions of causality is the need for a known temporal relationship to exist between the two variables under study, specified in terms of prediction in the first notion, or causal effect in the second. The longitudinal nature of the BCS70 ensures that this condition is met.

'Causality' is one of the key concepts contained within the research priority outlined above; the other is 'mechanism'. Here, it is important to differentiate between a risk indicator and a risk mechanism. Rutter et al., (1998) defined indicators as features that have indirect connections with causal processes, but which themselves, are not part of the mechanisms of causation. The example that Rutter and colleagues use as a risk indicator is parental marriage breakdown. While marital breakdown is associated with adolescent crime, it is the amount of parental conflict within the home and not parental separation, or as some have recently suggested, it is the conflict resolution style used by parents that is the main causal mechanism (Cummings & Davies, 2002). Therefore, it is possible to consider marital breakdown and adolescent crime as both being outcomes of marital conflict.

In effect, this could also be considered as a refinement of our understanding of what is the key aspect (or active ingredient) of marital breakdown that increases the risk of crime in dependant adolescents. It may be possible to untangle this causal process further, in particular by identifying the intermediate links in the causal chain through which marital conflict impacts on adolescent criminal behaviour. Is it the case that conflict within the home teaches children to be more aggressive or to adopt an aggressive approach to problem solving etc. Knowledge of the sequence of processes through which identified risk factors operate is important in the design and delivery of appropriate intervention strategies. Using the Rutter et al., (1998) example, an intervention aimed at reducing marital conflict would be more effective than one designed to keep couples together, although it would be hard to envisage an intervention that achieved this without addressing the roots of conflict between the couple.

It must be recognised, however, that within the study of human behaviour it is unlikely that simple bivariate causation (X causes Y) will be observed. The causes of a social behaviour such as drug use are known to be multifactorial (Hawkins, Catalano, & Miller, 1992). And given the range of processes that may influence behaviour, it is unlikely that individual studies will observe all the causes of a particular behaviour (Pickles, 1993). Rather, as Pickles concluded, studies are more likely to investigate *component causes* or *sufficient causes*, which account for only a proportion of the total causation, and are measured against *background factors* - unobserved risk factors. *Synergy* occurs when two or more component causes are required to generate a sufficient cause (Pickles, 1993). Neither component on its own could be considered a sufficient cause. For example, low parental supervision may only be a risk factor when young people are exposed to drug use on a regular basis. Neither the level of supervision nor the level of drug exposure in the local community is a sufficient cause on its own. A causal impact only occurs when there is synergy.

The study of comorbidity provides a useful example of the complex relationships that may exist between variables that require careful unpicking if the causal relationships are to be successfully understood. Fergusson, Poulton, Horwood, Milne, & Swain-Campbell (2003) identified six path models explaining the connection between two comorbid disorders (X, Y), only three of which resulted from a causal relationship. Here X caused Y, Y caused X or there was a reciprocal causative relationship between X and

Y. However, it is also possible that the association between X and Y was that they were both caused by Z, or caused by correlated factors Z_1 and Z_2 or that X and Y are indicators or manifestation of a more general common disorder G.

Menard (1991) summarised the three conditions necessary for the establishment of a causal relationship between two or more variables. First, the variables must co-vary in a way that is expected. Second, there must be an appropriate temporal relationship between cause and effect. The cause(s) must precede the effect or outcome. And third, the relationship between the variables must not be spurious. It must not be due to some other plausible explanation or common cause that jointly influences both the 'cause' and 'effect' under consideration.

Both cross-section and longitudinal research can be used to identify covariation between variables. However, only longitudinal studies, with the repeated collection of data from the same individuals over time, can be used to establish the temporal order between variables. For example, longitudinal studies have shown that alcohol consumption usually occurs before the use of illicit drugs (Chen & Kandel, 1995; Kandel & Logan 1984; Kandel, Yamaguchi, & Chen, 1992). While alcohol may be considered as a possible cause of later illicit drug use, drug use cannot be considered as a causal factor in drinking as drinking precedes it. However, as cross-sectional studies have a single data point during which all information is collected, they cannot be used to untangle the temporal order of behaviours or experiences (see Ramsay & Percy, 1996). With cross-sectional data, both cause and effect are observed simultaneously. As a result, cross-sectional studies, while meeting the first condition for the establishment of causality, fail to meet the second - the identification of which of the covariates is the cause and which the effect. Variables can be contemporaneous, or with an unknown temporal relationships. Here, the direction of the causation can be difficult to determine (Asher, 1983).

Once covariates have been identified and the temporal order specified, the next stage in making causal inferences is the elimination of other plausible rival explanations. Central to this is the examination of within-individual change over time in the covariates under consideration (Le Blanc & Loeber, 1993; Loeber & Farrington, 1994; Nesselroade & Schmidt McCollam, 2000; Rutter, 1994a). In experimental studies, the researcher manipulates the potential cause (or independent variable) and observes changes in the outcome, while controlling for other possible explanations. Random allocation of subjects is used as the principle method of control.

Within naturalistic longitudinal studies, other procedures can be employed to rule out spurious results including (a) the analysis of concomitant change, (b) long-term prediction from early child experiences (c) cross-lagged analysis (d) sequential analysis (e) sequential covariation (f) the analysis of life events and the stepping stones approaches (Le Blanc & Loeber, 1993). Causal testing can be further strengthened by pitting of one causal mechanism against a rival (Rutter, 1993; 1994a). The repeated application of this procedure over a number of studies can be used to effectively rule out spurious explanations within longitudinal studies that do not permit random assignment.

Each of the procedures listed above requires intraindividual data measuring gross change. This requires repeated observation of the behaviour of a sample of individuals over time. In other words, the same individuals are observed at each of the various age points. Cross-sectional research, which samples different individuals at each age point, only permits the study of aggregate change over time. As a result, causal inferences about developmental change are drawn not from an analysis of individual change but from differences in the mean, variance and covariance of factors across the different age groups in the sample (Weinhert & Schneider, 1993). The age of each age group is used as a proxy indicator of development. Instead of comparing the level of alcohol consumption of an individual at age 12 and the same individual at age 14, a single cross-sectional design study compares the mean level of alcohol use amongst young people aged 12 and the mean level amongst a different group of young people aged 14 at the same point in time. However, inter-cohort comparisons of this sort may not necessarily reflect true developmental patterns (Menard 1991).

Repeat cross-sectional studies, where change is measured across different samples drawn from the same population, may be indicative of causal processes but do not permit the analysis of the processes with the same degree of precision as individual-level data. Examining concomitant change, for example in alcohol consumption and unemployment, within repeat cross-sectional surveys or even population-level data sets proves a weak test of whether losing a job is a causal factor in problem drinking. Official statistics data sources such as the trends in the amount of alcohol released by Customs and Excise for home consumption, and trends in employment benefit claimant count, may show similar increases over time. However, it would not be possible to determine from such data sets whether it was the same people who were becoming unemployed and drinking more, or whether it was different individuals. While repeat cross-sectional surveys are able to link individual employment status and drinking behaviour at the individual level, this can only be done for one moment in time, as different individuals are included in the study at the next data collection. Therefore, it is not possible to assess whether earlier job loss affected later drinking. This requires the tracking of individual change over time.

Even with well-conducted longitudinal studies the identification of causal processes underlying developmental disorders, such as alcohol use, is far from straightforward. Researchers face a number of practical and methodological challenges relating to the sheer complexity of human behaviour and its influences. All behaviour is embedded within nested layers of social context or environmental influence including the neighbourhood, the school, the family, and the peer network (Bronfenbrenner, 1979, Lerner, Walsh, & Howard, 1998, Boyce et al., 1998). Risk factors for problem drinking have been identified at all levels of social context (Hawkins et al., 1992). Such environmental influences also interact with the internal resources or psychological processes within the individual, and individual differences in the cognitive processing of risk may exist (Rutter 1994a). It must also be appreciated that all environmental influences are embedded within these layers of social context, with interactions occurring between any single risk process and other environmental factors, as well as between risk and outcome (Cicchetti & Sroufe, 2000).

Given the above, single direct causal influences between risk and outcome are likely to be rare, rather risk processes are likely to operate though indirect causal chains both within and across the hierarchical levels of an individual's environment (Boyce et al., 1998; Rutter 1993; 1994a; 1999b; Rutter et al., 1998). For example, living in poor housing and negative local economic conditions may place increasing stress on the family system. Changes within family interactions in response to the stress, such as an increasing number of parental arguments or family break-up, may disrupt the family's ability to transmit pro-social norms and behaviours. These may interact with the child individual personality and characteristics leading to the development of antisocial norms, deviant peer group and adolescent problem drinking (see Oetting &

Donnermeyer, 1998; Oetting, Donnermeyer & Deffenbacher, 1998; Oetting, Deffenbacher & Donnermeyer, 1998).

Over recent years, there has been a resurgence of interest in the study of how local communities shape adolescent behaviour (Booth & Crouter 2001; Leventhal & Brooks-Gunn, 2000). Much of this may be due to the increasing primacy of ecological models of human development that emphasise the various levels of social context in which young people live (Bronfenbrenner, 1979, Boyce et al., 1998; Lerner, Walsh, & Howard, 1998). This has been coupled with the growth of statistical procedures that can successfully accommodate the natural social grouping in which young people live within longitudinal data analysis (Boyle & Willims, 2001; Moskowitz & Hershberger, 2001; Willet, Singer, & Martin, 1998). Traditional research methods are based on the assumption that individual observations are independent of each other, or in other words that the individual respondents in the study do not interact with one another in ways that influences the particular phenomenon under study. In contrast, multi-level modelling techniques, as they are called, do not have this independence assumption and can accommodate the fact that, for example, school children who attend the same school are likely to be more similar to each other than they are to children who attend another school.

While multi-level modelling offers exciting possibilities for the study of social context further work is required. To date, there has been little discussion of procedures for dealing with overlapping and competing levels of context (known as cross-classification), for example school children belong simultaneously to a) classes within schools within catchments areas, b) peer cliques within social groups/crowds within neighbourhoods, and c) families within neighbourhoods within towns. Most applications of multi-level models have been used to examine the main effects of different levels of context on behaviour (for example, Duncan, Duncan, & Strycker, 2002; Kumar, O'Malley, Johnston, Schulenberg, & Bachman, 2002; Hoffman, 2002; Kariouz & Adlaf, 2003). While these and similar studies are an improvement in statistical methodology over studies in which the various nested layers have been ignored, and have generated new knowledge on the risk factors of adolescent substance use, to date there has been few examinations of the interaction between the different levels. As O'Connor, Hetherington and Reiss (1998) stated, the goal of contextual research should be to examine how social contexts moderate and mediate risk processes operating across and within levels of social context. Curran and Willoughby (2003) refer to this as the study of the 'coaction' of different influences across development. While theoretically critical, they conclude that current statistical approaches, for example latent trajectory models, cannot test coaction. While there have been conceptual advances in this area (Boyce et al., 1998; Parke, 2004; Wilcox, 2003) further work is need to fully operationalise and model these systemic developmental processes.

Magnusson (1993) argued that the complexities of individual-environment interactions are best understood from holistic or dynamic systems perspective. The systems metaphor, while not a detailed empirical theory, is a general conceptual framework that helps to guide and organise our understanding of human development. A general systems perspective assumes that the system is (a) hierarchical in structure, comprised of interdependent subsystems operating within larger systems (b) dynamic (c) adaptive to change, and (d) involves reciprocal and circular transactions within and between subsystems (Cox & Paley, 1997). This final point is the appreciation that not only can the social context in which an individual lives alter their behaviour but also the individual can alter the social context (Boyce et al., 1998; Lerner et al., 1998; Magnusson, 1993). Reciprocal interactions may also exist at the behavioural level. For example, changes in alcohol use may impact on an individual's use of other substances, which in turn may alter their use of alcohol.

However, it must be accepted that no single research study can cover all interactions that may impact on the development of a particular behavioural disorder. What becomes important then are what are termed the boundary conditions of the study - what is outside the focus of the study (Pearl, 2000). Here, a systems perspective, because of the way it delineates complex multidimensional processes into series of systems and subsystems, may be useful in accurately specifying the boundary conditions, that is to say, those subsystems outside the study.

The three conditions required for testing causal processes outline above may still prove insufficient in determining causality in cases when the cause may be structurally, functionally and mechanistically similar to the outcome (Menard 1991). When this arises, the preceding variable may be more accurately described as a precursor rather than as a cause (Hay & Angold, 1993). While a causal risk factor increases the likelihood of the outcome, for example problem alcohol use, actually occurring, a precursor, such as early onset drinking, is an actual stage in the progression to problem alcohol use.

Pickles (1993) provided a number of pointers to distinguish precursors from risk factors. Precursors (for example, alcohol use) can be distinguished from certain risk factors (for example, being male) as precursors cannot be fixed over time. If the variable is fixed, it is a risk factor and not a precursor. Where risk factors do vary over time (for example, marital conflict), they can be distinguished from precursors as they will be *exogenous* to the outcome (has separate origins to that of the outcome) while the precursors will be *endogenous* (likely to share common risk factors with the outcome, such as gender, and be itself causally related to the outcome). For example, it is common for alcohol use to be preceded by tobacco use, and alcohol use itself to act as a precursor for later illicit drug use (Chen & Kandel, 1995; Kandel & Logan 1984; Kandel, Yamaguchi, & Chen, 1992).

In an attempt to assess causal relationships between risk and outcome, this study will employ regression models (multiple, logistic and multinomial logistic). These model permit examination of multiple predictors and a single continuous or categorical outcome. Multiple models can be estimated for multiple outcomes. Their primary benefit is that provide information on the relationship between a predictor variable and an outcome while statistically controlling from the effect of other potential predictors (this is where the counterfactual principle is covered, in part, by regression). While multivariate regression is a powerful method for examining causal relationships between variables, it does have limitations. In particular, it does not permit causal links (also refer to as paths) between predictor variables. Models that facilitate such linkages are known as path models (only contain manifest variables) and structural equation models (SEM: contain latent and manifest variables) (Loehlin, 1998). SEM permits a more detailed test of developmental theory, as the researcher is able to express and test the structural relationship between all variables. Variables within SEMs are not required to have a direct causal link with the outcome. For example, some predictors may act through a mediator, (variable A affects variable B which in turn influences the outcome Y). Likewise, some variables can act as moderators, in that changes in the moderator may affect the nature of the relationship between another risk and outcome (the

55

influence of variable A on outcome Y is moderated by the level of variable B). However, while SEMs can be seen as a powerful extension of regression models, this additional functionality does add considerable complexity to the statistical analysis. SEM analysis requires a well-defined theory on which to base the structural relationship between variables. If this is absent SEM can quickly become a simple a theoretic data mining exploration for significant links, not the most appropriate method for expanding developmental theory. Given the absence of existing UK studies in this area, and the current gaps within existing knowledge (see later chapters for a full review) it was decided that multivariate regression models, while having a reduced ability to fully test developmental theory, would be an appropriate first step in exploring the research questions outlined in chapter 1. This work can be extended into SEM at a later stage once this initial modelling has been completed. Multivariate regression modelling is not without its advantages. In particular, it can incorporate many of the developmental psychopathology core concepts including interindividual change in behaviour, the identification of comorbidity (both concurrent and successive), and the examination of alcohol use pathways.[3.2] The following analysis chapters attempt to apply the guiding principles of a developmental psychopathology framework within the confines of the BCS70 data and the statistical methods selected. Additional technical issues regarding research and statistical methods used are continued within the corresponding analysis chapters.

SUMMARY

This study utilises the power of existing longitudinal data to identify and test causal processes that may underlie the development of problem drinking amongst 16-year-old adolescents. Employing a developmental perspective this study examines both intraindividual differences in adolescent drinking behaviour (how individual drinking patterns vary across the population at age 16) and intraindividual change in drinking patterns over time (the extent to which early drinking behaviours predicts later drinking behaviours).

[3.2] This is possible due to the fact that the BCS70 data sweeps use in this study assess alcohol on only two points, at age 16 and at age 26. Additional repeated measurements of the outcome variable can facilitate growth-modelling approaches for the examination of developmental pathways.

The study draws on the rich history of developmental psychopathology to construct a conceptual and theoretical framework to inform the broad research aims of the study, and also the more specific research questions examined in subsequent chapters. Issues important to developmental psychopathology such as distinction between normal and abnormal behaviour, how young people may shift across this subtle boundary, and the environmental forces that appear to influence these shifts will be considered. While the complexities of undertaking causal testing are appreciated, existing guidance on the appropriate met examining causal relationships are employed where possible.

4 BCS70: BACKGROUND, DESIGN AND METHODOLOGY.

This study utilises data from the 1970 British Cohort Study (BCS70), one of the four national longitudinal birth cohort studies within Great Britain. This chapter provides an overview of the study's design and methodology. It will describe each of the five BCS70 sweeps, examining in turn sample size, informants, sampling and tracking procedures, data instruments, response biases, and data processing/cleaning procedures. In addition, it will outline some of the key methodological limitations of national cohort studies and discuss secondary analysis as a basic research strategy.

THE 1970 BRITISH COHORT STUDY

In 1970, data was collected on 17,196 babies and their families born between 5th and 11th April. These families were re-contacted on four further occasions, in 1975, 1980, 1986, and 1996. At each occasion a wide range of information was collected, from multiple sources, on the child's physical, social and educational development. As such it provides an important and valuable resource for social scientists, detailing the life histories of a representative cohort of children.

The following sections present a summary of the data collection exercises. It draws extensively from the five technical reports that accompany the survey. For a full account of the survey methodology the reader is referred to the appropriate technical report.

Birth

As indicated above, the target sample for the British Cohort Study 1970, originally known as the British Births Study, was all babies born (including stillbirths) within the United Kingdom, between 5th and 11th April 1970. This generated a sample of 17,196 cases. Estimating the level of missing data for the birth cohort is difficult due to

58

the inadequacy of hospital records in the 1970s, which did not permit the calculation of the number of births that actually occurred over this period. The BCS70 research team estimated that between 2% and 5% of mothers who gave birth during the study week did not participate in the survey (Institute of Child Health, not dated).

The attending midwife or other medical practitioner completed questionnaire forms in most cases. The questionnaire was composed of three sections. The first section, completed by means of an interview with the mother, collected information on basic family demographics; including age of parents, marital status, occupations, antenatal preparation, smoking history, and contraception. Section two was completed from medical records. This covered details such as previous pregnancies, antenatal visits, details of the delivery (location of labour, type of delivery, medical interventions etc.) and the outcome of the birth. Section three, also completed in consultation with the mother, looked at the first seven days of the birth. It specifically collected information on medical problems for either mother or baby, feeding, sleeping arrangements and medical interventions provided.

The five-year follow-up

The cohort size in 1975 was estimated to be in the region of 16,300, of which 13,136 (80.7%) were successfully traced and participated in the five-year BCS70 follow-up. Full details of the first follow-up were provided in the corresponding Technical Report (Golding, not dated). Data was collected via three schedules; a maternal self-completion questionnaire; a home interview; and a developmental test booklet.

The mother's self-completion questionnaire contained a sequence of attitudinal questions and more sensitive questions on the child's behaviour at home and maternal depression. The home interview, in most cases, also involved the mother (over 92% of interviews). The interview was used to collect details of the child's medical history and current heath condition.

Four developmental tests were constructed for use with the young children. The Human Figure Drawing Test ("draw-a-man test") asked the child to draw a man or a lady. The instructor emphasised drawing the whole person and not just the head or face.

In the Copy Design Test, the children were required to copy a series of shapes "as carefully as possible". The shapes included circles, squares, crosses and flags. Before starting the Reading Test the child's mother was asked if the child could read some words. If the mother replied that they could not, the test was omitted, otherwise the child was asked to read some simple words. The series of words increased in complexity. The test was stopped when the child failed to correctly answer five in a row. The final test was the English Picture Vocabulary Test. Here the child was presented with a series of pictures and asked to point to a named object. Again the test was stopped once the child had five consecutive incorrect answers. Test scores and drawings were returned to the Institute of Child Health for coding. Each test was coded by at least three coders with inter-rater reliabilities ranging from 0.7 to over 0.9 across the four tests.

The ten-year follow-up

The ten-year follow-up, originally entitled the Child Health and Education Study, was the second attempt to capture the full sample. A subsample was contacted at age 7, but not used in this study. The primary focus at this age was assessing educational progress, the development of specific and non-specific learning difficulties, and childhood health hazards (see technical report, Butler, Despotidou & Shepard, not dated).

Initial tracking of cohort members was undertaken by Local Educational Authorities (LEAs) in England and Wales, and their Scottish counterparts Regional Councils (RCs). Schools identified as containing cohort members on their registers were asked to supply pupil contact details to the research team. These new address details were merged with the existing address database amassed over the previous data sweeps. In addition attempts were made to track pupils through General Practitioner Registers, an exercise coordinated on behalf of the research team by Area Health Authorities (England and Wales) and Health Boards (Scotland).

Of the 16,135 respondents who completed one or more birth questionnaires (this does not include children from Northern Ireland who were dropped from the study after the birth sweep), 14,875 (93%) completed one or more survey instruments in 1980.

The 10-year-old follow-up consisted of 15 separate survey items, distributed over two packs, the Education Pack and the Health Pack. Table 4.1 gives details of the health pack components, respondent and completion rate. Packs were distributed through Area Health Coordinators located within each Health Authority/Board. A local Heath Visitor or Clinical Medical Officer completed the actual fieldwork. This involved contacting and visiting allocated families, undertaking the parental interview, leaving the maternal self-completion questionnaire (to be posted back to the study research team) and booking a medical examination for the child.

The parental interview contained a range of demographic items such as questions on family background and structure, parental education and employment, and family income. Details of child and family health were also collected during this interview. More sensitive items were allocated to the maternal self-completion form. This contained measures of child problem behaviours (including items from the Conners' Hyperactivity Scale (Conners 1970, Goyette, Conners & Ulrich, 1978); and Rutter A Scale, child skills and maternal malaise (Rutter Tizard, & Whitmore, 1970).

Table 4.1 Contents of the Health Pack (10-year follow-up)

Instrument	Respondent	Completed by	Cases
Parental Interview Form	Parent	Health Visitor	13,869
Maternal Self-completion Form	Mother	Mother	13,679
Medical examination Form	Cohort member	Community Medical Officer/ School Nurse	13,869

The medical examination focused on the identification and recording of physical and medical conditions. Basic height and weight measurements were completed as part of a systematic assessment.

The educational test pack consisted of a series of educational tests, together with pupil and teacher questionnaires. The tests were comprised of Pictorial Language Comprehension Test; the Friendly Maths Test; the Edinburgh Reading Test, and the British Ability Scales (selected subscales). The tests, completed within school, were administered and recorded by a teacher. The pupil's teacher also completed a short questionnaire. This instrument contained four sections: the child's educational status; social behaviour; developmental behaviour and school environment. Developmental behaviour was assessed by the Child Development Scale, which consisted of selected items from the Rutter B Scale, the Conners' Hyperactivity Scale and the Swansea Assessment Battery (Conners 1970, Goyette et al., 1978; Rutter et al., 1970). Appendix A gives details of an exploratory factor analysis of these items.

The final element of the educational pack was the pupil self-completion questionnaire. The teacher would read out individual items for those children with reading difficulties. The questionnaire contained Caraloc Locus of Control Scale (Gammage, 1975) and the Lawsec Self-Esteem Scale (Lawrence, 1981). The questionnaire also contained items on smoking and other health related behaviours. Table 4.2 provides details of the completion rates for the Educational Pack.

Table 4.2 Contents of the Education Pack (10-year follow-up)

Instrument	Respondent	Completed/Scored by	Cases
Pictorial Language Comprehension Test	Pupil	Teacher	12,701
Friendly Maths Test	Pupil	Teacher	11,685
Edinburgh Reading Test	Pupil	Teacher	11,685
British Ability Scales	Pupil	Teacher	11,685
Teacher Questionnaire	Teacher	Teacher	12,755
Pupil Questionnaire	Pupil	Pupil	12,699

The sixteen-year follow-up

The general aim of the sixteen-year follow-up, originally entitled Youthscan UK, was to review the health, educational and social development of the cohort in their mid-teens (see Goodman and Butler (not dated) for full details). Age 16 is an important juncture in the life course. It marks the end of compulsory education and the beginning of the transition into more adult roles and responsibilities.

Of the 16,500 target respondents, 11,622 (70%) cohort members were traced and completed one or more questionnaires. Tracing was undertaken by Local Education Authorities (LEAs) in England and Wales, and their equivalent in Scotland, the Regional Councils (RCs). Independent Schools outside direct control of LEAs/RCS were contacted directly by the research team at Social Statistics Research Unit (SSRU). For those children who could not be traced via LEAs and RCs, attempts were made to locate them through District Health Authorities and Scottish Health Boards. In total, over 13,000 children (78%) were traced.

In addition to self-completion questionnaire completed by the cohort members, data was also collected from parents and teachers. Cohort members were also asked to complete a diary and a series of standardised tests. The school doctor/nurse undertook a medical examination of cohort members. Supplementary questionnaires were distributed to respondents in two packs, a health pack and an education pack. The health pack consisted of five instruments (Table 4.3). The various District Health Authorities coordinated distribution of the packs via health visitors. The health visitor for each traced cohort members delivered the maternal and student self-completion questionnaires and the diary to the family, and undertook the completion of the Parental Interview Form. The Community Medical Officer usually conducted the medical examination at a local health clinic.

Table 4.3 Contents of the Health Pack (16-year follow-up)

Instrument	Respondent	Completed by	Cases
Parental Interview Form	Parent	Health Visitor	9,584
Maternal Self-Completion Form	Mother	Mother	8,993
Student Self-Report Health Questionnaire	Cohort member	Cohort member	6,898
Medical Examination Form	Cohort member	Community Medical Officer/ School Nurse	6,143
Leisure And Activities Diary	Cohort member	Cohort member	7,544
Family Follow-Up	Parent(s)	Parent(s)	7,336

The Parental Interview Forms collected details of the family composition, hospital admissions, current and past health problems, family health and smoking, family finance and the quality of the home living environment. In the Maternal Self-Completion Form mothers were asked about the cohort member's medical history, parent-school contact and relationship, and housing conditions. In addition, the questionnaire also contained the Rutter/Conners Behavioural Scale and the Rutter Malaise Health Inventory.

The cohort member's self-completion form asked further questions about the respondent's health. It also contained questions on self-reported drug use and criminal behaviour.

The medical examination form required a full medical examination to be completed by the Community Medical Officer or School Nurse. In addition, data on the cohort member's physical, mental, educational and emotional problems, health service utilisation, and disabilities were also collected.

Four months after the health pack was sent out, health visitors also delivered a follow-up questionnaire to parents. This collected socio-economic details of the family including the cohort member's qualifications and current employment status. The educational pack was distributed via LEAs and consisted of nine instruments (Table 4.4). The educational test materials consisted of standard vocabulary and spelling tests, and a series of psychometric scales including the GHQ12 (Goldberg, 1970), the Caraloc Locus of Control Scale (Gammage, 1975) and the Malaise Inventory (Rutter, et al., 1970).

The Health Related Behaviour Questionnaire was produced by an external body, the Health Education Authority Schools Health Unit. It covered such topics as self-reported sports activities, TV watching, smoking and pocket money. It also contained the Lawseq Self-Esteem Scale (Lawrence, 1981).

Questions about the number of friends the cohort members had, their sex, the activities undertaken together and their parents' interest and involvement were contained in the "friendship and the outside world" questionnaire. This section also contained questions of health in the past year, antisocial behaviour, and contact and attitudes towards the police.

Table 4.4 Contents of the Education Pack (16-year follow-up)

Instrument	Respondent	Completed by	Cases
Educational Tests	Cohort member	Cohort member	6,003
'Moving On' Questionnaire	Cohort member	Cohort member	4,433
Health Related Behaviour Questionnaire	Cohort member	Cohort member	5,265
'Home and all that' Questionnaire	Cohort member	Cohort member	6,349
'Friends and the outside world' Questionnaire	Cohort member	Cohort member	6,290
'Life and leisure' Questionnaire	Cohort member	Cohort member	6,417
Dietary Diary	Cohort member	Cohort member	4,693
Teacher Questionnaire	Teacher	Teacher	3,816
Head Teacher Questionnaire	Head teacher	Head teacher	N/a

The 'Teacher' and 'Head Teacher' questionnaire focused on education issues, with the teacher reporting on the cohort members' educational abilities and predicted examination grades. Head Teachers provided details of the school environment in which the cohort member was educated, including such aspects as the subjects offered within the school, the school's pastoral care plans, school's academic level and catchment area.

In total, 11,622 respondents completed one or more of the questionnaires described above. This is equivalent to 88% of traced respondents and 70% of the total eligible sample. Response rates for the individual questionnaires are given in tables 4.3 and 4.4. More details of the maximum response rates for respondents who completed two and three questionnaires are provided in Goodman and Butler (undated).

Preliminary examination of the alcohol measures at age 16.

The alcohol measures within the 16-year-old follow-up where located on two questionnaire components; document F (health related behaviour) and document H (friends and the outside world). Both questionnaire components were completed by 5,039 respondents. A further 226 completed section F only, and 1251 completed section H only, giving a total of 6516 respondents who completed a least one of the two sections.

Document F contained measures of the number of drinking days in the previou week [*"If you had an alcoholic drink since this time last week, on how many days did you do so"* (F56)] and the total number of units consumed in the previous week [*"Since this time last week, how much of the following have you drunk? Shandy (pints); Beer including larger (pints); Cider (pints), Wine (glasses), Martini, Cinzano, vermouth, port, sherry, spirits (gin, whiskey, vodka, brandy, Pernod, rum, Bacardi, etc.) (glasses)"* (F57_TOT)]. Examination of F57_TOT revealed that those cases who replied 'no drinking days' at F56 (n=1615) were set to 'not asked-missing'. To construct a valid estimate of the total units consumed over the previous seven days, these cases were recoded to zero (no units consumed) on F57_TOT.

Component H had a more comprehensive set of alcohol questions including measures of frequency [*"In the last 12 months, about how often have you had anything alcoholic to drink?"*](HD1), age of first use [*"Can you tell us how old you were when you started to drink alcohol?"* (HD4.1 - first ever and HD4.2 - first unsupervised)]; days alcohol consumed in previous seven days [*"During the last seven days, which actual days have you had one or more alcoholic drinks?"* (HD5.1 to HD5.8)]; brand preferences [*"Here are some alcoholic drinks. Which of these have you had to drink? {followed by a list of 17 drinks}"*(HD6A.1 to HD6Q.1)]; money spent on alcohol [*"Have you spent any money on alcoholic drinks or buying alcohol in the last seven days? If yes, how much did you spend?"* (HD8 and HD8.1)]; over-consumption [*"Do you think that you drink more than you should?"* (HD15)]; binge drinking [*"Think back over the last two weeks, have you during that time had four or more drinks in a row? If yes, how often did this happen in the last two weeks?"* (HD16.1 and HD16.2)]; and alcohol related problems [*"After drinking have you ever done any of the following?" {List includes activities such as fighting, breaking things, upsetting friends, parents or boyfriend/girlfriend, driving car or not going home}* (HD17.1 to HD17.7) and *"When people have too much to drink they sometimes come into contact with the police; has this ever happened to you?"* (HD18.1)]. It was decided that the 16-year-old sample would be limited to those respondents (N=6516) who had completed either section H or section F, or both. Cases that were missing on both of these two sections (n=5099) were excluded from the analysis as there were insufficient alcohol measures to estimate their drinking patterns.

The twenty-six-year follow-up

The twenty-six-year follow-up survey was conducted between April and September 1996, (full details of this sweep can be found in Despotidou and Shepard (Not dated)). For the first three follow-ups, schools were used as a vehicle for tracking and contacting cohort members. Between 1986 – the end of compulsory education for the cohort members – and 1991 no attempts were made to maintain contact with cohort members. However, with the transfer of the study to the SSRU at the City University in 1991, all respondents for whom a current address was available were contacted via a birthday card posted to their home. This was also used as an opportunity to confirm correct address information, to provide cohort members with feedback on the results of the study and to outline plans for future sweeps of data collection. A special tracing exercise was undertaken in the first half of 1996 to recontact those cohort members for whom address information was not available. This included a mail-out to cohort members by the Driver and Vehicle Licensing Authority, examining Family Health Service records, and extensive use of telephone and other directories. This resulted in tracing of some 13,500 of the original 16,000 respondents. Between April and September 1996 a single questionnaire was mailed out to all respondents where address information was known. Each questionnaire was accompanied by a covering letter and reminder letters were sent out 2-3 weeks after the mail-out of the questionnaire. A second reminder was sent out after a further 3-4 weeks. In the end, 13475 questionnaires in total were mailed out to respondents. Fully completed questionnaires were returned by 8798 respondents (65%). A further 205 respondents (2%) returned partially completed questionnaires, giving a total of 9,003 (67%) responses.

The main focus of the 1996 questionnaire was on contact with the labour market. Details of employment history including number of jobs, periods of unemployment, periods out of the labour force, and full details of any current jobs were collected. The questionnaire also asked about training, qualifications and skills gained since age 16. Other sections included 'relationship marriage and children' and 'health'. The former section covered details of current relationships/marriage, number of children, household composition, and household tenure. The latter section included self-reported health, experiences of medical conditions since age 16, accidents and injuries, disabilities, drinking and smoking habits, and depression symptoms.

METHODOLOGICAL AND PRACTICAL ASPECTS OF SECONDARY ANALYSIS

Secondary analysis is the re-analysis of existing social research data sets. It is now common place that large-scale multipurpose surveys are archived and made available to other social researchers for secondary analysis. The principal benefit of secondary analysis is that it incurs no data collection costs. As such, it offers excellent value for money. In the case of longitudinal research, the cost of collecting data from individuals over an extensive period of time is considerable. Few large-scale longitudinal studies are ever conducted, and the economic viability of those that are relies on considerable secondary analysis being undertaken. Not only does this maximize the research return on the funds invested in the data collection, but also, funders may welcome their initial investment being used to lever additional funding for secondary analysis studies. In a similar way secondary analysis also saves time. It can be used to provide longitudinal answers to research questions without the time needed to collect the data, which in the case of the BCS70 is 26 years. The avoidance of fieldwork costs, however, is not without a price. The secondary analyst has no control over any aspect of data collection including the sample, the data collection mode, and the measures used. They are restricted by the methodological decisions taken by the original research team. The feasibility of any secondary analysis is essentially the trade-off between reduced time and costs on the one hand and the limitations imposed by the data set itself on the other. With large-scale surveys such as the national birth cohort series, this has been borne in mind in the design of each survey sweep. As a result, these studies have been developed to minimise the restrictions or limitations placed on other researchers who may consider using the data.

Key to the success of any secondary analysis study, therefore, is the identification and selection of the data set to be used. It is essential that the quality of the data set be ascertained prior to the analysis. Singleton, Straits and Straits (1993) suggested that secondary analysts reconstruct the process of data collection to ascertain its limitations, possible errors and biases. In particular, as the secondary analyst has no control of the measurement of key concepts within the data set, it is important to ensure that the data set selected includes adequate measures of the key concepts under study, in this case alcohol consumption and related problems.

The utility of the BCS70, in this case, is bolstered by the fact that it contains multiple measures of alcohol consumption within the 16-year follow-up. Even then, however, measures from existing data sets may not reflect current technical developments in the measurement of key concepts. In addition, recent developments in statistical techniques, for example structural equation modelling (SEM), are not well suited to secondary analysis studies. SEM requires multiple observed indicators of key constructs that can then be used to construct latent variable measures (see Kline, 2004; Loehlin, 2004). However, older longitudinal studies tended to be designed before the advent of SEM technologies. As a result they rarely contain multiple measures of key constructs limiting the application of full SEM procedures. While the BCS70 contained multiple measures of alcohol consumption, thus permitting latent variable modelling, it did not contain multiple measures of other key indicators.

AGE, PERIOD AND COHORT EFFECTS

Cohort studies are the principle technique for the study of age effects, that is changes in social processes primarily due to ageing, maturation and development (Rutter, 1988). However other effects, in particular period and cohort effects, may influence responses. Cohort studies are prone to these potential sources of bias.

Period effects are those attributable to the particular period or historical context in which the cohort grew up. As can be seen from the historical trends in alcohol use presented in the previous chapter, the consumption of alcohol varies from one period to another. As a result, being born in a particular period, for example the 1960s will influence your alcohol consumption to a degree. People living during this period were likely to consume more alcohol than those living during the war years. With single cohort studies such as the BCS70, all cohort members are born within the space of one week. Therefore, their life experiences will be shaped by the period in which they grew up – the 70s, 80s and 90s. It is possible that these experiences, and hence the findings from such studies, are not fully generalisable to people who grew up in other periods. Because of the time it takes to complete a cohort study, data used to make inferences about current adolescent development may be some 10 to 15 years old. It may be the case that the period in which the data was collected differs from the period to which the results will be applied.

Cohort effects may further confound age effects under study within longitudinal cohort studies. Cohort effects can be conceptualised as characteristics of a particular cohort that influence the outcome variable under study, in this case alcohol use, independent of age or period effects. One of the most studied cohort effects is the Easterlin Cohort Size Hypothesis (Easterlin, 1987), which suggests that the size of a cohort relative to the size of its parent's cohort is related to social problems amongst the cohort. Put another way, large cohorts (the product of high birth rates) should have higher levels of alcohol consumption than smaller cohorts (the product of low birth rates), relative to the size of their parent's cohort. Menard & Huizinga (1989) found the existence of Easterlin cohort effects in relation to alcohol use. Cohort size was found to be associated with the frequency of drinking amongst cohort members. They estimated that in the USA a reduction in the absolute cohort size of about 100,000 birth was associated with a reduction in alcohol prevalence of around 3.6%.

Given the existence of period and cohort effects, it is important that the findings from a single cohort study are treated with care. However, this does not mean that cohort studies need to be endlessly repeated with each new generation of young people. It is possible to use cross-sectional data to assess the degree to which the causal processes identified within a single cohort study generalise to other cohorts or periods. This is what Rutter (1994a) terms the 'test of non-replication'. The causal relationships between environmental risk factors and developmental outcome observed within a longitudinal cohort study can be used to predict the nature of the causal relationship in other cohorts. If the predicted relationship between the variables under study is also observed in the cross-sectional data, while not a full test of the causal mechanisms, it does lend empirical support to the conclusion that the causal mechanisms may be applicable to the new cohort. If the predicted relationship is not observed in the cross-sectional data this may indicate that the causal mechanisms are misspecified, and that the misspecification may be due to period or cohort effects.

It must be recognised when evaluating the findings from this study that the adult outcome data is also now over 10 years old. The adolescent period observed in the BCS70 was some 20 years ago. This is undoubtedly a major limitation of the work. However, in defence of the analysis, The BCS70 is the most "recent" UK birth cohort study with adult outcomes in existence, and will continue to be so until the children of the millennium cohort study reach age 26 (something that will not occur for a further twenty years). No other UK study can be used to address the types of research questions posed in this study. While US and New Zealand studies provide comparable data from younger cohorts there is limited evidence that the findings from these studies are directly transferable to the UK population. Notwithstanding these advantages, the potential cohort effects surrounding the BCS70 must be treated seriously.

ATTRITION AND SAMPLE REPRESENTATIVENESS

Attrition, or the failure to maintain contact with respondents over time, is a major problem for longitudinal surveys such as the BCS70, and one of the principal sources of survey error. However, missing data, whether from attrition or from some other source, is not always a methodological problem. If the missing data is missing at random the level of bias introduced maybe limited, or at least overcome by the use of statistical procedures (see Schafer & Graham, 2002). However, in most cases attrition is not random but systematic; that is to say, the rate of attrition is not constant across all social groups. Certain subpopulations, for example young males, are more likely not to respond to a postal questionnaire than other populations. If those populations also have a differential level of alcohol use, attrition can lead to serious biases occurring. It is therefore appropriate to assess the level of bias introduced into the BCS70 by attrition, in particular the degree to which subsequent BCS70 sweeps are a representative sample of the total age cohort from which they are drawn.

Assessing the representativeness of the BCS70 data is complex for two main reasons. Firstly, each sweep of the BCS70 is comprised of a series of individual postal questionnaires, supplemented by medical assessments and contributions from different professions (for example, Teachers). Each of these survey components has a different response rate, and therefore a different level of missing data. Many of the key items on which comparisons could be made, for example gender, ethnicity and social class, are repeated on a range of the survey components. As a result, multiple versions of key variables exist, each with a different level of missing data. Multiple comparisons with the same variables are possible, each of which could yield a slightly different result. While 11,622 respondents completed at least one questionnaire, the highest number who completed a single questionnaire component was 9,584 for the parental questionnaire. It

71

was decided, therefore, to use this questionnaire component, where possible, as the base comparison of the component sections of the full 16-year-old follow-up data. Secondly, differences between the 16 or 26-year follow-up and earlier data sweeps may be due to real change having occurred in time-variant indicators such as family structure and household income. As the birth data sweep represents the most complete survey, it provides the benchmark against which all subsequent data sweeps should be compared. However, for the later sweeps there could be either a 16-year gap or a 26-year gap between the data sweeps. It is difficult then to distinguish between real change and measure bias due to attrition. However, comparisons between the survey sweeps on time-invariant variables such as gender, should give an indication of how far the later sweeps have deviated from the full birth cohort.

Comparisons between the 16-year-old follow up and both the birth and 10-year-old follow-ups are presented in Goodman and Butler (not dated). In general the 16-year-old follow-up has fewer males, and households where the father is in social class III (manual) to V than either the birth or 10-year-old follow-up. These differences exist across all survey items but are lowest for section O (parent's interview form).

16-year-old full sample – alcohol sample comparison

These differences are further exacerbated by the fact that not all respondents in the 16-year-old follow-up completed either one or both of the sections containing the alcohol questions. Table 4.5 compares the restricted 16-year-old alcohol sample (completed either section F or section H) with the full 16-year old-sample (completed section O). Again we see an under representation of boys and respondents from poorer family backgrounds. There are also fewer replies from stepparent and foster parents within the restricted alcohol sample. Mothers of young people who completed the alcohol questions are also less likely to smoke than those within the larger 16-year-old cohort.

Table 4.5 Response biases between the 16 year old full and alcohol samples

		Full sample, %	Alcohol sample, %	Relative bias[1]
Gender	Male	50.1	42.8	17.0
	Female	49.9	57.2	-12.8
Ethnicity	White	97.7	98.3	-0.6
	Black	0.8	0.6	33.3
	Asian	2.4	2.6	-7.7
	Other	0.9	0.9	0.0
Relationship to	Natural mother	95.3	96.0	-0.7
mother figure	Adoptive/foster	1.7	1.6	6.3
	Stepmother	1.0	0.7	42.9
	Other	2.0	1.7	17.6
Relationship to	Natural father	82.4	84.8	-2.8
father figure	Adoptive/foster	2.5	2.3	8.7
	Stepfather	6.7	5.8	15.5
	Other	8.4	7.1	18.3
Income	<£2600	2.5	1.8	38.9
	£2600-£5199	14.3	12.3	16.3
	£5200-£7799	14.0	13.7	2.2
	£7800-£10399	14.5	14.5	0.0
	£10400-£12999	11.6	11.6	0.0
	£13000-£15599	9.2	10.6	-13.2
	£15600-£18199	5.9	6.4	-7.8
	£18200-£20799	3.6	4.0	-10.0
	£20800-£23399	3.2	3.5	-8.6
	£23400-£25999	1.5	1.8	-16.7
	>£26000	3.7	4.3	-13.9
	Refused	15.9	15.4	3.2
House type	House	94.4	95.2	-0.8
	Flat	3.8	3.4	11.8
	Room	0.5	0.5	0.0
	Mobile home	0.2	0.2	0.0
	Other	1.1	0.8	37.5
House ownership	Yes	18.4	19.8	-7.1
	No	81.6	80.2	1.7

Notes.1. Relative bias = ((Full sample % - Alcohol sample %) / Alcohol sample %)*100. A negative value indicates an over-representation and a positive value an under-representation within the alcohol sample.

Significant tests were not performed on the response biases as the large sample sizes involved would ensure that even very small differences between the samples are significant. In this case statistical significance is of limited value in determining the substantive significance of the differences presented. Examination of the raw percentage biases, together with consideration of the prevalence of the characteristics being compared (small differences between rare characteristics can yield large percentage biases), should give a broad indication of the relative importance of the biases and the extent to which they need to be factored into subsequent analysis.

16 – 26-year-old sweeps comparison

Standard response bias calculations for the 26-year-old follow-up were completed by the SSRU research team at City University, London (see Despotidou & Shepard (not dated) for full details). For a range of socio-economic, educational, and social variables the distribution within the 1996 sample was compared with that recorded within the previous sweeps. Overall, the 1996 sample is a good representation of the target population. However, comparing the 1996 sweep with the original birth sweep in 1970, it can be seen that the 1996 sample is under-representative of people whose mother or father was born outside of the UK. Here, the differences between the achieved 1996 sample and the target 1970 sample are 1.3 percentage points and 1.6 percentage points respectively, equating to an under-representation bias of -16% and -18%. The 1996 sample also under represents people whose father was unemployed in 1970 (0.5 percentage points difference, bias -17%) who were raised by single mothers (0.6 percentage points difference, bias -15%) and who were born to teenage mothers (0.8 percentage points difference, bias 9%). In contrast the 1996 sweep over-represents individual whose mother completed education aged less than 15 (0.4 percentage points difference, bias +7%).

Similar differences can be detected when the 1996 follow-up is compared to the 1986 follow-up. Children born outside of the UK (0.3 percentage points difference; 13.04% bias), whose family are on income support (1.6 percentage points difference; 14.29% bias), whose father is manual social class (1.4 percentage points difference; 2.86% bias), and who has a disability (1.9 percentage points difference, 20.00% bias) are under-represented in the 1996 achieved sample.

There appears to be a response bias in relation to academic ability. Young people who had impaired reading ability in 1986 (3.2 percentage points difference, bias – 39.45%) were under-represented in the 1996 sample, while children who were assessed as top of the academic ability range were over represented (0.8 percentage points difference; 14.81% bias). Also children who had more than four separate addresses between 1980 and 1986 were under-represented (0.3 percentage points difference; 17.65% bias). This is a consequence of the postal survey data collection mode used in the 1996 follow-up.

There was also a small family structure bias apparent in the data. Children who had been 'in care' (0.3 percentage points difference; 23.08% bias) and children who wanted to leave home as soon as possible in 1986 (0.6 percentage points difference; 11.54% bias) were under-represented.

STRATEGIES TO ADDRESS MISSING DATA

To address the missing data contained within the BCS70, four separate missing data techniques were employed. These included: a) list-wise deletion of cases; b) the use of the EM algorithm for estimating unbiased maximum likelihood latent class parameters; c) the use of multiple imputation for models containing covariates, and d) the use of post-hoc statistical control for known sample non-response biases.

To date, the standard procedure for dealing with missing data has been to simply ignore cases with missing data, either through *pairwise* or *casewise* deletion. However, such procedures can lead to serious biases occurring (see Little & Rubin, 1987). With longitudinal studies involving repeated measures, the loss of cases due to missing values can quickly accumulate across multiple time points to a degree that may seriously compromise the viability of the research.

For those cases that did not contain responses to at least one or more of the teenage alcohol questions, listwise deletion was employed and these cases were excluded from the analysis. Given the centrality of the alcohol measures it was decided that respondents should have at least one alcohol indicator. Given the biases inherent in this approach, the use of listwise deletion was kept to a minimum. IT is also important to recognise that this is not standard listwise deletion, as cases with missing alcohol indicators were included if they had at least partial alcohol data (one of the four core indicators use – see chapter 5). Standard listwise would remove all cases with any missing data.

The software programme LEM was then used to estimate the latent class models with the partial alcohol data (see chapter 5 of full details). At the time these models were constructed, LEM offered greater functionality than other latent class programs, such as Mplus or WinLTA. In particular, LEM offered the opportunity to estimate models with random starting values and to estimate non-traditional models (i.e. model with local dependence). LEM also had specific procedures for dealing with missing data on the latent class indicators. The maximum likelihood estimates of the model parameters were computed in LEM by means of the Expectation Maximisation (EM) algorithm that successfully handles incomplete categorical data (Dempster, Laird & Rubin, 1977; Vermunt, 1997c).

The weakness of the EM algorithm is that it cannot handle missing data on model covariates. Fortunately, more recent versions of common statistical packages such as Mplus have included facilities to utilise "multiple imputation" (MI), which does facilitate the analysis of model where missing data is continued within the covariates (Rubin, 1987; Schafer, 1997; Schafer & Olsen, 1998). MI has been shown to reduce the bias associated with missing data compared to either listwise or casewise deletion (Schafer, 1997; Schafer & Graham, 2002). MI involves three steps. The first step is imputation. Here an EM algorithm is used to fill in the missing values with plausible values. The full available data (i.e. the non-missing data) is used to estimate the plausible values and the user can place specific limits on the values that can be estimated (range, decimal points etc.). This results in a reasonable approximation of the data set were it fully completed by everyone. To increase the accuracy of the imputations, it is replicated several times generating several imputed (full) datasets. In the analysis undertaken here, ten data sets were imputed for each analysis. While it is possible do undertaken valid MI with a little as three imputations (Rubin, 1987), ten were used due to the extent of missingness across the original BCS70 data set.

The next stage in MI is data analysis. The statistical model used, be it multiple or logistic regression, is estimated across each of the multiple data sets separately. In this case this results in ten sets of parameter estimates and standard errors.

The final stage in MI is to average the 10 sets of parameter estimates and standard errors across the imputed runs to produce a single overall set of estimates and associated standard errors. Rubin (1987) produced the rules for this averaging. For parameters estimates, the final overall estimate is simply the average of the 10 individual estimates. The standard errors, according to Rubin's rules, are computed using the average of the squared standard errors over the 10 datasets, and the between parameter estimate variation (Muthén & Muthén, 1998-2005b).

Here, the ten independently imputed datasets were constructed using the programme NORM (Schafer, 2000). The regression models were then estimated in Mplus using the IMPUTATION option (Muthén & Muthén, 1998-2005a; Muthén & Muthén, 1998-2005b). In the analysis of the adult outcomes (chapter 8) the large number of variables included within the NORM model and the high level of missingness, meant that a ridge prior (hyperparameter = 250) was required to stabilise the parameter estimation.

Finally, where biases are known to exist (for example gender) "control variables" were entered into regression models to provide statistical control for the biased factor. A similar procedure is used for modelling sample weights in complex survey designs (artificially induced sample biases). If the factor is significant, then the bias is controlled for within the model (and suitable adjustments are made to all other parameter estimates). If the factor is not significant then the biases can be considered to have little impact on the outcome measure and can be ignored.

SUMMARY

In summary, the BCS70 provides a highly valuable and important data resource for social science secondary analysis. A wide range of social, behavioural, educational and medical data is collected. No other more recent UK study can match the breadth of data collected over such a period of time (26 years). The data represents a powerful tool for examining the longitudinal developmental research questions posed earlier. While the study has clear and identifiable methodological weaknesses, in particular its period effect and level of attrition, steps can be taken to minimise the potential biases that could be introduced into the conclusion of the study from these two sources. These steps will

77

include the use of state of the art missing data techniques and careful consideration of the results of the study.

5 THE IDENTIFICATION OF HAZARDOUS DRINKING PATTERNS AT 16: A LATENT CLASS ANALYSIS

Using the multiple indicators of alcohol consumption contained within the BCS70 16-year-old sweep, this chapter presents a new typology of adolescent drinking patterns. To begin, it reviews the methodological issues surrounding the identification and classification of adolescent drinking behaviour. It introduces latent class analysis, a multivariate categorical data analysis procedure that addresses some of the outstanding concerns with more traditional methods. The results of the latent class model are presented, together with an extended examination of the validity of the typology created.

METHODOLOGICAL ISSUES

The assessment of alcohol consumption and the identification of problematic, abusive or hazardous drinking patterns amongst young people is a complex and difficult task (see Carroll 1995; Meyers et al., 1999). The first challenge relates to the fact that hazardous drinking behaviours are not directly observable within the confines of most research studies, that is, the researcher cannot scrutinize the young person drinking when they are out drinking with their friends. Therefore, alcohol consumption is usually assessed thorough indirect methods, typically retrospective self-report methods. As such, it is subject to standard measurement error resulting from deliberate over-reporting and under-reporting, memory errors, and other responses errors (Dawson, 2003; Del Boca, & Darkes, 2003; Percy, McAlister, Higgins, McCrystal, & Thornton, 2005). Research data on alcohol consumption, therefore, is subject, to varying degrees, to measurement error.

A second problem is caused by the complexity of the behaviour itself. It is possible to identify a number of distinct behavioural dimensions to alcohol consumption patterns (Dawson & Room, 2000; Room, 2000). These include, but are not limited to the following dimensions:

- The frequency of drinking;
- The quantity consumed (which together with frequency can be used to estimate total volume);
- The experience of alcohol related health and social problems;
- Duration of use;
- Temporal variability in drinking;
- Episodes of heavy drinking;
- The specific drinking repertoires favoured by the individual;
- The function of use and its cultural and social meaning;
- The social context of the drinking episode itself.

Using factor analysis, Bailey and Rachal (1993) identified three unique dimensions to problem drinking; the level of use (which is a combination of quantity and quality), problems related to use, and early symptoms of dependence. Kilty (1990) was able to operationalise a range of specific drinking 'styles' or 'situations' for young people, ranging from ceremonial /familial drinking, to drinking to alter one's mood. These styles were related to age at first consumption, quantity-frequency and alcohol related problems.

The multidimensional nature of alcohol consumption necessitates the use of a range of distinct measures, each attempting to observe one or more aspects of the behaviour. While the application of multiple measures of alcohol use within most research is relatively straightforward, it does, however, create problems in relation to the analysis of the data obtained from respondents. With multiple observations of the phenomenon, that is, multiple variables within the data-set, it can be difficult to identify meaningful patterns or relationships amongst the variables, or more specifically, to identify the relationship between the observed dimensions of drinking behaviour and the underlying unobserved phenomenon itself. In this situation there is a clear need to summarise the various dimensions of alcohol consumption, which are themselves often collinear, in a meaningful way that says something about the patterns of drinking that young people engage in, with as little loss of information as possible.

The heterogeneity of the behaviour under study is a further related issue. Within any given population of young people there will be a wide variation in drinking behaviours, and therefore wide variations in any behavioural dimensions observed. Most conceptualisations of problem drinking behaviours assume a basic single underlying continuum along which individuals can be placed or grouped, with one extreme consisting of limited users and the other consisting of individuals with a high dependence on alcohol (see Edwards, 1986; Heather and Roberston, 1984; Orford, 2001; Sanchez-Craig, 1986). What is central to this notion of a continuum is that the extreme ends of the spectrum are not fundamentally distinct from individuals on other parts of the continuum. Therefore, all individuals share, depending on the theoretical formulation, some degree of propensity to alcohol dependence, degree of appetite for alcohol, or possibility of learning problem-drinking behaviours. This poses a problem of how to deal with the heterogeneity in drinking behaviour that exists (for example variations in frequency, quantity and intensity of consumption), and how this heterogeneity relates to the proposed underlying continuum. This issue is not unique to adolescent drinking and has been identified in relation to other adolescent problem behaviours (see Rutter, 2001).

The traditional way in which various dimensional measures were combined to generate a single measure of an underlying continuum was through a simple summation or multiplication rule. Here, the scores on the particular measures used, for example the frequency of consumption, the quantity of alcohol used, the number of problems experienced, would be added together either in a raw or in an adjusted form (standardised) to produce an overall score. Arbitrary cut-off scores can then be applied to categorise individuals into various groups for subsequent analysis. Major diagnostic screening instruments tend to favour this approach to scoring. For example, the Alcohol Use Disorders Identification Test (AUDIT) (Bador, Higgins-Biddle, Saunders & Monteiro, 2001) employs a summation rule to aggregate the scores across 10 items assessing three domains (hazardous alcohol use, dependence symptoms, and harmful alcohol use). The various individual items include measures of the quantity and frequency of drinking, frequency of heavy drinking, impaired control over drinking, and drinking related problems and injuries. Total scores above a certain cut-off are recommended as indicative of hazardous and harmful drinking, and possibly dependency. Analysis of the individual subscales can be used to gain further insights into individual drinking practices. Other widely used scales such as the Michigan

Alcohol Screening Test (Pogorny, Miller & Kaplan, 1972), the Severity of Alcohol Dependency Questionnaire (Stockwell, Murphy & Hodgson 1983), Short Alcohol Dependency Data (Davidson & Raistrick, 1986) all employ similar data aggregation methods.

In the typology employed by Windle (1996) four of the five categories were based on arbitrary cut-offs on a standard multiplicative quantity-frequency measure. Here the number of drinks usually consumed when drinking (assessed over the previous 30 days) is multiplied by the usual number of days in which drinks are consumed over the previous 30 days, to give an average number of drinks consumed. For example moderate drinkers were defined as consuming greater or equal to 10 'standard' drinks, but less than 45 drinks, in the previous 30 days. Problem drinker category was defined as drinking above a certain frequency level (45 drinks in the previous 30 days) whilst also reporting alcohol related problems (5 or more).

While such scales demonstrate good validity and reliability (see Bador et al., 2001; Windle, 1996, Davidson, 1987) there are several technical weakness inherent in these aggregation methods. First, in many cases an equal weight is given to all items and dimensions. High scores on each item contribute the same value to the overall score irrespective of what the item is assessing. Within the AUDIT scale, for example, all items are scored on a 0-4 scale. Therefore a high score, or a low score, on the 'frequency of heavy drinking' item and the 'guilt after drinking' item, each contributes the same value to the overall assessment score. This would imply that each are equally important in the overall assessment of problem drinking. However, this may not be the case as some of the multiple dimensions that have been promoted as indicators of problem drinking may be more influential than others are and therefore should be given greater weight within the scale.

The second related problem with additive or multiplicative scales is that they are based on the assumption that the values recorded are real interval level values, when in many cases they are ordinal values. Even when information with a reasonably normal underlying distribution is collected, for example the number of drinks consumed, it is often recorded as a category (for example, 3-4 drinks) rather than as a normal value. Therefore, unit increases between and across variables are treated as being equal when in fact they are rarely so. As each variable contributes an equal weight to the overall scale score, a unit increase in feelings of guilt about drinking - from monthly (2) to weekly (3) – is equivalent within the summation or multiplicative rule to a unit increase in the frequency of heavy drinking – from never (0) to less than monthly (1). This is clearly not the case.

Unit increases within particular items may also not be equal, but may be treated as so for convenience. Again using the AUDIT as an example, an increase in the quantity of alcohol consumed from 3-4 drinks (score of 1) to 5-6 (score of 2) drinks produces a similar unit increase in this measure as does an increase in drinking from 5-6 drinks (score of 2) to 7-9 drinks (score of 3). However, the first spans a range of 4 drinks while the second spans an increase of up to 5 drinks. While this may be considered a rather small inconsistency in a unit increase, it is an inconsistency nonetheless.

Another approach is based on the assumption that the absence or presence of one or two key defining features can identify various adolescent drinking patterns. In the scale employed by Steinhausen and Winkler Metske (2003), problem drinkers were defined by drinking when lonely and drinking when they felt bad or had problems. In comparison, heavy drinkers were those who drank to get drunk, but who did not show the two problem drinking characteristics. This modified Guttman approach does appear to distinguish various adolescent drinking patterns with high concurrent validity, however, the loss of information is considerable. For example, in the Steinhauser and Winkler Metske (2003) study, data was collected on the lifetime use, the frequency of consumption, the frequency of drunkenness, and adverse social and health consequences. However, none of these were used to identify the drinking patterns, rather these were based on responses to seven additional items. Inconsistencies between the additional alcohol measures and the key indicator were not resolved with this approach. For example, 60% of the problem drinkers reported having been drunk less that four times in their lifetimes.

Various multivariate statistical methods have been employed to handle the multidimensionality in adolescent drinking patterns. Bailey and Rachal (1993) used factor analysis to reduce 28 alcohol measures into three unique dimensions of problem drinking that vary in level of severity across young people. As the authors note, before these continuous factors would be of practical use within the alcohol field they would need to be combined into a meaningful categories, that is, the application of arbitrary cut-off scores. Rehm and Gmel (2000) applied two simple techniques (dummy variables and interaction terms) to the aggregation of various alcohol dimensions within regression models. While these are valuable solutions to a specific statistical problem they have limited application outside of basic regression modelling, and when applied to more than two alcohol dimensions would produce results that were difficult to interpret.

The primary objective of the analysis presented in this chapter is to utilise multiple measures of adolescent drinking to construct a new typology of specific drinking profiles to which individuals can be assigned. In addition, this chapter will examine the demographical characteristics of the various drinking groups identified and will examine the construct validity of the typology generated.

The following chapter will then assess the relationship between the various drinking patterns contained within the typology and key social and behavioural characteristics also observed at age 16. Further analyses will then examine the precursors or antecedents that may shape the development of these observed drinking patterns at age 16 (chapter 7) and the extent to which these drinking patterns precede later problem drinking in adulthood (chapter 8).

Examining the relationship between the developed typology and other assessments of drinking behaviour gives an assessment of the convergent validity of the typology. It is therefore hypothesised that the typology should distinguish individuals on related, but independent, alcohol measures contained within the BCS70. These include the number of days on which alcohol was consumed in the previous seven days and the amount of money spent on alcohol in the last seven days.

Another key indicator of drinking behaviour is age of onset. Studies have consistently shown that problem drinkers have an earlier age of drinking onset than more social drinkers (DeWit, Adlaf, Offord, Ogborne, 2000; Fergusson, Horwood & Lynskey, 1995; Grant, Stinson & Harford, 2001; Gruber, DiClemente, Anderson & Lodico, 1996; Robins & Przybeck, 1985). While the studies listed above examine age of onset and drinking outcomes in adulthood, it is assumed that a similar relationship will be observed at age 16, although the strength of the association may not be as great as that which may be observed at a later (adult) follow-up. For example, Costello, Erkanli, Federman, and Angold (1999) detected a difference in age of onset between adolescents with and without alcohol abuse or dependence, but the difference was not statistically significant.

The assumption is that early onset marks a particular drinking pathway that is associated with a problem outcome in adulthood; one that is marked by a relatively continuous 'growth' in problematic drinking from onset to adulthood. If the pathway is assessed at an earlier time point, the differentiation between the problem and social drinking pathways on key dimensions of drinking behaviour may be less than at adulthood. However, the latent class typology should have sufficient validity to distinguish between individuals with different age of drinking onset.

METHOD
Latent Class Analysis

Latent class analysis (LCA) is an example of a class of statistical models known as latent structure models that include other specific techniques such as factor analysis, latent profile and latent trait models (see Bartholomew & Knott, 1999; Clogg, 1995; Lazarsfeld & Henry, 1968; for overviews of latent structure models and latent class models). Two core assumptions underpin LCA. The first is that is that the covariation observed between manifest variables arises because of their common association with a single latent characteristic that is not observed directly within the study. The second is that the latent characteristic, along which members of the population can be placed, is best represented by a categorical variable consisting of a number of discrete, but usually unknown, categories. These categories are referred to as 'latent classes'. Examination of the covariation patterns that exist between the manifest variables can, therefore, be used to make inferences about a respondent's position on the latent variable under study. While the related technique of factor analysis requires interval level observed variables and assumes an interval level latent variable, LCA models can be constructed with categorical level observed data and assumes a categorical latent variable.

When applied to this situation, it is assumed that the manifest variables contained within the study, that is, the various alcohol measures used, are a subset of all possible indicators of the latent variable (i.e. the full range of possible rating scales that could be developed to assess the known dimensions of drinking behaviour). Figure 5.1 presents a graphical representation of this latent class model. Here, adolescent drinking pattern is the unobserved latent behaviour. This behaviour is conceptualised as consisting of an unknown number of discrete categories of different drinking patterns (classes). These patterns give rise to the individual responses observed in the manifest variables, of which in this case there are four.

Figure 5.1: Basic latent class model

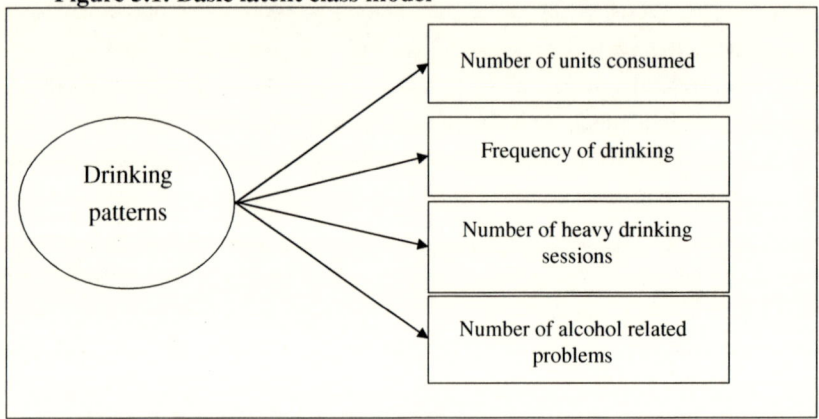

The latent classes generated by LCA are discrete and internally homogenous. Each respondent belongs to one and only one class, and the members of each class have a similar probability of reporting any of the possible combinations of scores on the observed variables. Each individual will have a probability of giving a particular score on each of the scales that is conditional on the latent class they belong to and members of the same class have similar conditional probabilities relative to the observed variables. By way of example, each respondent will have a probability of having no alcohol related problems, and for members of the same class this conditional probability will be the same. While the observed variables are correlated, it is assumed within LCA that this correlation is totally explained by the latent variable, or in other words, when the latent variable is controlled for, the correlation between the manifest variables will disappear (Bollen, 2002; Uebersax, 2000a). This is known as 'local independence' amongst the manifest variables. In relation to drinking behaviour, for this assumption to be met, the correlation between the frequency and the quantity of alcohol consumption arises because both are correlated with a latent variable that comprises a number of discrete drinking patterns. If this is taken into account there is no independent correlation between the two measures. Within general LCA models it is also assumed that any missing data within the manifest variables is either missing completely at random (MCAR) or missing at random (MAR).

The object of LCA, therefore, is to estimate:

- The optimum number of latent classes that explain the observed response pattern frequencies;
- The proportion of the population that belong to each identified latent class;
- The conditional probability of an individual who belongs to a particular latent class having a certain set of survey responses, known as a response pattern, based on the observed covariation between the manifest variables.

The output of LCA is two parameters. The first, the gamma parameter denoted by γ, represents the proportion of the population that is expected to be members of a particular latent class. The second parameter estimated, the rho parameter denoted by ρ, represents the probability of a respondent reporting a particular response dependant on the particular class they belong to.

The classical formulation of an unrestricted LCA model is given by:

$$P(Y) = \sum_{x=1}^{X} \gamma_x \prod_{q=1}^{Q} \rho$$

Where Y is the response pattern *a,b,c,d* on Q manifest variables (in this case q=1....4). X is the number of latent classes (x=1....X), γ_x is the probability of membership of latent class x - also referred to as a latent probability - and ρ is a matrix of $\rho_{a|x}$ $\rho_{b|x}$ $\rho_{c|x}$ $\rho_{d|x}$ probabilities for each *a,b,c,d* response condition on *x* class membership – also referred to as the conditional response probability, that is, $\rho_{a|x}$ is the probability for response *a* to item 1 conditional on membership of latent class *x*, and $\rho_{b|x}$ is the probability for response *b* to item 2 conditional on membership of latent class *x*). LCA estimates the gamma parameter for each latent class specified in the model, and a rho parameter for each response observed conditional on an assumed class membership. Therefore, the gamma parameters provide a link between respondents and latent classes, while rho describes the relationship between latent classes and the various response patterns observed. Alternative formulations of LCA, based on log linear analysis, are possible (Clogg, 1995: Hagenaars, 1993).

EM Algorithm

LEM employs a variant of standard Expectation- Maximisation (E-M) algorithm (Dempster, Laird & Rubin, 1977) for obtaining the maximum likelihood estimates of the model parameters with partially missing data (Vermunt, 1997b). The E-M algorithm is a two stage iterative process. In the first stage (Expectation) the missing data is estimated using the available data and initial starting values for the parameter estimates (either those provided by the researcher or those calculated at an earlier iteration stage). The completed data is then used in the second stage (Maximisation) to re-estimate the parameters. The parameters can then be fed into the next E stage. This iterative process is continued until the improvements gained by further iterations is deemed to be fall below some pre-set convergence criteria or a specific number of iterations has been achieved (usually 5000).

The E-M algorithm has two principal weaknesses. The first is that the E-M procedure does not always converge on the global maximum solution, that is, the single largest log likelihood, rather it may converge on one or more local maximum solutions. The principal solution to the problem of local maximum is to use multiple starting points in the E-M algorithm, or what Croon (1990) refers to as the brute force technique. If at least five runs, using random start values, converge on a single solution it can be accepted as the global solution (Uebersax 2000b).

The second weakness is that the E-M algorithm does not produce standard errors making it impossible to judge the precision of the parameter estimates. It is possible to use multiple imputation techniques to construct standard errors for LCA models (see Hyatt, Collins & Schafer, 1999) but these are not offered within LEM. As LCA is used here as a method for data reduction, rather than as a method for testing specific hypotheses, the lack of standard errors is less of a concern.

Respondents

The data used in this analysis is drawn from the 16-year-old follow-up (see chapter 4). The alcohol consumption measures were contained within the 'health related behaviour' questionnaire (n=5,265) and the 'friends and outside world' questionnaire (n=6,290). A total of 6,516 respondents completed one or both sections, therefore providing at least some alcohol data. Of these the majority completed both questionnaires (5,039), a further 226 completed the health behaviour questionnaire only and 1,251 completed the friends and outside world questionnaire only.

Alcohol use measures

At age 16, respondents were asked a range of questions about their drinking behaviour. From these, the following four alcohol use measures were constructed:

1. UNIT - *The number of units consumed in the previous week* (coded as a three category variable; 1 = none, 2 = 1-8 units, 3 = 9 units or more). In a series of questions respondents were asked to state the number of pints of shandy, pints of beer (including larger), pints of cider, glasses of wine, glasses of Martini, Cinzano, vermouth, port or sherry and measures of spirits they drank in the last week. The responses were converted to units and totalled across the various drinks to give a measure of the quantity of alcohol consumed.

2. FREQ - *Frequency of alcohol consumption in last 12 months* (coded as a three category variable; 1 = never, 2 = monthly or less frequently, 3 = weekly or more frequent). Respondents were asked how often had they anything alcoholic to drink in the previous twelve months. Seven answer codes were permitted including: 'I never drink', I drink only on special occasions', 'Once a month', 'About once a week', '2 to 3 times a week', '4 or 5 times a week' and 'Every day/most days'. These categories were collapsed into the three shown above.

3. PROB - *The number of alcohol related problems ever encountered* (coded as a three category variable; 1 = none, 2 = one, 3 = two or more problems). Respondents were asked whether they had ever done any of the following things after drinking alcohol: got into an argument or fight; got involved in breaking things; upset your boy/girlfriend; upset your friends; driven a car or a motorbike; upset your parents; thought it was better not to go home. In addition, respondents were also asked whether they had ever come into contact with the police when they had had too much to drink. The numbers of different problem-type experiences were added and categorised. The frequency of experiences of individual types of problem (for example, numerous fights) was not taken into account, rather, just the number of specific problem-types experienced were recorded and summed.

4. BINGE - *The number of heavy drinking episodes in the last two weeks* (coded as a three category variable; 1 = none, 2 = one or two times, 3 = three times or more). Respondents were asked whether they had consumed four or more drinks in a row during the previous two weeks, and if so, how many times this happened (once, twice, 3-5 times, 6-9 times or 10 times or more). These categories were recoded into three, as outlined above.

Validity measures

Age of first use: Two age of onset measures are constructed. The first is the self-reported age when alcohol was first consumed and the second is the self-reported age when alcohol was first consumed with friends, other than at special occasions. These two measures can be used to distinguish between those that were introduced to alcohol by their parents at an early age, but within a very controlled environment, and those that used alcohol in an uncontrolled way from an early age. The latter is more likely to be associated with drinking leading to intoxication. To achieve this distinction the two measures were combined to classify respondents into one of four categories (a) early supervised drinking but late unsupervised, (b) early unsupervised and unsupervised drinking, (c) late onset of supervised and unsupervised, and (d) never drank alcohol. Age 11 and age 13 were taken as the cut-offs for the respective measures. Children who drank alcohol at age 11 or before and who drank alcohol with friends at age 13 or before would be classified as category b.

Drinking days: Young people were asked to specify the number of days in which they consumed alcohol in the previous seven days. Respondents were also asked to specify on which actual days alcohol was consumed.

Spending on alcohol: The young people were asked to report the amount of money they spent on alcohol over the previous seven days. To avoid gratuitous over-reporting (resulting in large influential outliers), or errors occurring due to misplaced decimal points, alcohol spending was capped at £50. Values reported over this cap were recoded down to this upper maximum.

Brand preferences: Cohort members were presented with a predefined list of alcoholic beverages, from which they had to specify those which they never drank, sometimes drank and usually drank. The list was comprehensive covering 17 different drinks, ranging from larger and vodka to specific brands such as Cinzano and Bacardi.

Attitude to alcohol: Respondents are asked about their agreement with 17 alcohol related statement such as 'drinking makes you more at ease'. Responses were scored on a three point likert scale (agree fully/agree partly/disagree). Five of the 17 items are negative statements, such as 'drinking is bad for your health' and were therefore reverse recoded. A total attitude to alcohol score was calculated by summing the individual scores across the 12 positive items and the 5 reverse recoded negative items.

Reasons for drinking: Respondents who drank alcohol in the previous 12 months were presented with seven reasons why young people may drink alcohol. The list included both social reasons ('I drink to be sociable') and reasons more indicative of problematic drinking practices ('it helps me forget my problems').

Frequency of drinking more than they should: The young people were asked to specify how frequently that they thought they drank more alcohol than they should have. Response options included: don't drink alcohol/ NO/ YES sometimes/ YES occasionally/ YES frequently.

Frequency of intoxication: Respondents were asked to state the number of times that they had been 'really drunk'. The response codes were, NO never/ Yes, but only once/ YES, more than once? YES, every few weeks/ YES almost ever week/ I rarely or never drink.

Demographic measures

Ethnicity: Ethnicity codes were collapsed into four ethnic groups, white (comprising 96% of the sample), Black (0.6%), Asian (2.4%) and Mixed race (1%).

Family structure: Mothers were asked about the current structure of their family. Cohort members were allocated to one of four groups (1) Two natural parents (2) Single parents (3) Reconstituted family, and (4) Other (for example, living with grandparents or other relatives).

Family income: Parents were asked to estimate their combined income, excluding child benefit payments, but including all other earned and unearned income before tax and other deductions. This was originally recorded in 11 income bands. This was further reduced to 5 income bands: a) less than £5,199 per anum, b) £5,200-£10,399, c) £10,400-£15,599, d) £15,600-£20,799, e) more than £20,800.

Missing Values

Table 5.1 gives the number and proportion of cases with missing values on each of the four alcohol measures. On two of the measures, UNIT and PROB, the extent of missing data is relatively large (22.4% and 18.2% respectively). For the other two variables the proportion of missing data is less, but still at a level that warrants further consideration.

Table 5.1 Missing values analysis

Variable	N	Number of cases missing	Proportion of cases missing
UNIT	5055	1461	22.42
FREQ	6081	435	6.68
PROB	5327	1189	18.25
BINGE	6000	516	7.92

It is also possible to examine the pattern of missing values by considering the proportion of cases that are mismatched, that is, have a missing value on at least one variable) when two variables are considered (see Table 5.2). As expected when PROB and UNIT are examined the proportion of cases with missing data rises to 36%, over a third of all cases. When UNIT is considered alongside any of the other three variables the proportion mismatched does not fall below 26.24% of cases.

Table 5.2: Proportion mismatched on two variables

	FREQ	BINGE	PROB	UNIT
FREQ	6.68			
BINGE	3.33	7.92		
PROB	13.54	12.72	18.25	
UNIT	26.24	27.30	35.57	22.42

RESULTS

The frequency of responses to each of the four key alcohol use measures is presented in table 5.3. While the majority of adolescents consumed alcohol in the previous seven days, most did it with a degree of moderation, that is, eight or less units a week). However, there is some evidence that a sizeable population of young people is already drinking at levels that could be considered as hazardous.

Table 5.3: Measures of adolescent drinking behaviour

Measure	MALES		FEMALES	
	n	Valid %	n	Valid %
Number of units consumed in last week				
None	648	29.2	971	34.3
1-8 units	995	44.8	1527	53.9
9 or more units	577	26.0	337	11.9
Missing	568	-	893	-
Frequency of drinking in last 12 months				
Never	229	8.9	311	8.9
Monthly or less frequent	902	35.1	1501	42.7
Weekly or more frequent	1483	56.0	1700	48.4
Missing	219	-	216	-
Number of alcohol related problems				
None	1198	53.5	1810	58.6
1	470	21.0	594	19.2
2 or more	571	25.5	684	22.2
Missing	549	-	640	-
Number of heavy drinking episodes in last 2 weeks				
None	1630	64.5	2433	70.1
1-2	651	25.8	808	23.2
3 or more	246	9.7	232	6.7
Missing	261	-	255	-

Over half of the 16-year-olds drink at least once a week (56% of males; 48 % of females), while 26% of males and 12% of females had consumed at least 9 units in the last week. This is equivalent to nine measures of spirit, nine glasses of wine, or four and a half pints of beer or cider. A quarter of the sample had experienced 2 or more alcohol related problems (26% males; 22% females).

Table 5.4 gives non-parametric (Kendal's tau-b) correlations for the four alcohol measures. The strongest correlation is between the frequency (FREQ) and the quantity (UNIT) of consumption. Both are moderately correlated with the frequency of binge drinking (0.412 and 0.475) respectively. The number of alcohol related problems appears to have little correlation with the other variables.

Table 5.4 Correlations between the four alcohol measures

	UNIT	FREQ	PROB E	BING
UNITS	1	0.547	0.065	0.475
FREQ		1	-0.007	0.412
PROB			1	0.161
BINGE				1

Goodness of fit

A series of unrestricted latent class models were constructed for various numbers of latent classes (2 to 6 classes) using LEM (Vermunt, 1997a). A range of 'goodness of fit' statistics can be calculated to identify the optimal number of latent classes needed to provide an acceptable fit to the data (see Clogg, 1995; Magidson & Vermunt, 2003). The principal goodness of fit statistics are the Pearson chi-squared statistics (χ^2) and the likelihood ratio statistic (L^2). Within LEM these are given by the following:

$$\chi^2 = \sum \frac{(Y_{ijkl} - \hat{Y}_{ijkl})^2}{\hat{Y}_{ijkl}}$$

$$L^2 = 2 \sum Y_{ijkl} \ln \left(\frac{Y_{ijkl}}{\hat{Y}_{ijkl}} \right)$$

where Y_{ijkl} is the observed frequency of response patterns created by variables i, j k and l, and were $\hat{Y}_{ijkl}$ represents the frequency of response patterns predicted by the model. Degree of freedom for both is given by ***m-n-1*** where ***m*** is the number of observed response pattern frequencies and ***n*** is the number of parameters estimated. The distributions of both statistics are asymptotic chi-squared permitting a formal significance test of fit. The associated degrees of freedom are calculated by subtracting the number of (log-linear) parameters to be estimated from the total number of possible response patterns (including those patterns with missing values; S = *ijkl* = 4*4*4*4 = 256). As a general rule of thumb, models with χ^2 and L^2 values less than their corresponding degrees of freedom can be considered as possessing 'adequate' fit.

However, it has long been recognised that when applied to sparse data, that is, where there are numerous response patterns with little or no observations, as occurs with the BCS70 data, both the χ^2 and L^2 distribution may not adequately correspond to an asymptotic chi-squared distribution (Clogg, 1995). Similar problems have also been identified with χ^2 and L^2 as tests of model fit when applied to data containing missing data (Collins, Fidler, Wugalter, & Long, 1993) and LCA models with ordered latent classes (Croon, 1990).

Clogg recommends the index of dissimilarity statistic (*D*) as a replacement non chi-squared measure of fit. *D* has a lower limit of 0 and an upper limit of 1. This formula for *D* is given by:

$$D = \sum \frac{Y_{ijkl} - \hat{Y}_{ijkl}}{2n}$$

Other alternatives include bootstrap methods (both data-based resampling and Monte Carlo sampling) or parsimonious indices such as the Akaike Information Criteria or Bayesian Information Criteria (Collins *et al* 1993; Croon 1990; Magidson & Vermunt, 2003; Ubersax 2001). The AIC statistic is given by:

$$\text{AIC} = L^2 + 2p_h$$

where p_h is the number of unknown parameters to be estimated for the *h*th model. Macready and Dayton (1994) suggested that the $2p_h$ acts as a penalty against

95

complexity, as it is larger in models with a greater number of latent classes. They provide a simplified version of the AIC, which is used in this instance.

$$\text{AIC*} = L^2 + 2df$$

The BIC statistic is given by:

$$\text{BIC} = L^2 + df \log N.$$

With AIC and BIC, the smaller the value the better fitting the model in comparison with other possible models. Collins, Lanza, Schafer and Flaherty, (2002a) also suggested that the L^2 statistic is inflated when the manifest variables contain missing values, as is the case again with the BCS70 data. They suggest the calculation of a L^2 statistic that is adjusted for the occurrence of missing data by subtracting the L^2 value for a saturated model from the unadjusted raw L^2 value, as shown:

$$L^2_{\text{adjusted}} = L^2_{\text{raw}} - L^2_{\text{saturated}}.$$

The saturated model L^2 was estimated using LCA software `WinLTA` (Collins, Lanza, Schafer, & Flaherty, 2002b).

Table 5.5: Goodness of fit statistics for various latent class models

Model	χ^2	L^2_{raw}	L^2_{adj}	d.f.	CR	AIC*	BIC	D
1 latent class[1]	8297.8	5379.7	4949.8	232	6671.7	4915.8	3342.3	0.3244
2 latent classes	2292.9	1962.0	1532.1	223	2110.5	1516.0	3.6	0.1998
3 latent classes	883.0	860.6	430.7	214	859.0	432.6	-1018.7	0.1274
4 latent classes	552.9	534.3	104.3	205	532.3	124.2	-1266.1	0.0917
5 latent classes	488.1	466.9	36.9	196	468.0	74.9	-1254.4	0.0846
6 latent classes	468.4	461.1	31.1	187	456.1	87.1	-1181.1	0.084

Notes

1. Null model

The AIC values presented in table 5.5 indicate that a latent variable with 5 classes is the optimum fit for the data. A model with six classes sees an increase in AIC when compared with the 5-class model. Bearing in mind the two components to AIC, what we see here is the added complexity of the 6-class model being penalised beyond its modest reduction in G^2. The 5-class model can be considered a more parsimonious model than the 6-class option.

Collins and colleagues suggested that double cross-validation is also a possible remedy for the weaknesses in L^2 as a measure of fit, particularly when the data could be considered as sparse, that is, where many of the possible response patterns have few or no respondents reporting experiencing them (Collins, Flaherty, Hyatt, & Schafer, 1999). Double cross-validation involves dividing the sample into two random split halves (sample A and sample B) and fitting the models under consideration to both samples. First, each model is fitted to sample A (the calibration sample) where the predicted response frequencies are saved and a corresponding L^2 value calculated. The saved predicted response frequencies from sample A are then compared with the observed response frequencies when the model is run using sample B (the cross-validation sample) and another L^2 computed. The process can be repeated using sample B as the calibration and sample A as the cross-validation. The assumption with cross-validation is that well fitting models will produce the lowest L^2 across the various calibration and cross-validation estimations.

The results of the cross-validation exercise conducted on this data are presented in table 5.6. Again, these models were constructed in WinLTA as opposed to LEM. Apart from the 3-class model, all models perform best in sample B. The 6-class model produces the lowest cross-validation G^2 statistic in both sample A and B, however, the reduction in G^2 noted for the addition of an extra latent class is very small (<0.08). Therefore, the 5-class model is selected as the optimal model as it is more parsimonious than the 6-class model with little loss of model fit.

Table 5.6: Results of the cross-validation

Model	Sample A models		Sample B models	
	Calibrated on	Cross-validated on	Calibrated on	Cross-validated on
	Sample A	Sample B	Sample B	Sample A
2 latent classes	1093.021	1115.691	1107.248	1101.462
3 latent classes	508.266	500.229	483.313	525.338
4 latent classes	325.605	342.381	314.646	349.172
5 latent classes	283.199	334.572	291.744	309.310
6 latent classes	283.201	334.506	291.758	309.236

Goodness of fit L^2

Non-traditional LCA models.

In addition, to fitting traditional LCA models it is possible to fit non-traditional alternatives to see if model fit can be further improved. In particular, a series of models were fitted that assumed various patterns of local independence. Also, parameter restrictions, as recommended by Croon (1990) for ordinal latent classes were also performed. Table 5.7 summaries the AIC* model fit statistics for the various non-traditional models. The AIC* statistics suggest that the non-traditional models all have poorer fit that the 5-class model (AIC*=74.9).

Table 5.7 AIC* statistics for non-traditional LCA models.

Model	2 classes	3 classes	4 classes	5 classes	6 classes
AB local dependence	886.8	230.1	87.3	101.2	121.5
CD local dependence	132.7	427.0	124.4	143.2	115.3
AB+CD local dependence	821.6	216.7	111.1	130.2	157.6
ABD Local dependence[1]	289.5	101.2	117.5	131.1	151.1
ABD Local dependence[2]	287.1	86.9	104.7	114.9	128.9
Ordinal restrictions[3]	1514.1	710.9	620.4	587.9	593.1

Notes
A: UNIT; B: FREQ; C: PROB; D: BINGE

The ABD model has in fact two latent variables (X and Y). X remains the latent class under consideration, while Y is a discrete latent variable representing the local dependence between A, B and D. (see Uebersax 2000a for further details of how such multiple indicator models can be used to assess local dependence). The first ABD model is conducted with Y as a 6-class latent variable. The second ABD model has Y specified as a 5-class latent variable. This model places ordinal restrictions on the parameter estimates as suggested by Croon (1990).

Significance of effects

The next stage in assessing model fit is to test the differences within the conditional probabilities associated with each manifest variable. Variable I should be deleted from the model if the conditional probabilities ρ_{ilc} are equal. Table 5.8 gives the Wald statistic for each of the manifest variables. It shows that each of the four variables within the model is significant. That is, the probabilities of giving the three possible responses on each variable, conditional on membership of a particular latent class, differ across each of the five latent classes.

Table 5.8 Wald statistics for the significance of each variable.

	Wald	df	p
A|X	2243.7	8	0.00
B|X	2756.9	8	0.00
C|X	436.8	8	0.00
D|X	2740670.8	8	0.00

Parameter estimates

Rho parameters

Tables 5.9 to 5.12 provide the initial estimates for the rho parameters for each of the manifest variables. These represent estimates of the probability of a respondent giving a particular response conditional on their latent class. Respondents in latent class 1 (Limited use) and class 2 (Occasional use) have high probabilities of drinking zero units in the previous week, 0.9 and 0.7 respectively (Table 5.9). Class 3 members (Moderate use) have a high probability of drinking 1-8 units (0.9) and a low probability of drinking none (0.1). Heavy users (class 4) are evenly split across 1-8 units (0.5) and 9+ units per week (0.4), while hazardous users are associated to a large extent with drinking 9+ units in the previous week (0.8).

99

Table 5.9: Rho parameters for number of units consumed previous week.

Latent Class Label	None	1-8 units	9+ units
1. Limited	0.9879	0.0621	0.0000
2. Occasional use	0.7061	0.2939	0.0000
3. Moderate use	0.1452	0.8539	0.0009
4. Heavy use	0.0465	0.5389	0.4146
5. Hazardous use	0.0034	0.1796	0.8170

Conditional probabilities for the frequency of alcohol consumption display a similar pattern (Table 5.10). Given that the measure is based on the previous year's drinking, it is unsurprising that only the limited class has a high probability of never drinking in the previous year (1). Occasional users have a high probability of monthly drinking (0.9), while this frequency has a moderate probability amongst moderate users (0.4) and a low probability amongst heavy users (0.2). Hazardous users are more likely to be weekly drinkers (1) as are heavy (0.8) and moderate users (0.6).

Table 5.10: Rho parameters for frequency of drinking in previous 12 months

Latent Class Label	Never	Monthly or less frequent	Weekly or more frequent
1. Limited	1.0000	0.0000	0.0000
2. Occasional use	0.0474	0.9484	0.0041
3. Moderate use	0.0000	0.3628	0.6372
4. Heavy use	0.0000	0.1772	0.8228
5. Hazardous use	0.0000	0.0000	1.0000

For all classes except limited and hazardous users, the highest conditional probability is for zero alcohol problems (Table 5.11). Surprisingly, limited users have a high probability of having experienced two or more alcohol related problems (0.7). As the alcohol problems measure is a lifetime indicator, this may reflect a number of young people, who having experienced health or social problems as a result of their drinking, have decided to curtail their consumption. Their consumption may have been considerably higher in previous years contributing to the alcohol related problems. The other alcohol consumption measures have more limited time windows (one year, two weeks and one week) and therefore reflect recent reformed drinking patterns. It is also possible, however, to interpret these findings in terms of differences in perceptions amongst respondents. Limited users, due to their lack of experience with alcohol may be more likely to assign minor issues or incidents as problems, where more experienced drinkers may not. Amongst the hazardous use class the highest conditional probability is for 2 or more problems (0.5), although moderate probabilities were estimated for one or zero alcohol problems (0.2 and 0.3 respectively).

Table 5.11: Rho parameters for number of alcohol related problems.

Latent Class Label	None	1	2 or more
1. Limited	0.2900	0.0000	0.7100
2. Occasional use	0.6738	0.1470	0.1792
3. Moderate use	0.7153	0.1906	0.0940
4. Heavy use	0.4590	0.3278	0.2132
5. Hazardous use	0.2612	0.2380	0.5009

All respondents, except those in the heavy drinking or hazardous use classes, have high conditional probabilities of having no heavy drinking sessions in the previous two weeks (Table 5.12). Even amongst the heavy users the probability of having no heavy drinking sessions is moderate (0.3). Only heavy drinkers have a high probability of having 3 or more sessions (0.6).

Table 5.12: Rho parameters for number of heavy drinking episodes in last two weeks.

Latent Class Label	Never	1-2	3+
1. Limited	1.0000	0.0000	0.0000
2. Occasional use	0.9482	0.0454	0.0055
3. Moderate use	0.8752	0.1248	0.0000
4. Heavy use	0.3252	0.6342	0.0406
5. Hazardous use	0.0671	0.3395	0.5934

Gamma parameters

Gamma parameters (γ) represent the estimated unconditional probability of belonging to each latent class, and are presented in Table 5.13. The majority of

101

respondents were classified in classes 2, 3 and 4 (25%, 32% and 24 %). The extreme classes are relatively small in comparison. Only around one in 14 were classified as limited (8%) and just over one in ten were classified as hazardous drinkers (12%).

Table 5.13: Gamma parameters

Latent Class Label		Gamma (γ)
1. Limited	(2)	0.0779
2. Occasional use	(3)	0.2524
3. Moderate use	(1)	0.3157
4. Heavy use	(4)	0.2390
5. Hazardous use	(5)	0.1150

Predicting membership of latent classes

One of the key outputs of this latent class analysis is the prediction of respondents' latent class, dependent on their responses to the alcohol measures. The LCA maximum likelihood estimates of γ_c and ρ can be used to calculate the class probability *P(c|Y)* of an individual respondent belonging to class **c**, with a response pattern **Y** on the manifest variables **Q.** The standard modal assignment rule is that respondents are then allocated to the particular class for which *P(c|Y)* is greatest. The formula for *P(c|Y)* is given as follows:[5.1]

$$\hat{P}(c \mid Y) = \hat{P}(Yc) / \hat{P}(y)$$

Where the estimated probability of having response pattern **Y** is given by:

$$\hat{P}(Y) = \sum_{c=1}^{C} \hat{P}(Yc)$$

[5.1] The specific notation for the class probability formulation outlined below was kindly provided by Dr Amanda Sacker (2002).

The joint probability of an individual having response pattern **Y** conditional on class **c** is then:

$$\hat{P}(Yc) = \gamma_C \prod_{q=1}^{Q} \rho_{\gamma_i | C}$$

As mentioned previously, **Y** is the response pattern *i,j,k,l* on **Q** manifest variables (**q**=1....4). **C** is the number of latent classes (**c**=1....**C**), γ_c is the probability of membership of latent class **c**, and ρ is a matrix of $\rho_{i\backslash c} \, \rho_{j\backslash c} \, \rho_{k\backslash c} \, \rho_{l\backslash c}$ probabilities for each *i,j,k,l* response condition on **c** class membership.

Clogg (1995) and Hagenaars (1993) outline a number of weaknesses with this modal method of class assignment. First the parameter and resultant class estimates are only estimates of unknown true latent class scores for individuals. Except when the estimates are boundary values, that is they are 0 or 1, they are likely to contain measurement error resulting in a number of individuals being allocated to the wrong class.

Second, as the estimates are based on a sample population, they will also be subject to sampling error, adding further uncertainty not accounted for by the model predictions. And third, as the latent class membership scores are probabilities, it is not possible to identify a single 'true' score for an individual. Rather the individual has several sets of possible true scores that may be assigned. Again, modal allocation fails to adequately deal with this uncertainty.

The extent of such problems within the modelling depends on the parameter estimates. When they approach boundary values (1 or 0) there is considerably less uncertainty surrounding class allocation and therefore a lower allocation error rate. In contrast, the problems are considerably larger when parameter estimates and the associated latent class probability are equal across classes, that is, approaches 0.2 across each of the 5 classes. Here there is considerable uncertainty regarding actual class allocation and a resultant larger error rate. Clogg (1995) recommends the use of multiple imputation techniques, similar to those used in the data augmentation procedure, to produce a more reliable estimate of class membership. While both of these alternatives have considerable merit, technical constraints meant that it was not possible to implement them in this case. Therefore, the limitations outlined by the authors must be borne in mind.

The modal allocation procedure produces a summary statistic known as the estimated expected proportion of classification errors produced by modal allocation (E) (see Hagenaars, 1990; Vermunt, 1997b for details). This gives an overall estimate of the probability of being misclassified by the model. With the 5-class model $E = 0.22$. Therefore the model should correctly classify 78% of respondents (100-22=78).

Demographic and social characteristics of hazardous drinkers at age 16

There was a slightly higher proportion of males (11%) than females (7%) classified as hazardous drinkers (Table 5.14) (chi^2 = 75.271, df = 4 p <0.001).

Table 5.14: Gender by drinking status

Latent Class Label	Males %	Females %
Limited use	7.9	8.1
Occasional use	20.6	25.5
Moderate use	34.3	38.6
Heavy use	26.1	20.7
Hazardous use	11.1	7.0
Totals	100.0	100.0

Notes
1. Males, n = 2788; Females, n = 3728.

Also hazardous drinkers were exclusively White (English, Welsh, Scottish, Northern Irish, Irish or other European) or mixed race (defined here as 'mixed parentage' or any other ethnic group) (9% and 8.5% respectively). No Asian (Indian, Pakistani or Bangladeshi) or Black (West Indian or Guyanese) respondents were classified as hazardous drinkers, although 3% were considered heavy drinkers (Table 5.15). Almost 60% of Asian young people were considered to be limited drinkers on the basis of their alcohol scores. This compares to 16% of black respondents, 7% of white respondents and 6% of mixed race respondents.

Table 5.15: Drinking status by ethnicity

Latent Class Label	White %	Black %	Asian %	Mixed %
Limited use	6.5	15.6	59.2	6.4
Occasional use	23.5	46.9	21.5	29.8
Moderate use	37.0	34.4	16.2	27.7
Heavy use	24.0	3.1	3.1	27.7
Hazardous use	9.0	0.0	0.0	8.5
Totals	100.0	100.0	100.0	100.0

Notes

White, n = 5039, Black, n = 32, Asian, n = 130, Mixed, n = 47.

Hazardous drinkers were more likely to come from reconstituted families, that is, families that consist of one natural parent and one stepparent (Table 5.16) A limited use drinking pattern was most prevalent amongst young people living in single parent households (9%).

Table 5.16: Drinking status by family structure

Latent Class Label	Two biological parents %	Single parent %	Reconstituted family %	Other/ Unclassified %
Limited use	8.2	9.1	3.6	8.5
Occasional use	23.3	23.6	26.4	23.2
Moderate use	37.5	30.8	32.6	36.7
Heavy use	22.5	29.7	25.1	22.6
Hazardous use	8.5	6.9	12.2	8.9
Totals	100.0	100.0	100.0	100.0

Notes

Two biological parents n = 4,330; Single parents n = 276; Reconstituted family n = 386; Other n = 1,524.

Construct Validity

A key issue that warrants attention at this stage is the extent to which the limited use category, given the high probability of reporting alcohol related problems, actually represents two distinct populations of drinkers rather than a single relatively homogenous group. The level of reported alcohol related problems may indicate that a proportion of young people classified as limited users may be fact be 'past' heavy alcohol users (have used alcohol in the past but do not use now) and therefore quite distinct from those young people who have never drank alcohol. If this is the case, there is an argument that it may be appropriate to drop those respondents who have never consumed alcohol from the LCA, thus permitting comparisons to be made between past users and hazardous users. In particular, there may be some value in examining the similarities in past drinking patterns between the two classes, and why the past drinkers stopped and the hazardous drinkers did not. This is a key issue in the validation of the 5-class model.

Age of first use

In general, most young peoples' first drink of alcohol occurred after the age of 10 (67.4%). Only 14% had tried alcohol before the age of 8. Heavy and hazardous drinkers tended to try alcohol at a slightly earlier age than other adolescent drinkers (chi^2 = 3075.8, df = 20, $p<0.00$). Around 40% of hazardous drinkers had tried alcohol before the age of 10 compared with 26% of moderate drinkers and 18% of occasional drinkers (Table 5.17). This table gives an indication of the extent of past drinking amongst the limited use category. Around 30% of the limited use group had actually consumed alcohol. Of those that did, the age of onset profile appears closest to that of the occasional use or moderate use groups. Over one third of limited use alcohol users had an age of onset between age 14 and 15, and a further 20% tried alcohol for the first time after the age of twelve. However, there does appear to be a group within this larger category who report an early onset. Nearly 20% of those in the limited use category who had used alcohol by age 16 had an onset before age 8. This, however, is a relatively small minority of a small drinking category of adolescents (approximately 27 cases in total).

Similar patterns were also detected in relation to drinking with friends other than on special occasions (Table 5.18). As drinking with friends was generally a later occurrence, it suggests that most young peoples' first introduction to alcohol most likely occurred with parents on special occasions.

Table 5.17: Drinking status by age of first ever use of alcohol

Latent Class Label	Never used %	<8yr %	8-9yr %	10-11yr %	12-13yr %	14-15yr %	Total %
Limited use	69.4	6.1	3.1	4.5	5.8	11.0	100
Occasional use	2.9	10.6	7.4	17.3	25.1	6.7	100
Moderate use	0.7	14.0	11.6	20.5	27.3	25.9	100
Heavy use	0.0	16.9	13.0	21.9	26.5	21.6	100
Hazardous use	0.0	24.2	16.2	23.2	22.0	1.5	100
Total	7.1	14.3	10.7	19.0	24.2	24.2	100

Notes

1. N = 4978 (Limited use n = 445; Occasional use n = 1102; Moderate use n= 1757; Heavy use n= 1169; Hazardous use n = 505).

Around one in three hazardous drinkers had drunk alcohol with a friend before age 14. The comparable figure for moderate and occasional drinkers was around one in six and one in ten respectively. Few of the limited use group had drunk alcohol unsupervised with friends before age 14 (3.9% of total class). However, if the analysis is limited to just those that drank alcohol unsupervised in the limited use group (around 47 cases), around 36% had drunk with friends before age 14. This is similar to that found amongst hazardous drinkers (34%).

Table 5.18: Drinking status by age of first ever use with friends

Latent Class Label	Never used[1] %	<8yr %	8-9yr %	10-11yr %	12-13yr %	14-15yr %	Total %
Limited use	89.1	0.0	0.5	0.2	3.2	7.0	100
Occasional use	26.5	0.3	0.3	1.2	8.7	63.0	100
Moderate use	8.5	0.3	0.3	2.2	14.2	74.4	100
Heavy use	1.0	0.1	0.2	2.5	20.2	76.3	100
Hazardous use	0.2	0.2	0.6	3.8	29.3	66.0	100
Total	16.2	0.2	0.3	2.1	15.2	66.0	100

Notes

1. This column corresponds to never having drunk alcohol unsupervised with friends.

2. N = 5169 (Limited use n= 431; Occasional use n = 1077; Moderate use n= 1825; Heavy use n= 1303; Hazardous use n = 533).

3. As 30% of cells had expected values less than 5 the chi squared test is not reported.

Drinking days

Respondents classified as having hazardous drinking patterns also reported drinking alcohol on a greater number of days than other drinkers did (chi2 = 4137.733, df = 28, $p<0.00$) (Table 5.19). For limited drinkers the mean number of drinking days is almost zero (0.0095). For occasional users the mean is still substantially less than one (0.2). It is only with heavy drinkers that the mean number of drinking days approaches two days in the previous week (1.97). Moderate drinkers drank on average one day out of the previous seven (1.16).

In stark contrast to the other drinking patterns, young people classified as having a hazardous drinking profile reported an average of 3.35 drinking days in the previous week, or in other words, 1.3 drinking days more than the second highest class. Over 21% of the hazardous use class reported drinking on five or more days in the previous week, compared with around 5% of heavy drinkers and 1% of moderate drinkers (Table 5.19).

Table 5.19: Drinking status by number of days alcohol consumed in last seven

Latent Class Label	0	1	2	3	4	5	6	7
Limited use	99.2	0.6	0.2	0.0	0.0	0.0	0.0	0.0
Occasional use	84.7	12.2	2.0	0.7	0.3	0.1	0.0	0.1
Moderate use	31.8	36.9	20.5	7.1	2.4	0.8	0.3	0.2
Heavy use	11.1	30.9	28.4	16.3	8.5	3.3	0.5	0.9
Hazardous use	2.5	7.9	22.3	25.8	20.0	10.5	4.6	6.3

Notes
1. N = 6516 (Limited use n= 524; Occasional use n = 1527; Moderate use n = 2396; Heavy use n = 1500; Hazardous use n = 569).

The majority of both heavy and moderate users consumed alcohol on no more that two days out of the previous seven (71% and 89% respectively). Of the hazardous drinking class, only 33% achieved this. Most of the reported alcohol consumed occurred at the weekend as would be expected. Almost all of the hazardous drinkers drank alcohol on a Saturday night (85%) (Table 5.20). On any other night of the week around a third of hazardous drinkers would have been drinking. For heavy drinkers, the figure was about half this, with around 15%

drinking on midweek days, increasing to just under half on a Friday and two thirds on a Saturday.

Table 5.20: Proportion of drinkers consuming alcohol on each of previous seven days

Latent Class Label	Mon.	Tues.	Wed.	Thur.	Fri.	Sat.	Sun.
Limited use	0.2	0.0	0.2	0.4	0.2	0.0	0.0
Occasional use	1.7	1.5	1.6	2.3	4.5	7.8	3.5
Moderate use	8.1	8.6	10.0	9.9	27.6	40.7	24.2
Heavy use	16.3	14.5	14.4	16.0	48.8	65.8	30.5
Hazardous use	29.7	28.6	30.9	36.6	77.4	85.3	47.9

Note

1. This is a multiple response table so the marginals do not sum to 100.

2. Percentages based on the number of respondents and not on the number of responses.

Spending on Alcohol

The average money spent on alcohol in the previous week was only £1.70 (sd=£3.70) or £3.34 at 2005 prices[5.2]. As can be seen from the standard deviation, this cohort average masks considerable variation in individual spending patterns. As would be expected, heavy drinkers and hazardous drinkers spent more money than less frequent drinkers (F = 753.657, df = 4, p<0.000). Hazardous drinkers spent in the region of £7.50 (sd £6.70) in the previous seven days. This is equivalent to around £14.72 at 2005 prices. Moderate drinkers reported mean spending levels of only £0.90 (sd=2.70). The mean spending of heavy drinkers was around half that of hazardous drinkers (£3.00; sd=£3.49). For occasional and limited drinkers spending was negligible.

Attitude to alcohol

Table 5.21 provides the mean attitude scores across the five drinking categories. As expected hazardous drinkers had more positive attitudes to alcohol than other drinkers (F = 356.306, df = 4, p<0.001). The table almost shows a linear relationship between mean attitudes and drinking status.

[5.2] The equivalent price estimates were generated using the inflation calculator at eh.net http://eh.net/hmit/ppowerbp/

Table 5.21: Mean attitudes to alcohol by drinking status.

Latent Class Label	Attitude to alcohol
Limited use	23.7
Occasional use	25.8
Moderate use	27.5
Heavy use	29.2
Hazardous use	30.9
All	27.5

Notes

N = 5493 (Limited use n = 454; Occasional use n = 1306;

Moderate use n = 2041; Heavy use n = 1250; Hazardous use n = 442).

Brand Preferences

Respondents were asked to identify, from a predefined list of alcohol drinks, those that they sometimes or usually drank (Table 5.22). Hazardous drinkers had the widest brand preference, usually consuming on average around six different types of alcoholic drinks (*sd*=3.3). However, the difference between hazardous drinkers and more occasional drinkers, although statistically significant (F = 356.306, *df* = 4, p<0.001), was not substantive in real terms (mean 3.6, *sd*=2.7). Moderate and heavy drinkers fell between these values (4.6, *sd*=3.0; 5.5, *sd*=3.1).

In terms of the specific types of drinks reported, lager was the most popular drink amongst the cohort (45% stated a preference for this) followed by cider (32%), wine (21%), martini (17%) and vodka (17%) (Table 5.22). Some care must be taken in interpreting the figures presented in this table as only 18 of the limited use group answered this question. The very infrequent nature of their alcohol consumption may mean that they have not developed any preferences. Therefore, excluding this group, hazardous drinkers were the most likely to state a preference for beer (larger and bitter) and the main spirit groups (whiskey, Bacardi, gin and vodka). In contrast, occasional users were the most likely to state a preference for sweet drinks such as shandy, Babysham and cider, while drinks such as wine, Martini and Cinzano were more popular amongst moderate drinkers than any other group.

Table 5.22: Proportion of drinking status stating brand was their usual drink.

	Limited use	Occasional use	Moderate use	Heavy use	Hazardous use
Lager	33	29	38	53	63
Bitter	11	6	8	15	23
Home brew beer	28	2	3	4	6
Shandy	28	18	13	7	2
Wine	17	18	24	19	16
Home made wine	6	6	7	5	4
Babysham	6	9	5	3	2
Sherry	6	4	4	2	2
Martini	11	18	19	16	13
Cinzano	6	11	13	10	9
Port	6	2	2	2	3
Cider	39	42	35	28	25
Whiskey	6	3	3	5	9
Rum/Bacardi	11	7	9	1	14
Gin	6	4	4	6	9
Vodka	33	11	11	19	30
Brandy	6	2	2	2	3

Notes

1. N = 5169 (Limited use n= 18; Occasional use n = 581; Moderate use n= 1499; Heavy use n = 1234; Hazardous use n = 521).

2. This table is based on a multiple response question. As each respondent could answer more than once the proportions do not sum to 100. Percentages are based on respondents and not on responses.

Reasons for drinking

Most young people drink because they like it (54%-90%) or to be sociable (66%-70%) (Table 5.23). As the level of alcohol use increases so does the proportion of drinkers who respond positively to the various reasons for drinking. Hazardous drinkers are the most likely to give each of the seven reasons as justification for their drinking. What is of concern are the relatively high levels of hazardous drinkers who are drinking out of habit or in response to perceived problems.

Table 5.23: Drinking status by reasons for drinking alcohol.

Latent Class Label	To be sociable	Out of habit	Like it	To relax	To forget problems	To lose inhibitions	To pass time
Occasional use	66.2	1.3	54.2	19.4	6.4	6.1	9.3
Moderate use	60.0	2.3	75.1	26.8	8.2	6.5	9.1
Heavy use	67.0	5.8	83.9	37.6	14.5	12.2	13.3
Hazardous use	70.1	15.2	90.0	45.9	25.6	15.8	20.6

Notes

1. N = 5059 (Occasional use n = 1086; Moderate use n= 2012; Heavy use n= 1403; Hazardous use n = 558).

2. As this is a multiple response question the proportions do not sum to 100. Percentages are based on the number of respondents and not on the number of responses.

3. This question was only asked of drinkers.

Non-drinkers were asked the reverse of this question. The most popular reasons given for why they did not drink alcohol included not liking the taste (61%), none of friends drink (55%), waste of money (51%), it has a bad effect of people (44%). Around one in four non-drinkers cited parents or religion as the reason why they did not drink (20% and 16% respectively).

Frequency of drinking more than they should

Almost half of the young people who reported that they often drank more than they should were classified as hazardous drinkers, and a further 35% were classified as heavy drinkers (Table 5.24). In contrast, of those respondents who claimed not to drink more than they should, only 4% and 20% fell into these two categories of drinking. As the frequency of drinking too much increases, there is a similar increase in the proportion of respondents categorised as heavy or hazardous drinkers, which is highly significant (chi^2 = 3989.247, *df* = 16, p = 0.000).

Table: 5.24 'Do you drink more than you should?' by drinking status

Latent Class Label	Never/rarely drink	NO	YES occasionally	YES sometimes	YES often
Limited use	49.1	1.6	0.5	0.1	0.0
Occasional use	39.3	26.5	11.8	7.9	2.4
Moderate use	11.1	47.6	33.3	21.3	13.2
Heavy use	0.5	19.8	41.7	43.4	35.1
Hazardous use	0.0	4.4	12.6	27.2	49.3
Total	100.0	100.0	100.0	100.0	100.0

Notes
1. N = 6021 (never/rarely n = 870; no n=3275; yes occasionally n= 973; yes sometimes n = 698; yes often n = 205).

It is also possible to look at this relationship from the other angle. Of those respondents classified as hazardous drinkers, only 18% considered themselves to often drink more than they should. A further 34% considered themselves to do this sometimes. Only 5% of heavy drinkers reported that they felt they often drank too much. Almost half of heavy drinkers felt that they never drank more than they should compared with 25% of those young people classified as hazardous drinkers.

DISCUSSION

The LCA model categorised adolescents into five distinct alcohol consumption patterns. Within this model a small minority of young people were identified as reporting hazardous or problematic alcohol consumption patterns. These young people, around one in eight of the sample, were estimated to have drunk on a weekly basis (100%), to be highly likely to drink more than nine units a week, to report at least one alcohol related problem (73%), and to have experienced at least one binge session in the previous two weeks (93%). This hazardous pattern was also confirmed when the young people were compared across other alcohol measures. The hazardous drinking class spent more money on alcohol, drank alcohol on more days in the previous week, and had an earlier age of onset of alcohol use than those young people in other drinking classes. The level of hazardous drinking identified in this study is slightly higher than similar analyses.

While employing relatively similar alcohol measures, that is, measures of quantity frequency, binge drinking and related problems) in a LCA model, Fergusson and colleagues classified 9.3% of 16-year-old participants in the Christchurch Health and Development Study as hazardous drinkers (Fergusson, Horwood, & Lynskey, 1995). The small percentage difference in the size of the of hazardous drinking category between the two studies, may be due to a number of factors such as subtle differences in the measures used, cultural differences in adolescent drinking patterns (one is a UK sample and the other a New Zealand sample) and the time difference between the two surveys. However, it does suggest certain robustness in latent class categorisations of alcohol consumption. There does appear to be a small, yet sizeable, minority of 16-year-olds displaying alcohol consumption patterns worthy of public health concern.

One area where the models differed was in relation to the extent of alcohol related problems reported by the lowest alcohol consumption group, here referred to as the 'teetotal' group. Within this study a large proportion of this group reported two or more alcohol related problems coupled with very low consumption levels. It could be the case that this class contains a large proportion of young people who have been drinking heavily in the past at levels sufficient to trigger problems with the police, school or the family (the problems measure has an 'ever' reporting period), but have since reformed their drinking behaviour. Alternatively, young people with low levels of alcohol consumption could be more likely to label trivial arguments with parents around alcohol consumption as 'problems', than those more familiar with drinking alcohol. While both may be plausible, the former receives some support from the analysis of the supplementary alcohol measures. The teetotal group has a lower age of onset of unsupervised drinking than the hazardous drinking group while reporting very limited current consumption. The association between age of onset and later alcohol problems is well established (DeWitt, Adlaf, Offord & Ogborne, 2000; Grant, Stinson & Harford, 2001; Gruber, DiClemente, Anderson & Lodico, 1996). Also, the estimated probability of reporting one alcohol related problem for the teetotal group is 0, compared with 0.29 for no problems and 0.79 for two or more problems. If the observed levels of alcohol related problems were the result of a slight over-reporting of so-called 'problems,' rather than the existence of two distinct groups within the teetotal class (a group with little exposure to alcohol and a group who were past heavy drinkers but who now consumed very little), we would expect the probability of reporting one alcohol problem to be greater than zero. This is not the case.

The findings above strongly support the concurrent validity of the latent class typology of adolescent drinking patterns presented in the previous chapter. As noted by Windle (1996) unidimensional measures of adolescent drinking behaviours drinking are unlikely to discriminate between various drinking styles to the degree in which a multidimensional measure can.

Support was found for the each of the hypotheses presented in this section. Problem drinkers tended to have an earlier age of onset, both supervised and unsupervised (with friends) than other drinkers. Likewise, they spent more money on alcohol, drank on a greater number of days per week, were more likely to drink alcohol on days other than the weekend, drank a wider range of alcohol drinks, were most likely to drink high strength brands, were most likely to report specific reasons for drinking and were most likely to consider that they regularly drank more than they should. In all, such findings provide support for the discriminative power of the latent class model. There are clear associations between the latent class drinking patterns and other independent measures of drinking behaviour.

Findings from the age of onset analysis (the only long-term retrospective alcohol use measure) would give some support to the suggestion that the limited use category does contain some past alcohol users who no longer drink. These young people reported early onset patterns similar to those who were currently heavier alcohol consumers. This raises the possibility that these young people drank at a relatively high level ,before deciding to stop or reduce their consumption. However, there are no other retrospective alcohol measures that would permit a more detailed testing of this hypothesis. Also, the relatively small number of these 'past' drinkers means that there is little practical value in dividing the limited use group.

In addition, to the question of concurrent validity of the typology, the findings raise some further issues for consideration. The first of these is the nature of the relationship between age of onset and liability for adolescent problem drinking. There are a number of specific risk processes that may link age of onset and increased risk of problem drinking. For example, problem-drinking liability may be a direct function of time. The longer you drink the more likely you are to develop a drinking problem. Early onset users, therefore, have a longer drinking history and if this assumption is correct, are at greater risk of progressing into hazardous drinking patterns. Alternatively, problem-drinking liability may be a function of the developmental stage at which young people are first exposed to substances. Very young drinkers may not have acquired the social skills to learn to moderate their drinking practices when first introduced to alcohol. They may fail to adopt controlled drinking practices. Older onset drinkers may have developed the social skill required to manage and moderate drinking behaviours when they are eventually introduced to it. It may also be the case that the age of first use is simply an indirect indicator of some common liability factor, and that a by-product of this individual liability towards problem drinking is the early desire to try alcohol. Here both behaviours, early and problematic drinking, may be the result of some common shared set of risk processes which give rise to the observed correlation between two otherwise independent behaviours.

Finally, it is also possible, and most probable, that problem drinking is in fact a function of both time and developmental stage, where the development of harmful alcohol consumption patterns requires both a drinking history that involves the introduction to alcohol at a developmentally inappropriate age, and a reasonable period of time for the behaviours to emerge.

Unfortunately the construction of the alcohol variables within the BCS70 means that it is not possible for us to further test any of the possible mechanisms listed above. For us to do this, it would be necessary to determine the age of onset of hazardous drinking behaviours, as this would be required to estimate the length of time to problem onset (onset of hazardous drinking minus onset of first use).

In summary, the latent class model of adolescent drinking patterns appears to have performed well as a data reduction strategy for categorical alcohol measures common within a large-scale epidemiological study. This is further confirmation of the value of LCA as an approach for modelling multi-dimensional self-report health data (Sacker, Wiggins, Clarke, & Bartley, 2003). The five classes do appear to be a functional typology capable of distinguishing adolescents on a range of other alcohol related measures. Analysis of the covariates also confirmed existing known association between hazardous drinking and other adolescent characteristics.

While LCA does address some of the limitations inherent in more tradition methods for aggregating multiple alcohol measures, it is still not without its weaknesses. The most serious of these is that most variables require some manipulation or adjustment (usually some minor recoding) before inclusion within the LCA model. This involves subjective decisions being taken by the researcher that may alter the nature and structure of the variable, for example the number of categories or the cut-off points used. The exact influence that these arbitrary decisions have on the resultant model is difficult to determine. Also, the resultant model does not place individual within specific classes but rather provide a profile of conditional class membership probabilities. Therefore, the allocation of individuals to classes based on a modal rule involves some error, some 22% in this case. Whether the levels of error compromise the value of the allocation is difficult to determine. And lastly, the model is data driven. As a result, a different sample or different items may generate a different class model. This reduces our ability to compare results across studies when LCA approaches are used.

SUMMARY

This chapter set out to estimate and test a new latent class typology of adolescent drinking. The objective was to integrate a range of core indicators of drinking behaviour, contained within the BCS70 (four in total), into a single useable classification of adolescent drinking styles. The four alcohol dimensions employed were the frequency of drinking, the quantity consumed, the frequency of binge drinking and the number of alcohol related problems encountered. Data used were from the 1970 British Cohort Study sixteen-year-old follow-up. Partial or complete responses to the selected alcohol measures were provided by 6,516 cohort members. The data were collected via a series of postal questionnaires.

Multiple latent class models were estimated using LEM. The best fitting model was a 5-class model in which the corresponding classes were labelled as limited, occasional, moderate, heavy and hazardous drinking. Around 12% of the sample were classified as 'hazardous drinkers' reporting frequent drinking, high levels of alcohol consumed, frequent binge drinking and multiple alcohol related problems.

Bivariate analysis was used to assess the concurrent validity of the typology. The latent class typology exhibited good validity in terms of its ability to distinguish respondents across a number of alcohol and non-alcohol indicators. Notwithstanding a number of limitations, latent class analysis offers an alternative data reduction method for the construction of drinking typologies that addresses known weaknesses inherent in more traditional classification methods.

6 CORRELATES OF HAZARDOUS DRINKING AT AGE 16.

This chapter examines the relationship between adolescent drinking patterns and other various psychological, social and behavioural problems also assessed at this developmental stage (16-year-old data sweep). The aim of this analysis is to attempt to identify the characteristics of heavy and hazardous drinkers, in particular the extent to which problem drinking clusters other adolescent problems.

This analysis does not permit conclusions to be drawn about possible causal relationships between drinking patterns and individual characteristics, as both the potential risk and potential outcome are assessed at approximately the same point in time (there may be small differences in when respondents may have completed the various questionnaire components within the BCS, and some of the measures presented in this chapter may, in fact, be retrospective, however there is insufficient data to actually date the experiences reported). The logic underpinning causal relationships dictates that a cause must occur before an outcome. Therefore, for much of the data collected within a single BCS follow-up, that is, all non-retrospective data, it is not possible to identify the direction of any potential causal relationship. In other words, it is impossible with cross-sectional analysis to be certain as to what came first. Even if the data collected is retrospective, it still may not be possible to place it before the onset of the drinking patterns, given the difficulty in dating the actual onset of the actual drinking pattern. Therefore, the temporal relationship between retrospective risk and drinking patterns is still unknown.

Notwithstanding these limitations, the identification of key correlates of problem drinking is of importance for a number of reasons. First, correlations between drinking behaviour and other psychological or behavioural problems may be indicative of concurrent comorbidity. If alcohol problems co-occur or cluster with other behavioural or psychological disorders it would have substantive implications for the treatment of such disorders. At issue here, is not whether certain behaviour problems or psychiatric conditions increase the risk of problem drinking (although this may in fact occur), but

119

whether problem drinkers more likely to experience other problems than non-drinkers. Dealing with drinking problems amongst adolescents would be further complicated by the existence of other behavioural of psychiatric problems. The degree to which 'dual diagnosis' may exist within the adolescent drinking population is of importance to those who provide generalist and specialist services to young people.

Second, correlations can be used to test potential causal relationships (Rutter, 1994). As mentioned previously, cross-sectional analysis cannot be used to identify causal pathways or to build causal models. However, it can be used to identify key proximal factors that are not causally associated with the behaviour under study, or in other words, to rule out potential casual pathways. Simply put, if there is no correlation between a characteristic and behaviour they cannot be causally related. However, even if correlations do occur, it must be remembered that they do not provide evidence of the existence of causality, rather they may simply reflect no-causal co-occurrence.

Finally, the demographic characteristics of problem adolescent drinking are of intrinsic interest in their own right. The planning of treatment and support services requires intelligence on the nature and extent of the 'in-need population', that is, the population that would benefit from some support or intervention (Percy, 2000).

This chapter will examine the extent to which adolescent problem drinking is correlated with other adolescent problems after controlling for variations due to demographic differences. It will present a review of existing research, identify a number of gaps in the current knowledge base and present analysis that addresses these gaps and discusses the implications of the findings.

CONCURRENT ASSOCIATIONS WITH OTHER ADOLESCENT PROBLEMS

Both cross-sectional and longitudinal studies have consistently shown that young people with drinking problems also appear to be more likely to have other co-existing problems, such as other drug use problems, delinquency, and affective disorders (for reviews see Armstrong & Costello, 2002, Clark & Burkstein, 1998; Deas & Thomas, 2002; Gilvarry, 2000; Sher, Grekin, & Williams, 2005; Weinberg, Rahbert, Colliver & Glantz, 1998). Fergusson, Horwood and Lynskey (1994) estimated that in a large sample of New Zealand 15-year-olds, around 3% had experienced multiple problems including conduct disorder, contact with the criminal justice system, early onset cannabis use, early onset sexual activity and alcohol abuse. A further 5% (mostly female) displayed these characteristics without conduct/delinquent behaviours.

Other substance use

In a survey of adults, Dawson (2000b) found increasing levels of smoking with increasing alcohol consumption (frequency, quantity and frequency of heavy drinking episodes). Not only is smoking associated with the onset of alcohol consumption but Dawson also concluded that problem drinking was also a factor in preventing smoking cessation in adults.

Alcohol initiation has long been accepted as an initial precursor stage in the development of other drug use behaviour (Kandel & Yamaguchi, 2002, Kandel & Yamaguchi 1993, Kandel, Yamaguchi & Chen, 1993). Cross-sectional studies have indicated that heavy alcohol users are also more likely to use other illicit drugs, for example, Ramsay and Percy (1996). However, longitudinal studies would suggest that the actual relationship between alcohol and other drugs is complex. Chassin, Pitts and Prost (2002) found that later drug use was associated with early onset heavy drinking. While later drug use did not appear to be predicted by the age of onset of alcohol consumption (as distinct from the onset of heavy drinking), drug use did appear to predict later alcohol problems (Labouvie & White, 2002). Yamaguchi and Kandel (2002) also found that progression through the drug use sequence (alcohol use only; alcohol and cigarette use; alcohol and marijuana use; alcohol, marijuana and cocaine/heroin use in the last year, commonly referred to as the gateway model of drug use), was associated with substantively increased likelihood of being alcohol dependent, relative to all other preceding stages in the sequence. Bentler, Newcomb and Zimmerman (2002) proposed the existence of complex feedback effects, whereby changes in the *intensity* of either alcohol or drug use could influence similar changes in the other. This feedback model can be considered to be a further extension of the traditional stages model noted above, where a differentiation is made between simple alcohol consumption and problem use, and reciprocal interactions are permitted.

National surveys have also confirmed the strong correlation between the frequency of alcohol use, smoking and cannabis use amongst adolescents (Boys, et al., 2003; Greenblatt, 2000). After controlling for measurement error, Lynskey, Fergusson

121

and Horwood (1998) observed strong correlations between the largest amount of alcohol consumed by adolescents in last three months and their frequency of smoking (r=0.51) and their frequency of cannabis use in the last year (r=0.56). The authors concluded that these correlations were best explained by a single factor representing an individual liability for substance use. Recent studies have further supported this single factor liability (Morral, McCaffrey & Paddock, 2002; Vanyukov et al., 2003), which Clark (2004) termed the 'common risk model' of substance use disorders. Anthony (2002) argued for the combination of the traditional 'stepping stone' or 'gateway' model, in which alcohol leads to cannabis use which leads to hard drug use, with this common risk model. Within this approach the common liability to substance use manifests itself in a general stage-sequential unveiling of substance use behaviours or precursor stages (Pickles, 1993). Jackson, Sher, Cooper, & Wood (2002) in analysis of the National Longitudinal Study of Adolescent Health and the Adolescent Health Risk Study found evidence for both a common third factor and a bidirectional causation explanation of the comorbidity between alcohol and tobacco.

While numerous European studies have examined the association between adolescent drinking and other drug use (for example Sutherland & Willner, 1998; Sutherland, & Shepherd, 2001a; Wetzels, Kremers, Vitoria, & de Vries, 2003) most have only looked at the basic co-occurrence of substance use status. In other words, they have examined the relative prevalence of other drug use amongst drinkers and non-drinkers. There is limited non-US data on the relationship between different alcohol consumption patterns and the risk for other drug use.

Mental Health Problems

Estimates of the proportion of young people with a substance abuse problem who also have at least one other psychiatric condition range from 60% (Armstrong & Costello 2002) to 80% (Rohde, Lewinsohn & Seeley, 1996). The most common association were with conduct disorder and depression. Weaker associations were noted for anxiety and ADHD. However, research on the relationship between adolescent alcohol use and other mental health problems is rather inconclusive. While most studies are supportive of a link between problem drinking and mental health problems, in particular mood and anxiety disorders (Clark et al., 1997; Clark & Bukstein, 1998;

Kushner, Sher, & Erickson, 1999; Ragin, Rasinski, Cerbone, & Johnston, 1999; Rutter, 2001), contradictory findings do exist (Armstrong & Costello, 2002; Deas & Thomas, 2002).

Costello, Erkanli, Federman and Angold, (1999) found higher alcohol rates amongst young people with depression (boys only) and behaviour disorders (both sexes) but not anxiety (both sexes). Federman, Costello, Angold, Farmer, and Erkanli (1997) reported that amongst alcohol using boys no differences in the rates of anxiety or depression were detectable, however, they were observed amongst alcohol using girls. Poulin, Hand, Boudreau, and Santor (2005) found that both alcohol consumption patterns and age were significant predictors of depression but only for girls. Alcohol consumption was a particularly powerful risk factor for depression in young girls. As they grew older the additional protection provided by age, offset the risk associated with alcohol consumption. Cigarette smoking was also found to be associated with depression. Neither alcohol nor cigarettes were risk factors for depression in boys, however cannabis use was a significant predictor of depressive symptoms (Poulin et al., 2005).

Chassin et al., (2002) found lower levels of depression amongst male early onset heavy drinkers than moderate or non-drinkers. For females depression was associated with infrequent drinking. Greenblatt (2000), while confirming the contemporaneous comorbidity between heavy drinking, criminality and other externalising behaviours, found no evidence of a similar association with symptoms of anxiety or depression, thought problems, withdrawal, attentional or social problems. Boys et al., (2003) found that while depression (but not anxiety) predicted regular drinking, regular drinkers were no more likely than non-drinkers to have emotional problems or other psychiatric disorders. This relationship was also confounded by the joint comorbidity between alcohol use, emotional problems and regular smoking. Woodward and Fergusson (2001) found that while young people with DSM anxiety disorders reported higher levels of alcohol dependence, once confounding effects were controlled for this relationship became non-significant. Within the Early Developmental Stages of Psychopathology Study (EDSP) anxiety predicted alcohol consumption, and this relationship remained significant even after controlling for confounding factors (Zimmerman, Wittchen, Hofler, Pfister, Kessler, & Lieb, 2003).

Antisocial behaviour

One of the key difficulties in reviewing the relationship between problem drinking and antisocial behaviour (ASB) is that ASB is far from a single unified construct (Rutter et al., 1998). Three main approaches can be detected within the research literature. The first adopts a psychiatric or clinical psychology orientation that defines ASB in terms of psychosocial dysfunction or impairment. The Diagnostic and Statistical Manual of Mental Disorders, Fourth Edition, grouped together three related clinical disorders - conduct disorder (CD), oppositional defiant disorder (ODD), and attention deficit hyperactivity disorder (ADHD) - as 'disruptive behaviour disorders' or 'externalising behaviours' (see Clark, Vanyukov, & Cornelius, 2002).

ODD and CD have been shown to consistently predate and predict alcohol use and alcohol disorders (Clark & Bukstein, 1998; Clark, et al., 2002; Lynskey & Fergusson, 1995). Using a relatively low-level definition of heavy alcohol use, Kumpulainen (2000) concluded that externalising behaviour and hyperactivity in males at age 12 predicted the development of heavy drinking at age 15. Moss and Lynch (2001) found that adolescent alcohol use disorder symptoms were only associated with CD for females and CD and ADHD with males. Wilens (1998) commented that given the fact that both CD and ADHD are highly comorbid conditions themselves, CD might possibly mediate the observed relationship between ADHD and alcohol use disorders. A similar conclusion was reached by other studies (Biederman, Wilens, Mick, Faraone, & Spencer, 1998; Disney, Elkins, McGue, & Iacono, 1999). Smith, Molina, & Pelham, (2002) postulated that the twin dimensions of ADHD, namely inattention and hyperactivity might in fact contribute to two separate mediation pathways. The first, associated with hyperactivity and conduct disorders, leading to early onset alcohol problems and the second, associated with inattention and possible internalising problems, leading to later onset alcohol problems. Findings from the National Household Survey of Drug Abuse have shown higher levels of attention problems in heavy drinkers compared with other young people even after controlling for other known risk factors (Greenblatt, 2000), although this relationship did not vary with age or gender (Ragin et al., 1999).

The second approach to the study of ASB and alcohol defines ASB in terms of self-reported criminal or delinquent acts. While delinquents may or may not meet the

124

diagnostic criteria for the disorders outlined above, research within this criminological perspective has also confirmed the link between antisocial behaviour and alcohol use (Rutter et al,. 1998; Rutter et al., 1997). The National Household survey of Drug Abuse found a strong association between the level of drinking and the likelihood of having committed a range of criminal acts (Greenblatt, 2000). In general, ASB precedes the development of alcohol problems, and has been shown to predict the onset of drinking per se (Jessor & Jessor, 1977) and the frequency of drinking (Adalbjarnardottir & Rafnsson, 2002). Even though the onset of alcohol problem tends to post-date the onset of other problem behaviours, the association more likely reflects a shared liability (common set of risk processes) than the causal actions of one disorder on the other (Jessor & Jessor, 1977; Rutter et al., 1998). In particular, behavioural undercontrol has been cited as a key proximal developmental factor linking alcohol problems, hyperactivity, inattention and externalising behavioural in boys (Sher, 1994; Dawes, Tarter & Kirisci 1997).

Alcohol can also be a proximal environmental mediating factor in the perpetration of various, particularly violent, crimes due to its pharmacological effect of reducing inhibitions (Ito, Miller & Pollock, 1996). Here the link is with the quantity of alcohol consumed within a particular setting rather than problematic drinking per se. It could be argued that an individual with an alcohol problem would be drinking excessively on a more regular basis than less frequent drinkers, and therefore they may be more likely to commit alcohol related violence. White, Loeber, Stouthamer-Loeber & Farrington, (1999) provide support for this proposition. In a longitudinal study of adolescent males, they found concurrent and reciprocal associations between the frequency of violence and the frequency of alcohol consumption.

The final conceptualisation of antisocial behaviour focuses on the criminal justice system responses to adolescent behaviour. Self-reported delinquent acts will include both behaviours that are detected by the police and those that remain undetected, and also behaviours that meet the criteria from criminal justice action and those acts that are below a level that warrants police and court involvement. Therefore, employing an operationalisation of antisocial behaviour that considers only those behaviours which generated a Criminal Justice System (CJS) response will yield a much lower count than using a definition which is based on the act itself. However, the use of a criminal justice

125

definition provides a useful indicator of the seriousness of the offence, assuming it was detected by the police. The more serious the delinquent act, the further along the CJS it will have preceded. While behaviour based measures provide a more accurate count of offending behaviour it is difficult to assess the severity of the actual behaviour. Examination of a respondent's contact with the criminal justice system, provides some insight into the severity of their actions. Rutter et al (1998) provides an in-depth discussion of various measures of adolescent delinquency and the basic procedural stages within the CJS.

Academic performance

To date, surprisingly few studies have examined the relationship between alcohol consumption and academic performance. Hawkins et al., (1992), in their review of substance use risk factors, signposted academic failure as a potential risk, but this was not reaffirmed in other comprehensive reviews (Gilvarry, 2000; Petraitis, Flay, Miller, Torpy, & Greiner, 1998; Swadi, 1999). Most studies on this issue have examined the impact of academic failure, and in particular failing to graduate from high school, on adult drinking patterns (Mensch & Kandel, 1998).

Limitations in the existing knowledge base

Much of the knowledge base on alcohol comorbidity in adolescents is limited to clinical samples, case controlled studies, or studies of specialist populations, that is, children of alcoholics. As Armstrong and Costello (2002) noted, such evidence is limited in its generalisability. Young people with two or more conditions are more likely to enter treatment. A clinical sample may also be more severely affected by the disorders, may have distinct drinking trajectories, different risk factors and different temporal ordering of conditions. This predominance of clinical/treatment population studies of comorbidity is perhaps understandable given the real need for clinicians to take account of dual diagnosis in the provision of services to individuals with alcohol disorders. Clinicians should understand the needs and problems of their caseload, given the impact of a dual diagnosis on treatment planning (see Crawford, Crome, & Clancy, 2003, for a discussion of treatment of dual diagnosis cases). However, such research has considerable limitations when applied to the study of the developmental association between alcohol use and mental health and other problems.

126

In addition, clinical studies while being of limited generalisability tend to employ different conceptualisations of alcohol use than community studies. In many cases clinical studies focus on the psychiatric diagnosis to the detriment of any assessment of actual drinking behaviour. As a result young people tend to be allocated to one of two categories (disordered/non-disordered). While individuals who have a DSM classification of alcohol dependence or abuse (notwithstanding the validity and reliability of such classification with adolescents) undoubtedly are drinking at high levels, using a psychiatric conceptualisation of alcohol consumption means that such studies are unable to examine the relationship between mental health and lower levels of alcohol consumption. Questions around the extent to which more moderate drinking patterns increase the risk of other problems cannot be addressed in a study that dichotomise populations in relation to psychiatric diagnoses.

This problem of reducing the heterogeneity in adolescent drinking behaviour is not limited to clinical studies. Some large-scale prevalence studies of adolescent substance use, particularly when the study covers younger age ranges, have a tendency to look at adolescent drinking in terms of basic use, that is, to drink or not drink). No consideration is given to multiple dimensions of adolescent drinking such as frequency, quantity, related problems and binge episodes (see previous chapter). Again, such conceptualisations of alcohol consumption limit the ability to examine associations across the full spectrum of drinking patterns in young people.

Differences in the assessment of drinking behaviour may also give rise to much of the confusing evidence for the relationship between alcohol use and mental heath. For example, the onset of depression appears to follow the onset of alcohol use but to precede the onset of abuse or dependency (Armstrong & Costello, 2002; Brook, Brook, Zhang, Cohen, & Whiteman, 2002; Costello, et al., 1999). As a result, studies that examine mental heath problems relative to basic alcohol consumption (use/non use), such as community surveys of adolescent alcohol use, and those that examine the extent of mental health problems relative to alcohol disorders (disorder/no disorder), such as clinical studies, may generate different findings. In other words, the temporal ordering of the onset of the various behaviours and their progression into clinical disorders may explain why, when the rates of comorbid psychopathology are examined amongst

127

alcohol users relative to rates of alcohol use amongst young people with other disorders, different patterns of association are observed.

Of the limited number of community surveys of alcohol use and other problems, the majority are US based with a few noticeable exceptions. Few community samples of adolescent mental health comorbidity have been conducted within the UK. Fewer still have examined the relationship between alcohol use and mental health problems. There is limited information also on the numbers of young people within the UK who could be classified as having multiple serious problems, or the extent to which serious problems cluster within the school-age population. Therefore, replications of the US research within a UK context would be of value to assess the extent to which the associations observed within the US literature are bound by the specific cultural settings in which the research is conducted. Are the known associations between alcohol, other drug use, mental health problems and delinquency partly a factor of the US social context or are they also observed within the UK setting?

There is also a need for research that applies a conceptualisation and operationalisation of adolescent drinking patterns that goes beyond the use of unidimensional measures of alcohol consumption or limits comparisons to binary contrasts (use/non-use or disorder/no disorder). This would permit investigation of the nature of the relationship between problem behaviours and moderate drinking. As a result, questions around issues such as the potential thresholds of alcohol consumption, at which the risk for other adolescent problems becomes of practical significance could be addressed. Additional questions about the nature of the relationships between alcohol and specific other problems also remain unanswered. In particular, evidence of the role that ADHD and delinquency plays in drinking patterns is inconclusive and further work is needed.

METHOD
Respondents
The core sample used in this analysis is the 6,516 respondents who were allocated to a latent drinking class (see chapter 5). As the non-alcohol measures used in the analysis may be derived from items contained within sections of the BCS70 16-year-old follow-up other than those that provided the alcohol items, the actual working sample

with complete data may be somewhat smaller than this figure. Chapter 4 provides a discussion of the representativeness of the sample. To address potential biases that may result from the missing data, a statistical technique known as multiple imputation was employed (see chapter 4 for a full description).

Measures

Smoking age of onset: The age at which respondents first tried smoking. Coded into two-year bands.

Smoking frequency: Number of cigarettes consumed in a week. Responses were recorded on a seven-point scale ranging from 1 per week to 100+ per week. A non-smoker option was also provided.

Other drug use: Respondents were asked the number of times they had used each of 8 different substances. To minimise the possibility of someone observing the respondents' answers, the sensitive drugs questions were presented in two lists, mixed with non-sensitive questions. In the first list the drugs questions were the odd numbered items, in the second list they were the even. Respondents were then informed which list they had to use to answer the questions. These instructions were then to be destroyed by the respondent. The response codes were similar for all the questions and were contained within another section of the booklet. Responses were recoded to a single dichotomous variable representing use in the last year. One of the listed substances was Semeron, a fictional drug, used to estimate the extent of over reporting.

General Health Questionnaire: The General Health Questionnaire (Goldberg 1978) is a short 12-item screener for non-psychotic mental health problems.

The Rutter Malaise Inventory: A 22-item self-completion version of The Rutter Malaise Inventory (Rutter, Tizard & Whitmore 1970) was used to assess respondents' reported experiences of psychological symptoms, (for example, Do things worry you?) and somatic symptoms (for example, Do you suffer from indigestion?). The scale employed a three-point response code (not at all; some of the time; most of the time). Reports of 'most of the time' were considered to be evidence of symptom presence. Two items from the full malaise scale were not included in the 16-year-old follow-up. These were 'Are you troubled with rheumatism or fibrositis?' and 'Have you ever had a nervous breakdown?' The number of experienced symptoms was counted across the

129

various items. Convention would propose that scores over 8 are considered to indicative of high levels of malaise with the BCS70 cohort (Cheung, 2002).

Psychiatric or psychological referral: Within the parental self-completion form parents are asked to list any contact their child may have had with a specialist (psychiatrist or psychologist) regarding any emotional or behavioural problem.

Medical examiner reports of psychiatric or psychological problems: As part of their medical checks, the medical examiner was asked to record the presence of any psychiatric or psychological problems. Their knowledge was likely to be based on parental self-reports or on investigation of the young person's medical notes, if available. The protocol did not specify the use of any standardised test.

Delinquency: The young people were asked about the frequency of committing twenty-six different antisocial behaviours. These ranged from very minor incidents, such as watching a video nasty, to more serious offences, such as burglary. To minimise social desirability reporting, the behaviours were presented to respondents in two separate lists of which they had to complete only one. Each list contained all items. However, in the first list more serious offences were alternated with minor offences starting with a serious offence. The second list used a similar alternating pattern but started with a minor offence. Respondents were given instructions as to which list to answer. These instructions were then to be destroyed by the respondent.

The delinquency items were grouped into three main offence categories, based on the classification derived by Loeber and colleagues (Kelley, Loeber, Keenan, & DeLamatre, 1997). The first was an overt-offending pathway (repeated nuisance telephone calls, threats, and using force to get money). The second was a covert-offending pathway (criminal damage, shoplifting, theft, bike theft, theft of a car, theft from a cash machine, burglary, and selling stolen goods). The final category was lower level authority avoidance behaviours (watching video 'nasty', lying about age, watching an X rated film, going into a betting shop, spending £5 or more on a single visit to an amusement arcade, getting a tattoo, swearing at a teacher, reading a pornographic magazine, buying alcohol in a pub, and staying out all night). The frequency of behaviours was summed across each category.

Contact with the Criminal Justice System: Respondents were asked whether they had ever been in contact with the Criminal Justice System. Seven questions in total were included within this section, ranging from 'been moved on by the police' up to 'been found guilty by a court'.

Rutter A scale: A modified 19-item version of the Rutter A Scale (maternal completion) was employed. This scale assessed child behaviour problems. Exploratory factor analysis was conducted to explore the factor structure of the modified scale. Three factors were extracted (see Appendix A for full details), externalising problems (7 items), internalising problems (6 items) and hyperactivity (3 items). The items were scored on a three-point scale, from 'certainly applies' (scored as 3) to 'doesn't apply' (scored as 1). The scores on the various individual items were summed across the three scales. A total score was also calculated by summing all items. Three items did not load strongly on to any of the factors. While included in the calculation in the total score, the three items were excluded from subsequent subscale analysis.

Conners' Parent Rating Scale: As with the Rutter scale, a 19-item short form of the Conners' Rating Scale was used. The scale is primarily a measure of hyperactivity and attention problems; however, it does cover other behavioural problems (Conners 1970, Goyette, Conners & Ulrich, 1978). The items selected for use in the parental questionnaire were scored on a four-point scale (not at all/just a little/pretty much/very much). Exploratory factor analysis revealed a latent structure consisting of five factors (see Appendix A for full details). The five factors were; oppositional behaviour (6 items), impulsivity (5 items), gross motor problems (3 items), inattention (3 items), fine motor problems (2 items). Items were summed across the various subscales. A total ADHD index was also calculated by summing the subscale scores.

Family drinking patterns: Cohort members were asked to rate their perceptions of the drinking behaviour of family members. This was rated on a four-point scale (never, occasional, some days, most days). In addition, cohort member's mothers rated the drinking patterns of family members including the teenager.

Age of first menstruation: Mothers were asked to list the age at which female cohort members experienced their first menstrual period. Where this was recorded as "*before age 11*", this was recoded as age 10, although the actual age may have been earlier than this. Where mothers indicated that the young girls had not yet menstruated, this was coded as age 17, although the actual age may have been later than this.

Self-esteem: Esteem was assessed by the 'Lawseq', a 16-item self-report inventory (Lawrence 1981). Items were rated on a three point Likert scale (yes/no/don't' know).

Vocabulary test: Respondents were asked to complete a 75-item vocabulary test in which they were given a key word (identified in bold capitals) and a list of five alternate words from which they had to identify the word which meant the same as the key word (for example: FOREST: grass wood sleep grind judge). For the majority of respondents (n=3677) the vocabulary test was completed at school under test conditions. They were given 15 minutes to complete the task. A sizeable proportion of respondents completed the test at home (n=2059). As a result test scores from the "at-home" group may be less reliable than the "at-school" group. Respondents were given one point for each correct answer and correct answers were summed across the 75 items.

Spelling test: Respondents were given a spelling test consisting of 200 items presented in two 100 item lists. To reduce question order effects, on odd days list A was given first, and on even days list B was given first. The items consisted of a single word of which the respondent had to decide was spelt correctly or incorrectly. Items included words such as "thimble, seaze, pleasunt, charactor, and cystitis". One point was given for each correct answer and scores were summed across the two hundred items. As with the vocabulary test, some respondents completed it in school (n=3677) and some completed it at home (n=2059). The 'at-school' group was given ten minutes to complete each 100 word list.

Teacher assessment: In addition to the educational tests, teachers were asked to provide information on respondents including a rating of their performance in school and their underlying ability. By subtracting pupils' performance rating from their ability score it is possible to identify discrepancies between a teacher's perception of their ability and their work in class. Pupils were classified as over-performing (performance score higher that ability score), achieving at perceived ability level (performance score equal to ability score), and under-performing (performance score lower that ability score). Teacher rating of performance and ability are likely to be influenced by a wide range of classroom attributes and behaviours such as educational motivation, attitude towards the teacher, behaviour in class, attendance, interaction with other pupils, etc. As a result, this rating is likely to tap into a broad assessment of pupil behaviour in school.

Teachers were also asked whether pupils had been assessed for special educational provision, and whether they had ever been suspended from school.

Demographics: In addition to key behavioural measures the analysis also included a range of demographic indicators including ethnicity, gender, family structure and family income. Combined gross household income was recoded into six financial bands (under £2600; £2600 - £7799; £7800 - £12999; £13000 - £18199; £18200 - £23399; £23400 and above).

Analysis

Initial LCA model was estimated in LEM (Vermunt, 1997a,b) (see previous chapter). A modal assignment rule was then used to allocate respondents to the latent class that corresponded to the highest posterior conditional response probability across the observed indicators. Bivariate exploratory statistics and multinomial logistic regression were used to examine the relationship between covariates and assigned drinking patterns. It is worth noting that there is a small degree of error associated with a two-stage 'classify-analysis' procedure such as this, as it ignores the uncertainty associated with a probabilistic class allocation (Chung & Martin, 2001;). However, a two-stage procedure is more efficient, convenient and easier to estimate (see for example, Roeder, Lynch, & Nagin, 1999). Multiple imputation (MI) was employed to minimise biases in parameter estimates and standard errors due to item non-response (see chapter 4). Covariates were introduced into the regression models in a single block.[6.14]

RESULTS

Smoking

Table 6.1 clearly shows that young people who drank more were more likely to smoke as well (chi^2 = 602.617, df = 24, p < 0.001).

[6.14] An alternative option would be to arrange the covariates into multiple blocks, based on theoretical or psychometric criteria, and to enter the various blocks in a forward or stepwise method.

Table 6.1 Age of smoking onset by drinking status

	Never smoked %	>6 %	7-8 %	9-10 %	11-12 %	13-14 %	15 %	Total %
Limited use	71.7	2.3	3.5	3.5	6.9	8.5	3.5	100.0
Occasional use	54.8	1.2	4.0	5.5	11.8	16.1	6.5	100.0
Moderate use	43.8	1.8	3.9	7.8	14.6	20.5	7.5	100.0
Heavy use	26.8	2.0	6.5	11.3	22.3	22.7	8.4	100.0
Hazardous use	16.6	2.7	9.8	17.4	24.5	21.8	7.3	100.0
Total	42.3	1.8	5.0	8.6	16.0	19.1	7.1	100.0

Only 17% of hazardous drinkers never smoked. This compares to 72% of limited alcohol users. While only 6% of limited alcohol users had smoked before the age of 9, 13% of hazardous drinkers had done so by this age.

Those young people with the heavier patterns of alcohol consumption also report heavier current smoking (Table 6.2) (chi^2 = 747.609, df = 32, p < 0.001). While limited drinkers were almost all current non-smokers (94.1%), less than half of hazardous drinkers were. In fact, almost 5% of them were smoking over 100 cigarettes per week. As the intensity of drinking increased so too did the proportion smoking cigarettes at a high intensity.

Table 6.2 Frequency of smoking (number of cigarettes per week) by drinking status

	None %	1 %	2-5 %	5-10 %	11-20 %	21-40 %	41-70 %	71-100 %	> 100 %	Total %
Limited use	94.1	1.4	.2	.2	.4	1.6	.8	.6	.6	100.0
Occasional use	84.3	2.9	1.6	1.9	2.4	2.9	2.6	.9	.5	100.0
Moderate use	78.9	4.7	2.8	1.7	3.4	3.7	2.9	.8	1.0	100.0
Heavy use	61.0	5.2	3.8	3.6	6.4	9.2	6.7	2.9	1.3	100.0
Hazardous use	46.9	3.5	2.0	3.1	5.9	11.1	14.8	8.0	4.6	100.0
Total	74.4	4.0	2.5	2.2	3.8	5.3	4.6	1.9	1.2	100.0

Other drug use

Like smoking, the rate of illicit drug use was higher amongst heavy and hazardous drinkers than more occasional imbibers (Table 6.3). While the difference in drug use

134

prevalence between hazardous drinkers and limited drinkers was considerable, the difference between heavy drinkers and hazardous drinkers was still sizeable. In all drugs covered in the survey, hazardous drinkers were more than twice as likely to use the drug in the last 12 months than heavy drinkers.

Over one in five of hazardous drinkers had used cannabis in the last year. Not only were these respondents drinking at problematic levels but also their drinking could well have been accompanied by the use of cannabis. Other alcohol drug combinations were less common. It could be argued that the association between high levels of alcohol consumption and the consumption of other substances is due to response errors affecting both measures. In other words, those young people who exaggerate their alcohol use, also exaggerate their drug use as well. Examination of the responses to the fictional drug *semeron* would suggest that overt over-reporting was not an extensive problem (only 1.3% of hazardous drivers claimed to have used semeron). Such level of over-reporting would not be sufficient to account for the observed association between drinking and drug use.

Table 6.3 Prevalence of other drug use by drinking status

	Solvents	Uppers[1]	Downers[2]	Cannabis	LSD	Cocaine	Semeron	Heroin
	%	%	%	%	%	%	%	%
Limited use	1.7	0.6	0.8	1.1	1.1	0.3	0.0	0.0
Occasional use	2.9	0.9	0.3	2.9	0.9	0.3	0.3	0.1
Moderate use	2.8	1.6	1.0	4.1	1.2	0.2	0.5	0.2
Heavy use	6.0	3.0	1.4	9.2	2.4	1.0	0.4	0.6
Hazardous use	13.8	10.8	3.8	21.8	6.0	2.3	1.3	1.3
Total	4.5	2.5	1.2	6.3	1.8	0.6	0.4	0.4

Notes

1. Speed/whizz/amphetamines

2. Blues/tranks/barbituates

Mental health

While hazardous drinkers had, on average, higher General Health Questionnaire (GHQ) scores, the differences were not significant (Table 6.4). In contrast, significant differences across the five drinking patterns were observed for the number of reported symptoms of psychosomatic distress (malaise). Hazardous drinkers and those who used alcohol on a limited basis reported the highest scores. Moderate users reported the

135

lowest levels of malaise. This is also reflected in the caseness scores, where the rate of clinical malaise amongst hazardous drinkers was over twice the rate of moderate drinkers (Table 6.4).

Of the 5,343 parents who replied to the question on psychiatric or psychological referrals, 202 (4%) stated that their child had seen a specialist for an emotional or behavioural problem. The rate of referral to psychiatric or psychological specialists was slightly higher for those young people who reported hazardous drinking (6%). For other young people, that is, those in drinking classes 1 – 4, the level of referral was around 4%. However, it must be borne in mind that these are referrals only, and may not have resulted in an actual diagnosis being made. Also there may be considerable temporal variations in when the referrals occurred. To examine this latter point, the year of referral was considered. For latent class-5 - hazardous drinkers - the majority of referrals (60%) were in the five years just prior to the time of the interview (1986-1981). For other classes of drinking, referrals were slightly more frequent in the earlier years of the young person's life, with 43% (latent class 1 and 3), 50% and 51% (latent classes 4 and 2 respectively) occurring in the corresponding period.

Psychiatric data were also collected from the medical examinations that were completed on 3,782 (58%) respondents. Notwithstanding the limitations of this data, this information does provide some further insights into the comorbidity between hazardous drinking patterns and other emotional and behavioural concerns. First, medical examiners were asked whether the respondent had had any emotional or behavioural problem since the age of 10. Of the 3,707 respondents for whom this question was answered, 190 were reported to have had an emotional or behavioural problem. The rate of emotional problems was slightly higher amongst hazardous drinkers than other respondents. Almost 8% of heavy drinkers were considered as having an emotional or behavioural problem compared with around 5% for the other respondents (3.6% limited drinkers; 5.4% occasional drinkers; 4.8% moderate drinkers; 5.0% heavy drinkers). Second, medical examiners were asked whether there was any evidence that the respondent had a psychiatric or psychological problem. Positive replies were made for 169 respondents (4.5 % of respondents for which the medical examination was completed). Medical examiners identified 297 problems experienced by 8% of the 3,712 valid cases. Rates of psychological and psychiatric problems were again slightly elevated amongst hazardous drinkers (9%) compared with 8% of limited drinkers, 7 % of moderate drinkers and 8% of heavy drinkers. The similar rate of problems found amongst hazardous drinkers and occasional drinkers (9%), weakens any suggested relationship between the overall reported level of psychological and psychiatric problems and drinking patterns. It is also possible to look at the rate of specific conditions.

Table 6.4 shows the proportion of cases in each drinking pattern where the medical examiner reported a psychological or psychiatric problem. Those young people classified as having hazardous drinking patterns have slightly inflated risks of being labelled as also having depression and making suicide attempts or threats. However, none of these differences reached statistical significance across the five categories of drinking patterns. Table 6.4 also presents the Rutter A total scores. No significant differences were detected across the various drinking categories. Significant differences were detected, however, within the various Rutter subscales. Externalising behaviours peaked amongst hazardous drinkers. However, unlike other measures of antisocial behaviour, the mothers of the limited use young people reported high levels of externalising behaviour. In fact the relationship between drinking behaviour and externalising behaviours is best described as 'U' shaped, with the lowest level reported amongst moderate alcohol users. In contrast, internalising behaviours peaked amongst limited use drinkers. As drinking levels increased the mean level of parental reports of internalising problems decreased. No differences were detected across the levels of hyperactivity as assessed by the Rutter A scale.

Unlike the Rutter scale, significant differences were detected in relation to drinking and ADHD in young people when using the Conners rating scale (Table 6.4). On the total ADHD index maternal reports were highest amongst hazardous drinkers. Significant differences were detected on both inattention and impulsivity. Again, their mothers scored hazardous drinkers higher than the young people classified into other drinking patterns. Differences were also noted in relation to oppositional behaviour but not in relation to problems of gross or fine motor control.

Table 6.4 Association between adolescent characteristics (mean scores) and latent drinking classes at age 16

	Latent Class					
	Limited use	Occasional use	Moderate use	Heavy use	Hazardous use	*p*
Mean GHQ12 score	12.9	13.0	13.0	13.0	13.2	0.591
Mean Rutter Scale scores						
Rutter total score	23.3	22.9	22.7	22.8	22.9	0.125
Externalising behaviour	7.9	7.6	7.6	7.7	8.0	<0.001
Internalising Behaviour	8.6	8.4	8.2	8.1	8.0	<0.001
Hyperactivity	3.6	3.5	3.5	3.5	3.6	0.078
Mean Conners' Scale scores						
ADHD Index	5.6	5.2	5.3	5.8	6.5	0.001
Oppositional Behaviour	2.2	2.1	2.1	2.3	2.6	0.030
Hyperactivity	1.4	1.3	1.3	1.6	1.7	0.001
Gross motor problems	0.7	0.6	0.6	0.7	0.7	0.378
Inattention	1.2	1.1	1.2	1.2	1.6	<0.001
Fine motor problems	0.1	0.1	0.1	0.1	0.1	0.969
Mean malaise score	1.1	1.0	0.9	1.0	1.4	<0.001
Malaise caseness	2.0	1.4	1.2	1.5	3.2	0.041
(% with 8+ symptoms.)						
Medical examination						
% Behavioural problem	1.3	1.1	1.2	1.6	1.3	0.181
% Depression	1.7	2.4	1.8	2.3	3.0	0.683
% Aggression	2.0	1.0	1.3	0.8	1.7	0.743
% Eating disorder	1.3	2.2	1.1	1.1	1.4	0.328
% Psychosis	0.3	0.3	0.4	0.6	0.4	0.778
% Neurosis	1.0	1.0	0.6	0.7	0.3	0.565
% Suicide attempts/ threats	0.3	0.9	0.9	1.0	1.7	0.698

Antisocial behaviour

Hazardous drinkers followed by heavy drinkers report the highest frequency across the three delinquency pathways (Table 6.5). Heavier drinkers also had significantly greater contact with the police and the Criminal Justice System. Not only is heavier drinking associated with increased delinquency and greater risk of contact with the Criminal Justice System, but also it is associated with increased risk of being the victim of a crime. Hazardous drinkers suffer a significantly higher level of victimisation that those young people who drink less (Table 6.5).

Table 6.5 Association between adolescent characteristics (proportions) and latent drinking classes at age 16

	Latent Class					
	Limited use	Occasional use	Moderate use	Heavy use	Hazardous use	*p*
Mean freq overt behaviours	0.2	0.2	0.2	0.4	0.7	<0.001
Mean freq covert behaviours	0.9	0.7	0.8	1.4	2.6	<0.001
Mean freq authority conflict behaviours	2.7	4.8	6.7	9.8	13.9	<0.001
Mean self esteem	14.48	14.80	15.34	15.10	14.81	<0.001
Contact with the CJS						
% Moved on by police	11.4	21.7	24.5	38.9	57.6	<0.001
% Stopped by police	12.2	18.6	20.0	32.7	50.7	<0.001
% Stopped by Store Detective	4.4	6.2	7.2	10.7	20.1	<0.001
% Warned by police	7.9	12.3	12.8	22.1	35.8	<0.001
% Arrested	2.7	5.5	4.2	8.8	18.9	<0.001
% Cautioned	3.5	6.4	6.0	11.0	22.1	<0.001
% Found guilty in court	1.5	2.2	1.6	3.5	7.4	<0.001
Victimisation						
% Something stolen from you	12.6	14.5	17.9	20.0	26.4	<0.001
% Someone been violent to you	10.3	9.4	13.5	15.2	23.2	<0.001
% Someone threatened you	8.0	10.4	12.2	15.0	21.1	<0.001
% Unwanted sexual approaches	1.7	2.3	3.2	4.2	6.3	<0.001

Table 6.5 also presents the mean self-esteem score by drinking status. The table shows an inverted U shaped relationship between drinking and self-esteem. High self-esteem is associated with moderate alcohol consumption (15.34). As drinking both increases and decreases from the central point self-esteem level falls (F=8.412, *df* = 4, p<0.000). Limited use young people report the lowest mean self-esteem scores (14.48), followed by occasional users and hazardous users (14.80, 14.81, respectively).

Correlations were run to examine the strength of the relationship between hyperactivity, attention problems (both assessed by both the Conners and Rutter scale), mood problems (Rutter Malaise, Rutter A internalising behaviour) and offending behaviour (offending scales; overt, covert and authority conflict, Rutter A externalising behaviour) (see Table 6.6). In relation to hyperactivity, moderate correlations were observed between the inattention, externalising and oppositional behaviours. Hyperactivity was not strongly correlated with any of the measures of mood disorders, such as the Rutter A internalising behaviours subscale or the Rutter Malaise scale. It is interesting to note that hyperactivity appears not to be related to drinking behaviour when assessed by the Rutter items, but does when assessed by the Conners' subscale. Clearly, the subscales, while having the same labels, are assessing slightly different constructs. The correlation between the two subscales is 0.576.

Few mothers report frequent drinking amongst the cohort members (Table 6.7). Over 95% of mothers of the limited use group said that their young person had never used alcohol. Even amongst the hazardous use group, only a quarter of the mothers believed that they never used alcohol. Given the nature of most adolescent drinking it is not surprising that mothers appear to under-report the extent of adolescent drinking. Notwithstanding these limitations, significant differences in maternal reports of teenagers drinking were noted across the various latent classes (chi^2 = 1107.009, df = 20, $p < 0.001$). As adolescents' own reports of drinking increased, so too did their mother's reports. Over 40% of the mothers of hazardous drinkers reported that their teenager drank at least once or twice a week. This compares to 0.5% of mothers whose teenagers reported limited alcohol use. While only 9% of mothers of hazardous drinkers are aware that their teenager is drinking 3 or more times a week, less that 0.5% of mothers of limited or occasional alcohol users make similar claims.

Table 6.6 Correlations between behavioural and psychiatric morbidity scales

	Hyperactivity (Conners)	Inattention	Malaise	Overt	Covert	Authority avoidance	Externalising behaviour	Internalising behaviour	Hyperactivity (Rutter)	Oppositional behaviour
Hyperactivity (Conners)	1.00	0.558	0.101	0.079	0.123	0.085	0.434	0.355	0.576	0.585
Inattention	0.558	1.00	0.126	0.095	0.149	0.086	0.404	0.314	0.520	0.484
Malaise	0.101	0.126	1.00	0.093	0.107	0.006	0.136	0.175	0.079	0.195
Overt	0.079	0.095	0.093	1.00	0.593	0.074	0.122	0.041	0.049	0.090
Covert	0.123	0.149	0.107	0.593	1.00	0.114	0.171	0.047	0.099	0.110
Authority avoidance	0.085	0.086	0.006	0.074	0.114	1.00	0.107	-0.044	0.041	0.062
Externalising behaviour	0.434	0.404	0.136	0.122	0.171	0.107	1.00	0.381	0.407	0.476
Internalising behaviour	0.355	0.314	0.175	0.041	0.047	-0.044	0.381	1.00	0.345	0.564
Hyperactivity (Rutter)	0.576	0.520	0.079	0.049	0.099	0.041	0.407	0.345	1.00	0.376
Oppositional	0.585	0.484	0.195	0.090	0.110	0.062	0.476	0.564	0.376	1.00

Hazardous drinking is also associated with significantly higher levels of drinking amongst mothers (chi^2 = 345.585, df = 20, p < 0.001) and fathers (chi^2 = 288.790, df = 20, p < 0.001) (see Table 6.7). Around 40% of fathers and 23% of mothers of hazardous drinkers were drinking at least 3 times a week. In comparison only 20% of fathers and 8% of mothers of limited use drinkers were considered to be drinking at this level.

Table 6.7 Maternal reports of family members' drinking behaviour by teenager's drinking status.

	Limited use %	Occasional use %	Moderate use %	Heavy use %	Hazardous use %
Teenager					
Never	96.2	77.7	46.1	36.2	24.9
Once a month	1.8	9.4	13.4	11.7	8.5
2-3 times a month	1.3	8.1	18.7	19.3	16.6
Once or twice a week	0.5	4.7	20.3	28.8	40.8
3-4 times a week	0.3	0.1	1.3	3.4	8.1
Every day	0.0	0.0	0.3	0.6	1.1
Father					
Never	38.7	21.5	11.7	11.3	10.4
Once a month	9.5	9.8	6.2	6.4	3.9
2-3 times a month	9.5	11.5	11.4	11.2	10.4
Once or twice a week	22.8	35.7	37.9	37.3	35.8
3-4 times a week	11.7	13.0	20.0	20.5	22.8
Every day	7.8	8.5	12.8	13.4	16.7
Mother					
Never	59.7	35.4	24.4	24.0	18.5
Once a month	7.5	13.8	9.2	9.1	6.9
2-3 times a month	12.1	15.0	15.0	15.2	12.6
Once or twice a week	13.2	25.1	34.5	34.0	39.1
3-4 times a week	4.7	7.9	11.2	11.3	16.2
Every day	2.8	2.8	5.6	6.4	6.6

Academic performance

No significant differences were detected on either the scores for the vocabulary test or the spelling test across either the at-home completion group or the at- school

142

completion group. For the vocabulary test mean scores across the five alcohol categories ranged from 14.40 (sd =3.66) to 14.56 (sd =3.96) (F=0.239; *df* = 4; p = 0.916) within the at-school group. The results amongst the at-home group, while lower, displayed the same pattern. They ranged from 12.32 (sd =5.46) to 13.06 (sd =4.86) (F=1.28; *df* = 4; p = 0.275). Likewise no significant differences were recorded on the mean spelling test scores across the five alcohol patterns in either the at-school group (F=1.69; *df* = 4; p =0.150) or the at home group (F=1.45; *df* = 4; p =0.216). The range between the highest and lowest scores across the alcohol pattern was less than 3 points in the school group and 9 points in the home group.

Significant differences were found on teacher rating of educational performance and abilities across the drinking groups; however, the findings do not support the hypothesised relationship (Table 6.8). If anything the hazardous drinkers could be described as average. There are fewer hazardous drinkers in both the above-average bands and the below-average bands.

Table 6.8 Academic performance and drinking class.

	Latent Class					p
	Limited use	Occasional use	Moderate use	Heavy use	Hazardous use	
Assessment of academic performance, %						<0.001
Top 5%	5.8	5.2	6.1	4.6	2.9	
Bottom 5%	8.3	4.9	3.4	2.7	5.8	
Assessment of academic ability, %						<0.001
Top 5%	5.5	5.4	6.4	4.8	3.0	
Bottom 5%	2.9	0.6	0.6	0.3	0.0	
Been assessed for special education?						<0.001
Yes, action taken %	6.9	3.7	2.2	1.9	1.5	
Yes, no action taken %	1.8	0.5	0.6	0.4	0.5	
Discrepancies between performance and ability						<0.001
Under performing	11.0	10.5	12.7	22.9	30.0	
Performing at perceived ability	84.6	82.9	80.9	74.5	70.0	
Over performing	4.4	6.6	6.4	2.6	0.0	

Limited use drinkers, on the other hand, are more likely to fall into the extreme bands, both at the high ability and low ability ends than the other drinking categories. It may be the case that while heavy or hazardous drinking is less common among the more able young people, special educational needs may in some way mitigate against heavy alcohol consumption. These children may have less free time or may be under stricter parental supervision.

This conclusion is somewhat supported by the special educational assessments (Table 6.8). Such assessments are higher for those young people in the limited use drinking category. In contrast, the hazardous group was the least likely to experience educational assessment. However, when discrepancies between teacher rating of ability and current academic performance are examined clear differences emerge. While the majority of all pupils appear to be performing at a level equivalent to their perceived ability, a greater proportion of hazardous drinkers appear to be under performing.

Multinomial logistic regression

A weakness of examining association between pairs of variables (drinking pattern and a covariate) is that the relationship between any two variables may be due to their joint association with a third variable. In many cases, once the third variable is controlled for, the strength of the original association is reduced. With the number of potential covariates presented above, it is necessary to undertake a multivariate analysis. Multinomial logistic regression permits the examination of the relative contribution made by each of the various covariates to explaining the variation in the observed drinking patterns. As logistic regression can suffer from problems of multicollinearity, where covariates are not independent measures but also co-vary with each other or with subsets of each other, it is not possible to include all the potential covariates presented above. Therefore, the logistic regression was performed on only a selected number of covariates. Table 6.9 presents the parameter estimates, odds ratios and confidence intervals for the selected indicators. Hazardous drinkers were selected as the reference category for the logistic model.

The multinomial logistic regression procedure performs comparisons between the log odds of being in the hazardous drinking class relative to being in each of the other drinking classes in turn. Ethnicity differences were detected in the teetotal-hazardous drinking, occasional use-hazardous drinking and moderate use-hazardous drinking comparisons, but not for the heavy drinking comparison undertaken. In each case being non-white was associated with an increased likelihood of being in the lower drinking class. Gender differences were detected between hazardous drinking and the occasional and moderate use groups but not with the teetotal and heavy use groups. Females were more likely to belong in the occasional and moderate use groups than the hazardous use group.

While inconsistent findings were observed in relation to the effects of family structure on drinking patterns, parental drinking was associated with increased likelihood of being in the hazardous drinking groups. While the odds ratios for fathers drinking were significant across all comparisons made, significance was only reached for mothers drinking in the comparisons between hazardous use class and the teetotal and occasional use classes. In general, increased parental drinking, in particular paternal heavy drinking was associated with increased odds of being classified as a hazardous drinker.

Increased family income was also associated with increased odds of being classified as having a hazardous alcohol consumption pattern. Again the odds ratios were significant only for the teetotal and occasional use comparisons with the hazardous class.

Drug use and smoking were also associated with increased risk of being within the hazardous drinking class, as was the frequency of authority avoidance behaviours. While the frequency of overt offending distinguished between the hazardous use class and the other alcohol use categories, except the heavy use class, covert offending only reached significance for the hazardous–teetotal comparison. As with the other significant offending results, increased frequency of offending was associated with increased odds of also reporting a hazardous alcohol consumption pattern. No significant findings were observed across the GHQ, Conners' or Malaise rating scales.

Table 6.9 Adolescent characteristics associated with adolescent drinking patterns: multinomial logistic regression

	Limited use		Occasional use		Moderate Use		Heavy use	
	OR	Sig.	OR	Sig.	OR	Sig.	OR	Sig.
Ethnicity								
Non-white	13.82	**	3.45	**	2.18	**	1.46	
White	1.00		1.00		1.00		1.00	
Gender								
Females	1.02	*	1.32		1.36		1.08	
Males	1.00		1.00		1.00		1.00	
Family structure								
Single parent	1.34		1.34		1.36		2.02	*
Reconstituted family	0.60		1.27		0.90		0.95	
Other/undefined	1.44		1.25	*	1.26		1.11	
Two natural parents	1.00		1.00		1.00		1.00	
Father's drinking								
Heavy	0.07	**	0.02	**	0.27	**	0.54	*
Light	1.00		1.00		1.00		1.00	
Mother's drinking								
Heavy	0.56	**	0.61	**	0.88		0.87	
Light	1.00		1.00		1.00		1.00	
Family income	0.90	**	0.91	*	1.02		1.02	
Drug use								
Yes	0.41	**	0.53	**	0.53	**	0.64	**
No	1.00		1.00		1.00		1.00	
Smoking								
Heavy	0.17	**	0.20	**	0.24	**	0.46	**
Light	0.13	**	0.37	**	0.48	**	0.87	
None	1.00		1.00		1.00		1.00	
GHQ	1.00		0.99		0.98		1.00	
Conners' score	1.02		1.01		1.01		1.01	
Malaise score	0.99		0.96		0.95		0.95	
Overt offending	0.79	*	0.83	*	0.78	**	0.87	
Covert offending	0.95	**	0.93		0.97		0.99	
Authority Avoidance	0.76	**	0.82	**	0.88	**	0.94	**

DISCUSSION

The comorbidity between problem alcohol use and other drug use shown in this analysis is well established (Dawson 2000b; Jackson, Sher & Wood, 2000). Lynskey, Fergusson and Horwood (1998) found that the comorbidity between tobacco, alcohol and cannabis use in 16-year-olds arose from a shared set of common risk factors or source of vulnerability rather than any causal paths between the substances. However, class differences were also detected on the dummy drug 'Semeron'. Hazardous drinkers were the most likely to report the use of Semeron, even thought still in relatively small numbers. This may represent a small tendency to over report substance use, which may include alcohol, tobacco and illicit drugs amongst this group.

The ethnicity and gender differences detected in drinking patterns also support existing research (Best, et al., 2001; Fuller, 2005). While the hazardous class are more likely to be white compared with other drink classes, the gender gap is only observed when hazardous drinkers are compared with occasional and moderate users. It appears that while females in general drink less than males, they tend to be clustered in the non-extreme classes.

Children of problem drinkers have received considerable research attention, and this study confirmed the links between parental and child drinking behaviours (Jacob & Johnston, 1997; Johnston & Leff, 1999). Leib et al., (2002) found that paternal drinking, in particular, was associated with the transition from regular to hazardous drinking for adolescents. While this study did not examine the progressions in alcohol consumption, it did find that parental drinking distinguished between hazardous drinkers and heavy/moderate users beyond that accounted for by maternal drinking patterns. It may be the case that maternal drinking is influential in the early stages of adolescent drinking, possibly through reduced monitoring and supervision, while parental drinking plays a greater role in shaping later use and the development of problematic consumption patterns in late adolescence. However, this proposed pathway would require further longitudinal examination.

As with parental drinking, the association between adolescent alcohol consumption and delinquency is well established (Fergusson & Horwood, 2000; Fergusson, Lynskey & Horwood, 1996; Jessor & Jessor, 1977; White et al., 1999). Within this study the association between alcohol consumption and offending frequency was also confirmed. The association wasmost pronounced for authority avoidance and overt behaviours, that is to say the frequency of offending behaviour of these types, was related to an increased likelihood of being a hazardous drinker, relative to other high consumption groups. While the frequency of covert offences, in contrast, distinguished between hazardous drinkers and teetotallers, it failed to reach statistical significance for the other class comparisons. This suggestion that hazardous drinking has a greater effect on violent offences (overt) than property offences (covert) has been demonstrated in longitudinal studies (Fergusson & Horwood, 2000; Fergusson, Lynskey & Horwood, 1996). Increased alcohol consumption is associated with increased risk of delinquency, contact with the Criminal Justice System and victimisation. Not only are adolescent drinkers more likely to commit offences and to be prosecuted for them, they are also more likely to be the victim of a crime. Cross-sectional victimisation survey such as the British Crime Survey have shown that a high proportion of violent crime is committed by young men on other young men in and around locations serving alcohol (Mirrlees-Black, Mayhew, & Percy, 1996). The evidence presented here would suggest that this association between violence in young men (and women to a lesser degree) and alcohol, exists before young people are legally permitted to drink.

One interesting set of findings was the lack of association between drinking patterns and mental health problems. No subgroup differences were observed in general psychopathology, attentional problems or malaise. While studies have estimated that between 60% to 80% of young people with alcohol problems had at least one other psychiatric problem (Armstrong & Costello 2002; Rohde, Lewinsohn & Seeley, 1996) most of this is accounted for by conduct disorder, here operationalised in terms of offending behaviour. The evidence for a comorbid relationship between alcohol and other disorders is relatively inconclusive. While Federman et al., (1997) found that amongst alcohol using boys no differences in the rates of anxiety or depression were detectable, they were observed amongst alcohol using girls. Costello, et al., (1999) also found higher alcohol use rates amongst young people with depression (boys only) and behaviour disorders (both sexes), but not anxiety (both sexes). Greenblatt, (2000), while confirming the contemporaneous comorbidity between heavy drinking, criminality and other externalising behaviours, found no evidence of a similar association with symptoms of anxiety or depression. Chassin et al., (2002) found lower levels of depression amongst male early onset heavy drinkers than moderate or non-drinkers. For females depression was associated with infrequent drinking. Boys et al., (2003) in a major survey of psychiatric morbidity amongst UK adolescents, found that while depression (but not anxiety) predicted regular drinking, regular drinkers were no more likely than non-drinkers to have emotional problems or other psychiatric disorders.

Therefore, the evidence for a concurrent relationship between alcohol problems and other mental health problems is rather inconclusive. There are a number of reasons why these findings may have occurred. First, the relationship between alcohol use and mental health problems may only exist for psychosomatic problems and not for other psychological or psychiatric conditions. Second, the relationship between alcohol use and mental health problems may not be concurrent but developmental, with mental health problems preceeding but not always co-existing with alcohol use. This possibility will be examined in a later chapter. Third, the relationship between alcohol problems may exist but may be relatively subtle, and as a result the research design may not be able to detect the small effect, either because the sample size is too small or the measures are not sensitive enough. While this may be the case, from a purely statistical perspective the actual differences observed in the GHQ scores, for example, would not suggest substantive clinical significance warranting consideration. Even the statistically significant finding for malaise may not reach substantive clinical importance. Fourth, the relationship between drinking and mental health may be confounded by some third variable, for example gender. Here, a substantive association may only exist for one sex. When the findings are examined where both sexes are combined, the non-significant sex may weaken any association observed. Finally, the findings may have been biased by the extent of the missing data on some of the measures, in particular those on the psychiatric and psychological services and the medical examination. If those young people who were classified as problematic drinkers were more likely to experience mental health problems, but were also more likely to not complete the various questionnaires provided, this would weaken the findings. However, examination of the distribution of the missing values would suggest that they are relatively evenly distributed across the five drinking patterns. In conclusion, there is little evidence found in support of the general hypothesis that problem drinkers are more likely to suffer other concurrent mental health problems.

In conclusion, adolescent problem drinking is not evenly spread across the population; rather it tends to be clustered within certain groups. Young white males tend to be the main constituents of the hazardous drinking group. Alcohol consumption in adolescents is also associated with heavier drinking within the family. Adolescents who drink tend to have fathers and mothers who drink as well. Finally, drinking is also associated with other poor adolescent outcomes including poor performance at school, offending behaviour, smoking and drug use.

This analysis further confirms the validity of the LCA typology constructed here. The model successfully distinguishes adolescent drinkers across a range of non-alcohol variables confirming existing known associations between hazardous drinking and other adolescent characteristics.

SUMMARY

This chapter utilised the previously developed (chapter 4) latent class typology of drinking styles to examine the social, demographic and behavioural characteristics of problematic adolescent drinkers. Multinomial logistic regression (with multiple imputation) was the statistical procedure employed to test the various covariates considered within the model.

These findings were consistent with a common vulnerability model of adolescent problem behaviour. However, the relationship between drinking and offending was not constant across all offences. This analysis supported the hypothesis that hazardous drinking has a greater association with violent offences (overt) than property offences (covert).

This study also confirmed the links between parental and adolescent drinking behaviours. Here, however, paternal drinking distinguished between hazardous drinkers and heavy/moderate users beyond that accounted for by maternal drinking patterns. Hazardous drinkers were more likely to have a frequent drinking mother than occasional or limited drinkers, and were also more likely to have a frequent drinking father than all the other drinking classes. This difference may indicate a variation in the mechanisms through which parental drinking influences adolescent behaviour as well as differences in the proportion of parents within the two drinking categories used here.

One interesting set of findings was the lack of association between drinking patterns and mental health problems. While studies have estimated that around 60% to 80% of young people with alcohol problems have at least one other psychiatric problem, most of this is accounted for by conduct disorder/offending behaviour. The lack of a relationship between hyperactivity and alcohol use may reflect the developmental nature of the association. While childhood hyperactivity may predict later adolescent drinking, the age related decline in hyperactivity symptoms across adolescence, may result in a reduced association when examined in cross-section. It is worth bearing in mind when considering these findings that the association between alcohol consumption and mental health may have changed in the intervening years since these data were collected.

Even though the survey data used in this study are dated, it does demonstrate that latent class analysis is a viable analytical strategy for the identification of subpopulations of drinkers. The five classes do appear to be a functional typology capable of distinguishing adolescents on a range of other related alcohol measures.

While LCA does have some limitations, it does address weaknesses inherent in methods where the allocation of individuals to drinking subgroups is not based on an underlying statistical model. A better identification of drinking patterns amongst adolescents should contribute to current epidemiological knowledge on adolescent health behaviours and provide insights for the development of public health programmes for the reduction of alcohol related harm. Further analysis of the available data will examine the antecedents (chapter 7) of these drinking patterns and their consequence (chapter 8) for the successful transition to early adulthood.

7 ANTECEDENTS OF HAZARDOUS DRINKING

This chapter examines childhood characteristics and experiences that may influence individual vulnerability towards the development of hazardous drinking patterns at age 16. As such it deals with risk processes that occur before those examined in the previous chapters (5 & 6). However, as the examination of the correlates was essential for establishing the validity of the typology (chapter 5) and for describing the characteristics of the various drinking classes at age 16 (chapter 6), it was undertaken and presented before this chapter on the antecedents of drinking behaviour.

The chapter will begin by reviewing existing theoretical and empirical evidence on putative risk factors. It will also consider the methodological limitations of the existing knowledge base, in so far as they could be addressed within this study. From this a number of key research questions will be outlined, addressing both identified knowledge gaps and shortcoming. The chapter will then present the methods, analysis and findings of further empirical analysis of the BCS data, this time covering not only the 16-year-old sweep, but also the earlier data sweeps (birth, age 5 and age 10).

A CAUSAL MODEL OF ADOLESCENT PROBLEM DRINKING.

A large number of risk factors for adolescent substance abuse have been identified (see Gilvarry, 2000; Hawkins, Catalano, & Miller, 1992; Petraitis, Flay, Miller, Torpy, & Greiner, 1998; Swadi, 1999 for recent reviews). These multiple intraindividual and environmental factors interact to influence an individual's vulnerability to substance use problems (Glantz & Leshner, 2000). A consistent recommendation of these major reviews is the need for further theoretical progression that organises and integrates the existing complex body of empirical evidence, as a focal point for the development of new research priorities.

Sher (1994; Sher & Gotham, 1999) suggested that it is possible to identify subtypes of alcohol problems based on the underlying etiological pathways. He proposed that different constellations of risk factors operating together may give rise to

152

drinking problems, and as a result it may be possible to categorise alcohol problems on the basis of these etiological pathways. A distinction must be made between this theoretical typology and the empirical typology presented in previous chapters, which is based on differences in drinking behaviours. The use of the term 'pathway' is also somewhat different from the developmental pathway, as described earlier, which documents the change in individual drinking behaviours over time. Pathways within Sher's model refer to the way in which factors may mediate and moderate the influence of other factors, generating an overall liability for problem drinking. They are the etiological linkages between distal and proximal risk, and in this respect are similar to what others have termed causal chains (Boyce et al., 1998; Rutter, 1993; 1994a; 1999b Rutter et al., 1997). While most risk factors are involved in all forms of antisocial behaviour, their relative importance varies considerably across its many different variations (Rutter et al., 1998).

Deviant proneness pathway.

Behavioural undercontrol

Sher identified two main etiological pathways. The first of these is referred to as the deviant proneness pathway. At its core is individual 'behavioural undercontrol' or 'disinhibition'[7.15], a pattern of behaviours and personality traits characterised by impulsivity, sensation seeking, inattention and aggression, where the young person is unwilling to inhibit internal motivations and impulses to try new experiences (Dawes, Tarter, & Kirsci, 1997; Dawes et al., 2000; Sher, 1991). This is somewhat similar to Zucker's (1994, 2006) conceptualisation of 'antisocial alcoholism' (associated with adult problem drinking outcomes) and its variant 'developmentally limited alcoholism' (not associated with adult problem drinking outcomes).

[7.15] This cluster of behaviour problems is also referred to as problems of 'behaviour self-regulation' (for example, Dawes et al., 1997), or as 'antisocial propensity' (Gottfredson & Hirschi, 1990; Lahey, Waldman & McBurnett, 1999). This should not be confused with the term 'self-regulation' as used within addiction treatment research. While the former relates to general behaviour patterns, the latter refers specifically to an individual's ability to *control* or *regulate* their alcohol consumption (see Mitchell, 1992).

Empirical evidence supports behavioural undercontrol as a precursor for the development of alcohol disorders (Dawes et al., 1997; Iacono, Carlson, Taylor, Elkins & McGue, 1999; Sher & Gotham, 1999; Tarter, Kirisci, Habeych, Reynolds, & Vanyukov, 2004). This research would also suggest that while behavioural undercontrol is associated with underlying neurological/ physiological anomalies, which have a high heritability (Iacono et al., 1999), it is also subsequently moderated by parental behaviour and other sources of socialisation (Dawes et al., 1997; Dawes et al., 2000; Tarter et al., 1999). Links here can be made with the wider literature on causal processes underlying other forms of adolescent problem behaviour which also identify behavioural undercontrol as a major risk (see Rutter et al., 1998 for a comprehensive review, and the comorbidity literature reviewed in the previous chapter).

As discussed in chapter 5, ADHD is an often-used indicator of externalising behaviours and behavioural undercontrol. However, the relationship between ADHD and alcohol use has been found to be somewhat inconsistent across studies. In a case controlled study, Biederman and colleagues (2003) found no difference in the risk of later alcohol use disorder amongst teenagers with and without ADHD diagnosis. In contrast, Kumpulainen (2000) found that hyperactivity in childhood predicted alcohol consumption in adolescence. One possible reason for the inconsistent research findings may be due to the fact that ADHD (or hyperkinetic disorder as it is labelled under the International Classification of Diseases) is itself comprised of three core dimensions, namely inattention, impulsivity and hyperactivity (Biederman & Faraone, 2005; Swanson, et al., 1998). It is possible that these dimensions are related to behavioural undercontrol, and therefore to drug use behaviour, in different degrees. In a study of ADHD and smoking behaviour, Burke, Loeber and Lahey (2001) found that when conduct disorder was controlled for, full ADHD was not associated with tobacco use. However, when the dimensions were considered separately, inattention was significantly associated with smoking even after controlling for conduct disorder and other known predictors of substance use. Further support for inattention as a risk factor for smoking is provided by Barman, Pulkkinen, Kaprio and Rose (2004). Molina, Smith and Pelham (1999) in contrast, found that it was hyperactivity and impulsivity, and not inattention, that were associated with tobacco use. The difference between these two studies may be due to the conceptualisation of antisocial behaviour/conduct disorder, and how this was controlled for in the two studies. This is important as there is evidence that hyperactivity and antisocial behaviour can be considered as two points on the same developmental process (hyperactivity is a childhood manifestation of poor socialisation, and antisocial behaviour an adolescent manifestation of the same process) rather than two distinct, but comorbid, conditions (Patterson, DeGarmo, & Knutson, 2000). Following this, Smith and colleagues (2002) argued that hyperactivity and conduct disorders may lead to early onset alcohol problems, while inattention may be associated with internalising problems, and lead to later onset alcohol problems. To date there have been very few studies of the association between the early manifestation of the three dimensions of ADHD and the development of later alcohol problems.

Socialisation processes and alcohol disorders

In a major review of the socialisation literature, Oetting and colleagues identified three main sources through which pro-social norms and behaviours are learnt: the *peer group,* the *family,* and the *school* (Oetting, 1999; Oetting & Donnermeyer, 1998; Oetting, Donnermeyer, & Deffenbacher, 1998; Oetting, Deffenbacher, &, Donnermeyer, 1998; Oetting, Donnermeyer, Trimble, & Beauvis, 1998). Their model postulates a number of theoretical arguments. First, that socialisation agents can be sources of both pro-social and deviant norms, however, the family and the school are the most likely to be pro-social while the peer group is the most common source of deviant norms. Second, the transmission of norms and behaviours requires a strong bond or attachment with the socialisation source. If this bond is not in existence the transmission of norms and behaviours cannot occur. Third, weak bonds between the young person and their family and school increase the likelihood of the development of bonds with a deviant peer cluster. Finally, distal factors such as personality traits and secondary socialisation sources, such as neighbourhoods, impact on alcohol use thorough their effects on primary socialisation processes.

Peer alcohol use is one of the most consistent predictors of adolescent alcohol use (see Hawkins et al., 1992; Swadi, 1999). This association appears to result from two main processes, *social selection* (whereby adolescents choose to belong to friendship networks with similar drinking habits to themselves) and *social influence* (whereby social networks influence the behaviour of individual members through drinking offers,

155

modelling and perceived drinking norms - see Borsari & Carey, 2001; Coggans & McKellar, 1994 for general reviews). Although recent longitudinal studies have confirmed these effects in adolescents, the findings are inconsistent on which of the socialisation processes is the most influential (Bray, Adams, Getz, & McQueen, 2003; Dishon, & Owen, 2002; Ferguson, Swain-Campbell, & Horwood, 2002; Schulenberg et al., 1999; Sieving, Perry, & Williams, 2000; Urberg, Degirmencioglu, & Pilgrim, 1997; Urberg, Luo, Pilgrim, & Degirmencioglu, 2003; Wills & Cleary, 1999),

The degree of similarity between friends' peer alcohol use has been shown to vary across different social contexts (Cleveland & Wiebe, 2003). In schools with a higher base level of alcohol use (with greater opportunities for deviant peer selection) adolescent-to-peer similarity in alcohol use was higher than in schools with a lower base level of alcohol use (with less opportunities for deviant peer selection).

Much of the research on family socialisation processes has suffered from major methodological weaknesses, in particular the over-reliance on cross-sectional designs, which have overestimated the socialisation effect through their failure to take account of possible genetic causation in family influences on adolescent behaviours, and studies which have discounted the influence that children have on their parents behaviour (Harris 1995, 1998). However, more recent research has begun to address these weaknesses, and has shown the family socialisation effects still arise (Collins, Maccoby, Steinberg, Hetherington, & Bornstein, 2000; Galambos, Barker, & Almeida, 2003; O'Connor, 2002).

At the core of family socialisation is the transition of parental norms and behaviours to the young person. Oetting and colleagues (1998) argue that a strong attachment relationship between parent and child is essential to ensure successful socialisation, and it is this that is susceptible to poor parenting practices. While this has initial appeal, however, the research base supporting this proposition is surprisingly limited, both in terms of the impact that the quality of attachment has on the effectiveness of parental socialisation attempts and on the impact that poor parenting practice has on formation and maintenance of adolescent-parent attachment bonds. While there is a small body of research that confirms the association between parent-child attachment quality and child competencies (for example, Armsden & Greenberg,

1987; Bell, Forthun, & Sun, 2000) much of it is cross-sectional in design, and therefore of limited power in testing developmental hypotheses.

Something that has received more research attention is the impact that parental monitoring and supervision, another key socialisation process, has on adolescent behaviour. A lack of adequate parental supervision of adolescent behaviour is associated with substance use and other problem behaviours (see Kumpfer, Olds, Alexander, Zucker, & Gary, 1998 for review). Not only may parental monitoring limit adolescent opportunities to engage in unsupervised alcohol consumption, but it may also mediate the influence of deviant peers through limiting opportunities for contact. Dishon & McMahon (1998) argued for a broad conceptualisation of parental monitoring that includes both parental structuring of the child's social environment and their tracking of the child's behaviour in those environments. More recently Stattin & Kerr (2000; Kerr & Stattin, 2000) have begun to take account of the contribution that the young person makes in the effectiveness of parental attempts to monitor their behaviour. Here, evidence is provided that indicates that parental knowledge of child behaviour, particularly amongst older adolescents, is determined more by the child's spontaneous disclosure of information, than by their active attempts at tracking and surveillance. The relationship between parental knowledge and child behaviour is likely to be reciprocal in nature, with low knowledge leading to increased antisocial behaviour, which in turn precipitates a further decline in parental knowledge, possibly via the increasing reluctance of the antisocial child to disclose their own behaviour (Laird, Pettit, Bates, & Dodge, 2003).

A range of more distal environmental factors, such as poverty, marital conflict and family breakdown, may impact on the likelihood of a young person developing hazardous drinking behaviour through partly disrupting the parent-child socialisation process (Jacob & Leonard, 1994; Oetting & Donnermeyer, 1998: see also Bradley & Corwyn, 2002; Cummings & Davies, 2002 for more general reviews). Children raised in single parent households have consistently poorer outcomes than children raised with two biological parents (Duncan & Brooks-Gunn, 1997). Such an indicator of inflated risk may be a marker for a number of specific risk processes involving family conflict prior to separation, increased poverty and family stress, or decreased parental

157

monitoring (Duncan & Brooks-Gunn, 1997; Galambos & Ehrenberg, 1997; Rutter et al., 1998).

Parental separation is only a risk where the parent is a positive socialisation force as separation leads to a break in the parent child bond. Where the parent may be a negative influence (for example, is highly antisocial themselves) separation may decrease risk (Jaffee, Moffit, Caspi, & Taylor, 2003). As a result, divorce and parental separation can be both a health risk (reduced monitoring, increased poverty, absence of parental influence etc.) and an opportunity (removal of abusive parent, reduction in family conflict, promotion of psychological maturity) (Galambos & Ehrenberg, 1997).

Poverty is linked to a wide range of negative social and health outcomes in young people (Bradley & Corwyn, 2002; Duncan & Brooks-Gunn, 1997). However, the relationship between poverty and adolescent drinking is rather inconclusive (Johnstone, 1994). In relation to other problem behaviours the impact of poverty on child behaviour is indirect, and is mediated by parenting practices (Bradley & Corwyn, 2002; Linver, Brooks-Gunn, & Kohen, 2002). Poverty reduces family social resources and increases family stress, both of which can restrict parenting capacity. If poverty does influence drinking patterns in young people, a similar mechanism would be expected to that observed for other problem behaviours.

In addition to the peer group and the family, the school is the third primary socialisation agent in adolescent development (Oetting & Donnermeyer, 1998). Here, the school can be considered a protective agent, where bonds to a pro-social organisation are established in the absence of others (for example, with the family). Schools, as recognised by Oetting and colleagues, are not uniformly effective in achieving this, where poor teaching, high class sizes, poor discipline, and a unsatisfactory learning environment may contribute to pupil disengagement from the school. Pupils' characteristics may also contribute to the establishment of weak school bonds. Behavioural problems, hyperactivity, attentional problems and aggression may contribute to poor school performance, academic failure and decline in educational motivation (see Rutter et al., 1998 for discussion of this issue).

While there is a developing knowledge base on the deviant proneness alcohol pathway, gaps in our understanding still exist. Many of the studies examining behavioural undercontrol and problem drinking have employed less than optimal methods such as case-control design (for example, Dawes et al., 1997; Tarter et al., 2004), restricted to a particular gender (Dawes et al., 1997; Tarter et al., 2004) or restricted to offspring of alcoholic parents (Sher & Gotham, 1999) and small numbers (Tarter et al., 2004). The majority of community-sample risk studies in this area, which address these types of methodological weaknesses, by and large have focused on the onset of alcohol use or its social use (for example, Cleveland & Wiebe, 2003). Very few UK, or in fact European, studies have examined early childhood psychosocial processes associated with the development of more problematic drinking patterns in adolescence, which may differ from those that initiate drinking or maintain consumption levels at non-hazardous levels. Rather, UK studies have tended to rely on cross-sectional research designs (for example, Foxcroft & Lowe, 1997; Ledoux, Miller, Choquet & Plant, 2002; Sutherland & Shepherd, 2001a,b).

There is also considerable inconsistency in the research evidences on behavioural undercontrol. It is argued here that much of this may be due to differences in the definitions of behavioural undercontrol employed within studies. A wide range of different behavioural dimensions has been used to define this construct across different studies including antisocial behaviour, impulsivity, and hyperactivity, and this may contribute to the differing research findings produced. Examination of the association between the various individual dimensions of the broad construct of undercontrol and later drinking behaviours may give insights into the actual processes underlying the development of drinking problems in adolescence.

Given the limitations of sampling outlined above, few studies have failed to provide adequate control of background demographic covariates such as poverty. While an association between poverty and alcohol use is accepted (Goodman & Huang, 2002; Hawkins, et al., 1992) there is little evidence that the effect remains significant when more proximal factors are taken into consideration, for example antisocial behaviour.

Negative Affect Pathway

Sher (1994; Sher & Gotham, 1999; Sher et al., 2005) also suggested a link between drinking and negative affect (anxiety and depression) regulation, where the mood altering properties of alcohol are used to self medicate an emotional problem. Zucker (2006) also included a negative affect pathway within his classification of comorbid alcoholisms, suggesting that this was more associated with female drinking and occurred with a later onset (in young adulthood).

A long-term reciprocal relationship between alcohol use disorders and anxiety disorders has been observed amongst college students (Kushner, Sher, & Erickson, 1999), in which alcohol consumption induced short-term anxiety reduction, but increased longer-term anxiety, which itself led to increased chronic alcohol use (Kushner, Abrams & Borchardt, 2000). Amongst adolescents, however, there is inconsistent evidence for a both a concurrent (see previous chapter) and a longitudinal association between negative affect and alcohol consumption. Studies can be found that support a positive relationship (where high negative affect predicts high levels of drinking, for example, Rohde, Lewisohn & Seeley, 1996) a negative relationship (where high negative affect predicts low levels of drinking, (for example, Caldwell et al., 2002; Rodgers et al., 2000) and refute the relationship between alcohol and negative affect in adolescents (for example, Degenhardt, Hall, & Lynskey, 2001) It is possible that the inconsistencies in the existing knowledge base are due to the fact that the etiological pathway may be gender specific, where low levels of anxiety or depression in childhood is predictive of problem drinking in young adult males, while high negative affect is predictive of problem drinking in young adult females (Chassin, Pitts, & Prost, 2002; Pulkkinen & Pitkanen, 1994). It is also possible that the separate dimensions of negative affect are associated with alcohol in different ways. Kaplow, Curran, Angold & Costello, 2001) found that overall anxiety was not predictive of later drinking, however children with early symptoms of generalised anxiety were at greater risk of starting alcohol use, and children with separating anxiety were at a lower risk of early onset alcohol use. Zimmerman et al. (2003) identified social phobia and panic attacks as predictors of hazardous drinking amongst adolescents. While such findings may suggest a tension-reduction drinking process, Zimmerman et al. (2003) suggested that their findings were more suggestive of a shared common cause generating both the anxiety disorders and the hazardous drinking.

The inconsistencies in the relationship between negative affect and alcohol use may also arise from methodological differences, in particular the short-term nature of the relationship between affect regulation and drinking and a lack of third variable controls. For example, Colder & Chassin, (1993) found that negative affect, and not behavioural undercontrol, mediated the relationship between stress and alcohol use, however, later work indicated that impulsivity moderated the relationship between negative affect and alcohol use, in that depressed impulsive children drank more than depressed non-impulsive children or non-depressed children (Husson & Chassin, 1994). Likewise, Jackson et al., (2000) found that depression significantly predicted alcohol use disorder in bivariate analysis, but was no longer significant when other variables were entered into the model.

Additional Risk factors

Cognitive functioning

It is widely acknowledged that acute alcohol ingestion impairs cognitive functioning. In particular, it reduces planning, verbal fluency, memory, complex motor coordination, and executive functions, even after controlling for expectancy (Peterson, Rothfleisch, Zelazo & Pihl, 1990; Weissenborn & Duka, 2003). Chronic ingestion can also contribute to cognitive impairment in both adult and adolescent drinkers (Brandt, Butters, Ryan, & Byog, 1983; Brown, Tapert, Granholm & Delis, 2000; Clark, 2004, Moss, Kirischi, Gordon, & Tarter, 1994; Tapert & Brown, 2000; Tapert & Schweinsberg, 2005). However, it has been noted in other studies that the relationship between alcohol consumption and cognitive decline may not be linear but U shaped, with non-drinkers and heavy drinkers reporting the lowest cognitive scores and moderate drinking showing reduced cognitive decline (Britton, Singh-Manoux & Marmot, 2004; Rodgers et al., 2005).

In relation to the potential role cognitive deficits may play in the development of adolescent alcohol disorders, the research evidence is more limited. Most studies in this area have focused on case-controlled studies with the offspring of alcoholics. In one of the few community studies on this topic Fergusson, Horwood and Ridder (2005), using data from a New Zealand cohort, found a bivariate association between intelligence and later substance abuse. However, this relationship was non-significant once behavioural and family background were introduced into the model. Short term working memory capacity and general intelligence may independently moderate the impact of deviance proneness on later alcohol problems (Finn & Hall, 2004).

161

It is worth noting at this point, that prenatal exposure to alcohol can also induce cognitive executive functioning impairments (Noland et al., 2003). Therefore, in examining the predictive relationship between cognitive impairment and later alcohol consumption, it would be necessary to control for family history of drinking as a possible common risk factor for both cognitive impairment and adolescent drinking.

Parental substance use

When compared to demographically matched controls, studies have found that children of substance abusers tend to exhibit more behavioural and emotional problems, less socially adaptive behaviour, higher rates of psychiatric disorder and greater use of substances, although there is still a degree of inconsistency in the research results (Johnston & Leff, 1999). While inherited vulnerability (genetic transmission) appears to account for a significant proportion of this association (Sher et al., 1996; Vanyukov et al., 2003), increased risk of negative outcomes associated with having a substance using parent is also partially mediated largely through behavioural undercontrol (Sher & Gotham, 1999, Tarter et al., 1999). Other social processes may also play a major part in the increased vulnerability of the children of substance users, including prenatal exposure, family disruptions, family conflict, family alcohol and drug use norms and poor parenting practices (Jacob & Johnson, 1997; Johnston & Leff, 1999; Lynskey et al., 2002; Sher, Grekin, & Williams, 2005).

Family capital and parenting resources

Family capital can be defined as the human, social and financial resources available within the family for the undertaking of its core functions, in particular the socialisation of dependent children. While family human capital comprises the individual skills, attitudes and norms of parents and children, family social capital is determined by the quality and quantity of interactions and attachments between family members, (Parcel & Menaghan, 1993) and is associated with parental investment in their offspring (time and effort) (Coleman, 1990; Wright, Cullen, & Miller, 2001). Family financial capital refers to the monetary resources that parents can access to complete their parenting duties.

162

There exists a wide range of family capital indicators that have been examined in relation to child and adolescent outcomes. Poverty (or its indexes - socioeconomic status and household income) have long been associated with drug use and a range of other problem behaviours in young people (Bradley & Corwyn, 2002; Duncan & Brooks-Gunn, 1997; Zucker & Harford, 1983). For young children the link between poverty and poor developmental outcomes appears to be linked with the family's ability to provide a stimulating environment for the child (Linver, Brooks-Gunn, & Kohen, 2002; Yeung, Linver, & Brooks-Gunn, 2002). For adolescents, links between poverty and poor outcomes may be mediated by a range of possible within-family processes, including increased stress and distress amongst parents leading to poor parenting control and compromised parent-adolescent relationships (Felner et al., 1995). Magnuson and Duncan (2002) found that harsher and less responsive parenting was more common amongst low-income families. Lower job status and parental levels of education are also significantly related to higher rates of parental rejection towards their adolescent children (Felner et al., 1995).

Socioeconomic status (SES) may also be mediated by non-parenting indirect effects such neighbourhood characteristics (for example, poorer people tend to live in areas that have increased availability of illicit drugs), poor teacher expectations, and contact with a more deviant peer group (Bradley & Corwyn, 2002). Social and financial capital within the family is in part determined by family structure. Single parent families, parental separation and divorce, and reconstituted families have all been identified as indicators of poorer adolescent outcome including increased levels of substance use behaviours (Hawkins et al., 1992; Hetherington, Bridges, & Insabella, 1998; McLanahan, 1999; McLanahan, & Sandefur, 1994; O'Connor, Dunn, & Jenkins, 2001;Wells & Rankin, 1991).

One of the key debates within the literature is whether parental absence or poverty is more influential in determining adolescent outcomes. McLanahan (1997) concluded that overall, parental absence is more important than poverty for adolescent problems behaviour. For cognitive ability and school achievement the reverse is observed. Citing the evidence that children of "never-married" mothers tend to have the poorest outcomes even when compared to divorced parents, McLanahan (1997) suggests that it is absence itself rather than the cause of the absence that has the greater impact on children.

Additional support is provided by the finding that while remarrying may put reconstituted families on an equal financial footing with intact families they still seem to display outcomes not better than those for children from single parent families (Amato & Keith, 1991; Ginther & Pollack, 2001). McLanahan (1999), meanwhile, posited three main reasons why children in single parent homes have more negative outcomes than those from intact homes. Firstly, there are fewer resources within the family. Secondly, there is less available time for a single parent to monitor and supervise children. And, finally, there may be reduced access to community resources that can act as an extra support to parents. Importantly, she suggested that economic instability accounts for half of the disadvantage that accompanies being raised by a single parent. However, this does not suggest that the reason for parental separation is of little importance. Within families undergoing disruption, outcomes for children are poorer where parental conflict is higher (Rutter, 1994b). Also, children exposed to parental separation have been found to be at slightly increased risk of later conduct problems, mood disorder and substance abuse even after controlling for socio-economic effects of the separation (Fergusson et al., 1994); therefore there are effects beyond increased financial strain. Those children who lost a parent through death do not have the same degree of adverse social and psychological outcomes as those who lost a parent through divorce (Amato, 1993). Therefore, the cause of the absence appears to be an important risk factor in child outcomes, in addition to the impact of the actual separation.

Given the frequency of parental separation therefore, increasing numbers of children now have non-resident fathers and the significance of this for the child-father relationship and for the child's adjustment is an area of considerable interest (Dunn, 2004; Dunn, Cheng, O'Connor, & Bridges, 2004). Father involvement is a particularly important mediator that partially explains the greater behavioural problems observed among adolescents living in single parent households. Involvement by biological fathers is associated with improved behavioural scores for all adolescents regardless of living arrangements, although involvement by residential fathers seems to have greater effect than involvement by non-residential fathers. In their research on children in fatherless families, MacCallum and Golombok (2004) found that single parenthood following a marital separation in infancy might involve consequences other than just father absence, including financial hardship, low socio-economic status and lack of social support.

164

Family structure may also impact on family social capital. Mothers and fathers operate both as a parenting team and as individual parents (Deal et al., 1999; McHale & Rasmussen, 1998). This additional parenting dynamic is unavailable to single parents. Likewise the introduction of a stepparent may significantly alter family subsystems. Because reorganised systems are not necessarily more stable, new vulnerabilities may be created (Sameroff, 1983).

Early maturation

Research has consistently shown that the likelihood of substance use is increased amongst those young people with early onset puberty independent of age (Aro & Taiple 1987; Dick, Rose, Viken, & Kaprio, 2000; Patton et al., 2004; Stattin & Magnusson 1990; Wichstrom, 2001). A U shaped curve may best represent the relationship between age of maturation and alcohol with early and later maturers reporting the highest levels of consumption relative to their normally maturing peers (Andersson & Magnusson, 1990). Interestingly, Robe, Robe and Wilson (1980) found that maternal heavy alcohol consumption was associated with later puberty onset, however, this was not confirmed in a later study (Windham, Bottomley, Birner & Fenster, 2004).

Research questions

This analysis has a number of objectives. At a broad level it is an exanimation of the early childhood predictors (assessed at age 5 and 10) of adolescent drinking patterns. At a more detailed level it addresses a number of specific research questions regarding the differentiation of separate etiological pathways.

1. Are the findings from the predominantly US risk factor research literature (given the recognised methodological limitations of the knowledge base, in particular its over-reliance on clinical sample case control studies) replicated in a UK general population sample?
2. Does behavioural undercontrol (here defined as a broad construct) in childhood predict adolescent alcohol consumption when other factors are controlled?
3. Do the different dimensions of behavioural undercontrol (antisocial behaviour, inattention, hyperactivity and impulsivity) differ in their association with alcohol use?

165

4. Does family socialisation contribute to increased risk in addition to a behavioural undercontrol main effect?

5. Is there a predictive association between negative affect/internalising problems and later drinking?

6. Is there evidence for the influence of additional risk factors in addition to the two main etiological pathways (behavioural undercontrol and negative affect), for example cognitive executive functioning and demographic factors?

METHODS

Respondents

The core sample used in this analysis is the 6,516 respondents who were allocated to a latent drinking class (see chapter 5). As other measures used in the analysis are derived from items contained within earlier sweeps of the BCS70 the actual working sample with complete data may be somewhat smaller than this figure. Chapter 4 provides a discussion of the representativeness of the sample. To address potential biases that may result from the missing data, a statistical technique known as multiple imputation is employed (see chapter 4).

Measures

Behavioural undercontrol (age 5 and age 10) maternal rating: Versions of the Rutter Scales were utilised at age 5 and age 10. At age five mothers completed a modified Rutter A scale. Four items were dropped from the scale due to high levels of missing data relative to the other items. These items were a) biliousness, b) tears on arrival at school, c) stammers and stutters, and d) other speech difficulties. For this analysis a subset of 19 items similar to those used in the 16-year-old questionnaire (see chapter 5) was selected. Three subscale scores (hyperactivity, externalising behaviours and internalising behaviours) were calculated using the factor scores derived from the analysis of the 16-year-old data. This was used to ensure comparability across the various data sweeps. The mean score for hyperactivity was 4.94 (sd=1.61), and for externalising behaviour the mean was 9.29 (sd=2.08). Within the 10-year follow-up instrument the Rutter A items were measured along an analogue scale rather than a three-point likert scale. Mothers were asked to make a mark along a line between 'certainly' (scored 0) and 'doesn't apply' (scored 10). The reversal of direction of scoring with the 10-year-old follow-up was taken into account within the allocation to ensure equivalence. The mean score for hyperactivity was 8.73 (sd=6.83), and for externalising behaviour the mean was 12.04 (sd=8.08)

Negative affect (age 5 and age 10) maternal rating: As outlined above, the Rutter scale used at age 5 and 10 also included a measure of internalising behaviours. This subscale consisted of items such as "Often worries about many things?" and "Often appears miserable, unhappy, tearful or distressed?".

The mean score for internalising behaviours at age 5 was 8.69 (sd=2.10), and at age 10 it was 16.77 (sd=10.02).

Behavioural undercontrol (age 5 and age 10) teacher rating: In addition to parental rating of the child's behaviour, teachers were also asked to complete what was termed the Child Behaviour Scale. This was a combined scale comprising items selected from the Rutter B (Teacher) Scale, the Conners' Teachers Scale, and items on specific behaviours not covered by the two main scales (items relating to anxiety, and fine and gross motor coordination, etc) (Butler, Haslum, Barker, & Morris, 1982).

A maximum likelihood factor analysis (with Kaiser varimax rotation) was used to identify eight subscales within the main child behaviour measure (see Table A.3 in appendix). The subscales were as follows:

1. Antisocial behaviour	5. Gross motor problems
2. Inattention	6. Extraversion
3. Anxiety/neurosis	7. Toileting
4. Fine motor control	8. Hyperactivity

Scales 1, 2 and 8 represent the three dimensions of attention-deficit hyperactivity disorder, namely impulsivity (here combined within a larger antisocial behaviour construct), inattention and hyperactivity (Biederman & Faraone, 2005; Swanson, et al., 1998). DSM classification permits three symptom-based subtypes (mainly inattentive, mainly hyperactive-impulsive or both combined). However, as Biederman & Faraone, (2005) comment, the existence of a pure inattentive disorder distinct from a combined ADHD has not been widely confirmed.

167

Negative affect (age 5 and age 10) teacher rating: As outlined above the child behaviour scale includes a measure of negative affect in addition to those assessing behavioural undercontrol. Items within this subscale include "Is fearful or afraid of new things or situations?", "Behaves nervously?" and "Is worried or anxious about many things?".

Parental monitoring (age 10): Mothers were asked to rate the frequency in which their child tells them where they are going before they go out (*Child disclosure*). Frequency was rated on a four point likert scale (rarely or never/yes-occasionally/yes-usually/yes-always). They also provide the time at which the child is usually in at night. This was collapsed into a binary variable (rarely or never/yes). Parents were asked to state the *time* their child was usually in at night.

Child's education at age 10: A number of indicators of the child's primary education were obtained from the maternal self-report, including, *difficulties in maths, reading and writing* (these were rated on a three point scale (no difficulties/ some difficulties/ great difficulties) and *receipt of free school meals* (yes/no). Additional information was also obtained from the young person's teacher. This included:

a. *Special education provision* (attends special school or receives specialist therapeutic input at school);

b. *Level of concentration, fidgeting, and serious behaviour aberrations* (rated percentage of class time spent on each listed activity);

c. *Parental engagement in education* (teachers asked to rate both maternal and paternal interest in the child's education on a four point scale – very interested/moderately interested/very little interest/uninterested).

d. *Popularity with peers within school* (teachers asked to rate children on an analogue scale, rated between 1 and 47 in relation to the four dimensions - child's popularity with peers, number of friends, shyness, and cooperation with peers. Items scores were summed).

Locus of control and self-esteem: Pupils undertook a short self-completion questionnaire containing a measure of both self-esteem (LAWSEQ, Lawrence, 1981) and locus of control (CARALOC, Gammage, 1975).

168

Auditory working memory (British Ability Scale Forward Recall of Digits – 34 items): Detailed descriptions of the BAS subscales presented here were sourced from the BAS Technical Manual (Elliot, Smith & McCulloch, 1997). In the forward recall of digits test the child was given a series of numbers and asked to recall the series back to the teacher. The number sets start with two digits, and after five consecutive sets the sequence is increased by one digit, up to a maximum of eight digits. A point was given for each correct recall. Forward digit recall reflects the child's short-term auditory memory, concentration, attention and verbal expression, and is considered part of basic storage, search and retrieval cognitive processes.

Fluid reasoning ability (British Ability Scale Matrices - 28 items): In this subtest the child was presented with a self-completion task in which they had to complete a pattern by drawing the appropriate shape in an empty square in a matrix depending on the pattern presented in the completed squares of the matrix. The matrices ranged from 2x2 squares (3 cells completed 1 uncompleted) to 3x3 squares (with 8 squares completed and 1 uncompleted). To solve the problems the child had to first deduce the relationship between figures in the completed cells and then devise and draw the solution. Matrices scores reflect visual-spatial analysis, and non-verbal inductive reasoning, including the identification of rules governing abstract figures and the formulation of hypotheses about those rules.

Verbal knowledge and expressive language skills (British Ability Scale Word Definitions – 37 items): For each item of the 37 items in this subscale, the child was presented with a single word (for example collect) and asked, "What does XXXX mean?" The child's answers were recorded by the teacher verbatim and scored later by the BCS research team. The Word Definitions module is part of the verbal ability scales within the BAS, and measures comprehension of words and fluency in expressing definitions.

Verbal reasoning (British Ability Scale Verbal Similarities – 42 items): The Word Similarities module is a further component of the verbal ability scale. Here, children were presented with three words (for example orange, strawberry, banana) and asked to give another word that would go with these three (for example apple –referred to as a group example). If no response was forthcoming the child was prompted. The child was then asked "Why do orange, strawberry, banana and apple go together?". An example answer would be "because they are all fruit" (superordinate answer), or "because they have skin" (subordinate answer). The child's answers were recorded by the teacher verbatim and scored later by the BCS research team. Superordinate answers were scored higher than subordinate answers. This scale reflects children verbal reasoning and language skills. Low scores may indicate a reluctance to speak or poor working memory.

Shortened Edinburgh Reading Test (self-completion): This shortened version of the Edinburgh Reading Test (ERT) was comprised of 67 items selected to assess overall reading ability (vocabulary, syntax, sequencing, comprehension and retention) across the ability range, from age 7 to age 13. Particular attention was given to ensuring the assessment of poor reading abilities.

Friendly Maths Test: This was a test specifically devised for the BCS70 ten-year-old sweep. It consisted of 72 multiple-choice items covering the essential rules of arithmetic, number skills, fractions, algebra, geometry and statistics.

Maternal malaise (age 5): A 24-item self-completion version of The Rutter Malaise Inventory (Rutter, Tizard & Whitmore 1970) was used to assess maternal reported experiences of psychological symptoms (for example, Do things worry you?) and somatic symptoms (for example, Do you suffer from indigestion?). The version of the scale used at age 5 employed of a two-point response code (Yes, No). Two items from the full malaise scale that were not included in the 16-year-old follow-up ('Are you troubled with rheumatism or fibrositis?' and 'Have you ever had a nervous breakdown?'; see chapter 5) were contained within the maternal scale used at age 5. The number of experienced symptoms was counted across the various items.

Medical history at age 10: Mothers were asked a series of questions about the child's medical history to age 10. These include whether a) the child had any major or minor *congenital abnormalities* or defects (for example, Down's Syndrome, hydrocephalus, congenital heart problems); b) they had <u>ever</u> had *a fit or convulsion* or other turn in which they lost consciousness or any part of their body made abnormal movements; c) they had <u>ever</u> been referred to *family guidance or child psychiatry*; d) they had been *seen by a social worker* in last <u>12 months</u>; e) *how much time they had missed school* in the last <u>12 months</u> due to ill health or emotional disturbance (coded on a four point likert scale - none or less than 1 week/ over one week and up to one month, over a month and up to three months/ over three months); f) they had <u>ever</u> been *in care* .

Medical examination: In addition to the maternal self-report children underwent a medical examination at age 10. Relevant information taken from this examination included;

a. the existence of *emotional or behavioural problems*;
b. *motor coordination* - children were asked to complete a series of motor tests including throwing a ball in the air, sorting matches, and figure drawing on the palm of hand. Children were classified into one of four categories – normal limb coordination, questionably clumsy, mildly clumsy, and moderate to markedly clumsy;
c. *body mass index*- a ratio of height to weight was calculated in a similar way to that of the parent's body mass index (see below).

Early puberty: Mothers were asked, within the 16-year-old maternal self-completion section, to indicate the age at which their teenage daughter had her first period.

Parental health behaviour in 1980 (child age 10): A number of indicators of parental health behaviour were constructed. These included a crude *body mass index score* for both fathers and mothers. This was calculated by dividing paternal weight in kilograms by the square of their height in meters. Mothers were asked to recall their *alcohol consumption during early and late pregnancy*. This was reported on a four-point likert scale (most days/2-3 times per week/once a week or less/not at all). This was recoded into a binary variable (not at all/ once a week or more often). And finally, mothers were asked to record the *smoking behaviours* of themselves, the child's father and other household members.

Maternal and paternal education in 1980 (child age 10): Mothers were asked to list their own educational qualifications, and the qualifications of the child's father. Each of the series of responses was subsequently recoded into a single multiple response variable for each parent.

171

Social Class in 1980 (child age 10): On the basis of current and previous employment status both mother and fathers were allocated a social class category. This provides alternative family social class indicators. Social class categories are based on the 1980 census classification. Households are classified into one of six categories ranging from Class I to Class V, with Class III being divided into two subcategories Class III – non-manual, and Class III – manual.

Receipt of benefits in 1980 (child age 10): Mothers were asked to indicate whether the family was in receipt of any of the following benefits: child benefit increase for single parents, family income support, supplementary benefit, widows benefit, retirement pension, sickness/invalidity benefit, disability pension, attendance/mobility allowance, unemployment benefit. Receipt of such income support benefits provides another indicator of family poverty. Child benefit, due to its universal coverage across the sample was not included within this measure. This indicator is more likely to reflect benefit uptake rather than entitlement.

Gross family income in 1980 (child age 10): Mothers were asked for the range in which the family's total gross weekly income fell. The range was to include all earned and unearned income for both mother and father before deductions for tax and national insurance but was to exclude earnings by other household members and child benefits.

In addition to basic chi-squared tests and ANOVAs, a multinomial logistic regression was conducted, where assigned latent class membership was regressed onto a set of selected predictor variables. Multiple imputation was used to reduce biases due to missing data on the covariates (see chapter 4).

RESULTS
Table 7.1 and 7.2 provide bivariate analysis of the associations between early child and family characteristics and drinking patterns at age 16 (as indexed by latent class membership).

Behavioural undercontrol
While high externalising behaviour as young as age five, as reported by mothers, was associated with later drinking behaviour, hyperactivity was not significantly different across the latent classes at age 5, but was at age 10. At this age higher levels of

hyperactivity predicted higher levels of drinking. The association between these elements of behavioural undercontrol and later drinking behaviour was confirmed by the teacher reports. Again, hazardous drinkers at age 16 had higher levels of reported antisocial behaviour, higher level of extraversion and poorer attention. However, while hyper-kinesis was not significantly different across the five latent drinking classes, teachers report that these young people with later alcohol problems spent more time fidgeting in class than other pupils. In addition, teacher identified those young people in the hazardous drinking category as the most popular with their peers. Limited drinkers, in contrast had the lowest popularity. As the assessment was made at age 10, popularity cannot be a function of drinking behaviour, but rather it is due to other social characteristics of this group, such as their extraversion, and rebellious behaviour. The medical examinations recorded the highest rates of behavioural problems amongst the limited use and hazardous use groups. Here, over 5 percent of the limited use group and nearly four percent of the hazardous use group had a defined behavioural problem.

Negative affect pathway

While internalising behaviours (as reported by mothers) and anxiety problems (as reported by teachers) were both significant in the bivariate tests, in general negative affect was associated with lower levels of adolescent drinking (Table 7.1). Heavy and hazardous drinkers were considered to have the lowest mean negative affect, while the limited use alcohol group was rated as having the highest levels of internalising problems.

To test the possibility that a negative affect etiological pathway was gender specific, in that it may exist for girls but not boys, separate ANOVAs were estimated for each gender group. Amongst boys and girls teacher reports of anxiety problems were significantly different across the various latent drinking groups (Boys: $F= 7.295$; $df = 4$; $p = <0.001$) (Girls: $F= 3.27$; $df = 4$; $p = 0.011$). However, as noted above the higher levels of anxiety were reported for those young people who drank less when older. For maternal reports of internalising problems the difference did not reach significance for either gender.

An alternative method for identifying behavioural and emotional problems in children is to assess the level of specialist psychiatric or support services. No differences in the proportion of children attending family guidance or child psychiatry services before the age of 11 were reported (around 2% in each drinking class) (Table 7.1). However, there was a difference in the proportion of children seen by social workers in the 12 months previous to the 10-year-old follow-up data wave. The rates of social work intervention amongst the limited and occasional use group were double that of the other three groups (around 2% compared with 1%).

Menstruation

Girls classified as hazardous drinkers had a significantly earlier age of onset of first menstruation although the differences in actual age were relatively small. A difference of less that half a year was observed between hazardous drinkers and limited use drinkers (12.5 compared with 12.8 respectively). Unfortunately the BCS70 did not contain a similar measure of age of puberty in boys so this analysis is single gender only.

Cognitive ability and attainment at age 10

All the cognitive tests utilised within the BCS70 were significantly different across the drinking classes. In general, the limited and occasional use groups scored lower in the ability and attainment tests than the other three higher levl drinking classes. Of the six tests employed, heavy drinkers scored highest in three (digit recall, ERT and FMT), while hazardous drinkers scored highest on two (word definitions and similarities), and moderate drinkers scored highest on one (matrices).

The differences in the test scores were confirmed by parental rating of the child's performance at school. Young people in the limited use group were more likely to be rated by their mothers as having great difficulties with maths, reading and writing at age 10 than the other drinking classes. Generally, the heavy drinking group was the least likely to be rated in this way, followed by the hazardous drinkers. It is unsurprising therefore, that the limited use group was the most likely to be receiving special educational provision (22%) followed by the moderate use group. There was little difference in the levels of special educational input across the other three drinking categories. This relationship was also observed in relation to teacher reports of parental engagement and interest in the child's education. The highest levels of disinterest were observed within the limited use and moderate use groups.

Family capital

A range of family financial capital measures was incorporated within the BCS70 at age 10. These included paternal and maternal education, social class (based on employment), weekly income, and receipt of free school meals and other state benefits. In general the lowest levels of family capital were recorded amongst those households where the young person would be later classified as having a limited or occasional drinking pattern at age 16. These families had the highest level of free school meals uptake, and state benefits, and the lowest weekly incomes. They also reported the lowest levels of paternal educational attainment and social class. The highest levels of family capital were recorded amongst the moderate and heavy drinking young people.

Similar levels of maternal separation were observed across the five latent class groups at age 5. In contrast, however, paternal separation at age 5 was more common amongst hazardous drinkers than the other categories of young people. In particular, having a stepfather (6.0%) was more common amongst the hazardous drinkers than other groups (ranging from 1.8% to 4.6%).

Parental behaviour at age 10

Both parents were asked about their smoking behaviour, and mothers were asked about their consumption of alcohol during pregnancy. Around about half of fathers and a third of mothers smoked in 1980 (Table 7.2). Smoking rates were highest amongst the parents of those young people who were later classified as drinking at a hazardous level (56% of fathers and 42% of mothers. Smoking rates were lowest in the limited use group (42% of fathers and 28% of mothers). However, the likelihood of an non-parental figure smoking in the house was not associated with later drinking patterns in the young people. As with maternal smoking behaviour, drinking during pregnancy was more common amongst the heavy drinking group than the other categories, and again the limited use group mothers reported the lowest rates of drinking during pregnancy.

Table 7.1: Association between child characteristics at age 5 and 10 (mean scores) and latent drinking classes at age 16

	Limited use	Occasional use	Moderate use	Heavy use	Hazardous use	p
Maternal report						
Hyperactivity at 5	4.86	4.91	4.78	4.86	4.84	0.253
Externalising behaviour score at 5	9.16	9.00	8.91	9.07	9.13	**0.023**
Internalising behaviour at 5	8.62	8.72	8.68	8.61	8.51	0.336
Hyperactivity at 10	8.00	8.12	7.73	8.24	8.80	**0.011**
Externalising behaviour score at 10	11.97	11.41	10.40	10.94	11.58	**<0.001**
Internalising behaviour at 10	17.44	17.36	16.29	16.28	15.78	**0.001**
Age of menarche (girls only)	12.82	12.70	12.69	12.60	12.47	**0.032**
Maternal malaise	4.08	4.16	3.84	3.98	3.80	0.095
Father's BMI	24.19	24.43	24.42	24.32	24.42	0.554
Mother's BMI	23.97	23.31	23.19	23.27	23.33	**0.003**
Time child is in at night	7:09	7:23	7:20	7:25	7:30	**<0.001**
Medical examination						
Child's BMI	16.62	16.80	16.89	16.93	17.05	**0.020**
Teacher report						
Time spent on concentration on school work	71.23	72.25	72.13	71.35	69.65	0.133
Time spent on fidgeting	3.95	4.29	3.89	4.33	5.06	**0.010**
Time spent on serious behavioural aberrations	0.08	0.10	0.18	0.13	0.22	0.516
Popularity with peers	102.76	103.18	104.75	105.67	105.75	**<0.001**
Mean scores on the Child Developmental Behaviour Scale						
Antisocial behaviour	9.06	9.18	8.83	9.52	10.46	**<0.001**
Inattention	15.60	17.76	18.73	17.93	16.24	**0.022**
Anxiety	15.28	14.52	13.70	12.90	13.13	**<0.001**
Fine motor control	49.02	49.28	50.59	51.44	49.98	**<0.001**
Gross motor problems	9.54	9.18	8.21	7.35	7.83	**<0.001**
Extraversion	3.54	6.16	9.31	11.12	12.41	**<0.001**
Toileting	1.99	1.81	1.80	1.74	1.70	0.393
Hyper-kinesis	5.62	5.80	5.29	5.22	5.74	0.113

Table 7.1 (Cont.)

	Latent Class					
	Limited use	Occasional use	Moderate use	Heavy use	Hazardous use	*p*
Educational tests						
BAS word definitions	9.52	10.48	11.13	11.41	11.48	**<0.001**
BAS word similarity	27.30	28.32	28.89	26.20	29.12	**<0.001**
BAS matrices	17.42	17.16	17.90	17.79	17.41	**0.005**
BAS digit recall	21.69	22.54	22.78	22.97	22.60	**<0.001**
Edinburgh Reading Test	38.25	41.08	41.98	42.56	41.22	**<0.001**
Friendly Maths Test	42.64	45.05	47.12	48.09	47.73	**<0.001**
LAWSEQ (low self esteem)	1.91	1.66	1.32	1.31	1.11	0.072
CARLOC (external locus of control)	5.69	4.71	4.22	4.17	4.21	**<0.001**

Other factors

Other factors found to vary significantly across the five latent drinking classes were external locus of control (higher in limited drinkers), maternal BMI (U shaped relationship with BMI highest in limited and hazardous drinkers), child BMI (highest in hazardous drinkers), motor coordination problems (highest in limited drinkers), time in at night and the child's willingness to tell the parent what they do with their free time (hazardous drinkers were both in latest at night and least willing to disclose) (Tables 7.1 and 7.2).

Table 7.2: Association between child characteristics at age 5 and 10 (proportions) and latent drinking classes at age 16

	Latent Class					
	Limited use	Occasional use	Moderate use	Heavy use	Hazardous use	*p*
Natural father (%)	92.2	85.1	88.5	85.1	83.9	-
Natural mother (%)	97.0	96.7	97.3	96.8	97.1	-
Been 'in care' before age 11 (%)	1.9	2.0	1.4	1.6	1.0	0.515
Abnormality (%)	7.4	8.9	7.6	6.7	6.2	0.208
Convulsions before age 6 (%)	8.7	11.3	10.6	11.3	10.6	0.600
Referred to family guidance before 11 (%)	2.1	2.1	1.4	2.0	2.2	0.545
Referred to child psychiatry before 11 (%)	2.1	2.2	1.6	1.5	2.0	0.684
Seen by social work, last 12 mths (at 5) (%)	1.7	2.0	0.9	0.9	0.8	0.032
One week or less off school (%)	60.8	61.5	64.1	61.9	66.3	0.298
Father educated to degree level (%)	12.8	13.0	17.7	16.8	15.9	NA
Mother educated to degree level (%)	3.1	3.2	3.8	3.3	3.3	NA
Social class V (father's occ.) (%)	5.4	4.5	2.5	3.2	2.2	0.050
Social class V (mother's occ.) (%)	11.2	10.6	7.7	7.1	8.5	0.156
Gross weekly income below £35 (%)	1.5	2.0	1.3	1.1	0.6	<0.001
Receipt of benefits	22.7	23.8	17.9	19.1	20.9	<0.001
Alcohol in early pregnancy (%)	28.5	42.1	49.9	51.4	57.0	<0.001
Alcohol in late pregnancy (%)	26.3	39.4	46.7	46.3	52.2	<0.001
Father current smoker (%)	47.5	52.7	49.4	50.4	56.0	0.033
Mother current smoker (%)	28.3	38.9	34.6	37.8	42.1	<0.001
Other household members smoke (%)	7.0	7.5	6.2	7.4	7.2	0.584
Behaviour problems (med report) (%)	5.3	2.6	1.9	1.5	3.6	<0.001
Motor coordination problem (med report) (%)	2.4	1.5	0.8	0.6	0.2	0.017
Child self-disclosure YES - always (%)	71.6	71.7	72.0	66.7	63.9	<0.001
Great difficulty with maths (%)	3.4	3.4	2.3	2.3	2.4	0.048
Great difficulty with reading (%)	2.5	2.0	2.0	1.2	1.8	0.010
Great difficulty with writing (%)	3.2	2.4	1.6	1.3	1.8	0.004
Free school meals (%)	17.8	14.6	9.9	11.2	10.7	<0.001
Receives special educational provision (%)	21.9	13.0	10.6	10.6	9.7	<0.001
Mother uninterested in child's education (%)	3.5	2.3	1.6	1.8	1.2	0.002
Father uninterested in child's education (%)	5.8	3.7	3.0	3.2	2.8	0.217

Notes: – chi squared test unstable due to small counts for many of the contingency table cells; NA not applicable as a multi-response variable.

Multinomial logistic regression

To control for the impact of various confounders on the bivariate associations outlined above, a multinomial logistic regression was conducted to assess the relative importance of the predictor variables within a multivariate framework. Given potential problems of co-linearity (high level of correlation between variables included within the model) not all covariates identified as significant in the bivariate analysis presented above were included within the model. Rather one indicator was selected to represent the broad construct assessed by the multiple covariates. Table 7.3 presents the parameter estimates, odds ratios and confidence intervals for the selected indicators. Hazardous drinkers were selected as the reference category for the logistic models.

There was little association between adolescent drinking behaviour and child cognitive ability and performance at age 10, family socioeconomic status, social characteristics (parental interest in education, child disclosure, peer isolation, and locus of control) at age 10 and contact with social services. None of these indicators were significant predictors of drinking status across the four comparisons made, once other indicators were controlled for, that is, hazardous drinkers compared with each of the other drinking categories in turn).

Limited use drinkers were more likely to have a lower body mass index, to be in receipt of special education support, and to have a mother who smokes, at age 10. High extraversion and antisocial behaviour at age 10 and maternal drinking in pregnancy were predictive of being in the hazardous drinking group six years later when the two groups were compared (hazardous and limited use). When the occasional users were compared with hazardous drinkers, higher levels of childhood body mass index, antisocial behaviour, and extraversion, along with maternal drinking in pregnancy remained significant predictors of being in the hazardous category. In addition, a gender difference was detected, with girls being more likely to be classified as occasional drinkers than hazardous drinkers in adolescence, after controlling for the other significant childhood predictors of drinking outcomes.

Childhood antisocial behaviour, extraversion, maternal drinking and gender remained consistent predictors of adolescent drinking status when hazardous drinkers were compared with moderate drinkers. Again, boys, those with high levels of antisocial behaviour, extraversion, and those whose mother drank in early pregnancy were more likely to develop hazardous drinking patterns by age 16. When the logistic models were compared for only hazardous and heavy drinkers, only one indicator was found to be significant. Alcohol consumption during early pregnancy was again predictive of the development of hazardous drinking patterns in teenagers. No other indicator significantly differentiated these two groups beyond maternal drinking.

To test the possibility that the lack of evidence for a negative affect pathway may be due to the gendered nature of anxiety as a causal mechanism, a further multinomial logistic model was estimated with an anxiety gender-interaction term included. All three interaction terms (anxiety; gender; anxiety*gender) were only significant within the occasional and hazardous drinking class comparison. The revised interaction terms coefficients for this comparison are as follows (anxiety = 0.087; gender = 0.937; anxiety*gender = -0.031). When gender is zero (male) an increase in anxiety is associated with an increased log odds (0.087) of being in latent class 2 (occasional drinker). When anxiety is constrained to be zero, a unit increase in gender (female) is associated with an increase in the log odds (0.937) of being an occasional drinker. With an increase in gender (switching from male to female) the slope of the anxiety effect is also slightly reduced (-0.031); however this effect is not large enough to result in anxiety being associated with an increased risk of being a hazardous drinker at age 16. While anxiety is still associated with a reduction in the risk of being a hazardous drinker, it is just that the effect is less for females than for males.

Table 7.3 Predictors associated with drinking pattern: multinomial logistic regression

	Limited drinkers vs hazardous drinkers			Occasional drinkers vs hazardous drinkers			Moderate drinkers vs hazardous drinkers			Heavy drinkers vs hazardous drinkers		
	OR	95% C.I.	Sig	OR	95% C.I.	Sig	OR	95% C.I.	Sig	OR	95% C.I.	Sig
Gender												
Male	1.00	-		1.00	-		1.00	-		1.00	-	
Female	1.33	0.99, 1.79		1.68	1.33, 2.12	**	1.51	1.22, 1.86	**	1.19	0.94, 1.51	
Social worker contact												
Yes	1.00	-		1.00	-		1.00	-		1.00	-	
No	0.61	0.16, 2.30		0.43	0.14, 1.31		0.74	0.24, 2.30		0.82	0.25, 2.68	
Child BMI	0.92	0.86, 0.99	*	0.95	0.90, 1.00	*	0.97	0.93, 1.02		0.98	0.93, 1.03	
Received special education support												
Yes	1.00	-		1.00	-		1.00	-		1.00	-	
No	0.59	0.39, 0.90	*	0.80	0.55, 1.17		0.84	0.57, 1.22		0.80	0.53, 1.20	
Isolation	1.01	0.97, 1.06		0.99	0.96, 1.03		1.00	0.96, 1.03		1.00	0.96, 1.03	
Child Developmental Behaviour Scale												
Antisocial behaviour	0.97	0.95, 1.00	*	0.97	0.95, 0.99	*	0.97	0.95, 0.99	**	0.99	0.97, 1.01	
Inattention	1.01	1.00, 1.02		1.01	1.00, 1.02		1.00	0.99, 1.01		1.00	0.99, 1.01	
Anxiety	1.01	0.98, 1.04		1.01	0.99, 1.03		1.01	0.99, 1.03		1.00	0.98, 1.02	
Gross motor	1.01	0.99, 1.04		1.01	0.99, 1.04		1.01	0.99, 1.03		1.00	0.98, 1.02	
Fine motor control	1.00	0.99, 1.02		1.00	0.98, 1.01		1.00	0.99, 1.02		1.01	1.00, 1.03	
Extravert	0.99	0.98, 1.00	**	0.99	0.99, 1.00	**	1.00	1.00, 1.00	**	1.00	0.99, 1.00	
Hyperkinesis	1.02	0.99, 1.04		1.02	1.00, 1.04		1.02	0.99, 1.04		1.00	0.98, 1.02	
British Ability Scale												
Word definitions	0.98	0.94, 1.02		0.98	0.95, 1.01		0.98	0.96, 1.01		0.99	0.96, 1.02	
Recall of digits	1.00	0.96, 1.04		1.02	0.98, 1.05		1.01	0.98, 1.04		1.02	0.99, 1.05	
Word similarities	0.97	0.92, 1.02		0.99	0.95, 1.02		1.00	0.96, 1.03		1.01	0.97, 1.04	
Matrices	1.03	0.99, 1.07		1.00	0.97, 1.03		1.01	0.98, 1.04		1.00	0.97, 1.04	

[1] Hazardous drinkers are the reference category. * = $P < 0.05$; ** = $P < 0.01$. Maternal interest in education was collapsed into a binary variable for the regression analysis.

Table 7.3 (Cont.)

	Limited drinkers vs hazardous drinkers			Occasional drinkers vs hazardous drinkers			Moderate drinkers vs hazardous drinkers			Heavy drinkers vs hazardous drinkers		
	OR	95% C.I.	Sig	OR	95% C.I.	Sig	OR	95% C.I.	Sig	OR	95% C.I.	Sig
Friendly Maths Test	0.98	0.96, 1.00		0.99	0.97, 1.00		0.99	0.98, 1.01		1.00	0.98, 1.02	
Edin. Reading Test	1.00	0.99, 1.02		1.01	0.99, 1.02		1.00	0.99, 1.01		1.00	0.99, 1.02	
Locus of Control	1.01	0.98, 1.04		1.00	0.98, 1.03		1.00	0.98, 1.02		1.01	0.98, 1.03	
Income												
Income 1	1.00	-		1.00	-		1.00	-		1.00	-	
Income 2	0.84	0.33, 2.16		1.05	0.50, 2.22		0.92	0.44, 1.91		0.86	0.41, 1.82	
Income 3	1.00	0.54, 1.86		0.91	0.54, 1.54		0.88	0.52, 1.50		0.95	0.55, 0.63	
Income 4	0.99	0.54, 1.83		0.87	0.52, 1.47		0.98	0.59, 1.64		1.04	0.61, 1.79	
Income 5	0.76	0.39, 1.49		0.77	0.44, 1.35		0.84	0.50, 1.43		0.97	0.56, 1.67	
Income 6	0.68	0.30, 1.54		0.80	0.39, 1.62		1.17	0.60, 2.27		1.15	0.57, 2.33	
Income 7	0.83	0.37, 1.87		0.58	0.30, 1.12		1.04	0.57, 1.91		0.95	0.50, 1.79	
Drinking in pregnancy	0.40	0.31, 0.51	**	0.60	0.49, 0.75	**	0.75	0.62, 0.91	**	0.79	0.64, 0.98	*
Interest in education	0.79	0.59, 1.06		0.79	0.62, 1.00		0.80	0.63, 1.00		0.86	0.66, 1.11	
Paternal smoking	1.26	0.96, 1.67		1.10	0.88, 1.38		1.17	0.95, 1.45		1.15	0.93, 1.42	
Maternal smoking	1.51	1.15, 2.01	**	1.08	0.86, 1.36		1.18	1.95, 1.47		1.09	0.87, 1.36	
Child disclosure	0.86	0.48, 1.52		1.11	0.70, 1.76		1.21	0.76, 1.93		1.02	0.63, 1.66	

[1] Hazardous drinkers are the reference category. * = $P < 0.05$; ** = $P < 0.01$. Maternal interest in education wa collapsed into a binary variable for the regression analysis.

DISCUSSION

From the bivariate analysis it is possible to construct a stereotypical picture of the various types of young drinkers when they were aged 10. The limited use group appeared, in general, to have lower educational ability and attainment together with a higher likelihood of attending special educational provision. They also were more anxious, introverted and clumsy, with fewer friends than their school peers. As adolescent alcohol consumption is a social activity, the limited alcohol consumption of this group may be a function of poorer social skills. In contrast, the hazardous and heavy drinkers, performed well at school, came from wealthy families, were popular, extrovert, and had fewer worries or anxieties than the others. In a longitudinal study of early adolescents, Allen et al., (2005) found that popular adolescents displayed positive markers of social development, however, they also tended to display increased behaviours associated with growing peer approval, including alcohol and drug use.

Moderate to hazardous drinking appears to be associated with successful adjustment in adolescence. In most respects, poor adaptation at age 10 is associated with lower levels of alcohol consumption in later years. This may reflect, to a large degree, the role that alcohol plays in modern adult society. Alcohol consumption, even though it is legally forbidden at age 16, could be considered a normal part of the transition from adolescence to young adulthood. It is those children with the higher levels of social problems, as indexed by cognitive ability, internalising problems, coordination problems and social isolation, who appear to be the ones least likely to engage in drinking behaviour.

The one bivariate finding that is contrary to this summary is the higher levels of antisocial behaviour amongst heavy and hazardous drinkers. Childhood problem behaviours, such as bullying, fighting, teasing others and breaking things, predicted those young people who progressed beyond moderate drinking to heavier problematic drinking. While alcohol consumption at age 16 could be considered as a normal part of the transition to adult roles and responsibilities, for some young people this consumption occurs at a level that raise concerns about future health and social consequences.

Amongst girls there was evidence that alcohol consumption and antisocial behaviour was tied up with early maturation. Moffit and colleagues (2001) found that the link between alcohol problems and early menarche was associated with joining older more deviant peer groups. However, girls, in general, were more likely to be in the moderate or occasional drinking class than the hazardous drinking group. No gender difference was detected when hazardous drinkers were compared with either heavy or limited drinkers. It is assumed that these groups are predominantly male.

The bivariate and multivariate analysis lends strong support to the deviant proneness pathway of adolescent alcohol problems. This study found that behavioural undercontrol was a key predictor of adolescent drinking patterns across all types of drinking with the exclusion of the highest end of the spectrum. Between heavy and hazardous drinker no differences could be found on the behavioural undercontrol indicators.

In relation to the relative importance of the various dimensions of undercontrol that have been suggested as etiological mechanisms, antisocial behaviour appears to be the main predictor of adolescent drinking rather than hyperactivity or attention problems (here labelled as behavioural disorganisation). The analysis presented would indicate that any associations between alcohol consumption and hyperactivity or attention problems are likely, in the main, to be due to their common association with antisocial behaviour. This is similar to the findings of King et al., (2004) who concluded that amongst externalising disorders, ADHD was the weakest predictor of adolescent alcohol consumption, and conduct disorder the strongest. ADHD was predictive of smoking behaviour and cannabis use, but not alcohol use. These findings contrast, however, with a recent study, Niemelä et al., (2006), where the frequency of drunkenness at age 18 was predicted by teacher reports of both conduct disorder and hyperactivity at age 8. Although, when parents reports were considered, only conduct disorder was found to predict drunkenness. While it could be argued that the divergence in these findings is due to the fact that teachers are better able to identify ADHD as a result of ready comparisons with their class peers, this study also used teacher ratings of hyperactivity.

Little support was found for a negative affect pathway in adolescent drinking behaviours. In the bivariate analysis higher levels of anxiety were associated with lower levels of alcohol consumption rather than higher. In the multivariate analysis, anxiety did not differ significantly across the various drinking classes once other predictors were controlled for. This conclusion did not alter even when a gender*anxiety interaction term was introduced to the model. In fact, the multivariate analysis indicates the reverse, a higher teacher rating of extraversion (also referred to as positive emotionality) was predictive of later alcohol consumption. Extrovert children tend to be outgoing, expressive, popular and active and one possible explanation for these findings is that high levels of alcohol consumption in adolescents is an extreme manifestation of this positive sociable personality. It is also possible that the outgoing nature of these young people results in their greater exposure to situation where the unsupervised consumption of alcohol with peers is possible (environmental selection or manipulation processes) (see Shiner & Caspi, 2003, for a discussion of these processes). However, it must be recognised that the relationship between extraversion and psychopathology has received little attention relative to the negative emotionality (Nigg, 2006).

This lack of association between early negative affect and later adolescent drinking confirms the findings of other community-based studies (King et al., 2004; Niemelä et al., 2006). It is possible that a negative affect pathway represent etiological mechanisms that do not emerge before the transition to adulthood. Zucker (2006) in a major review suggested that negative affect pathway, while it had many childhood antecedents, emerged in early adulthood rather than early adolescence, as is common with a deviant proneness pathway. Kurger, Caspi and Moffit (2000) found that amongst older adolescents (aged 18) negative emotionality did predict alcohol abuse three years later (at age 21). In a large-scale high-risk case controlled study Chassin, Pitts and Prost (2002) also found that early onset high frequency drinkers were characterised by parental drinking, antisociality, externalising behaviour, low depression and peer drinking. This study confirms and extends these findings within a community sample.

In addition to those variables that were significant predictors of later drinking status, it is also worth considering those indicators that were not significant given the large sample size (and associated statistical power) involved in this analysis. In particular, adolescent drinking behaviour was not predicted by childhood cognitive functioning or family socioeconomic status once other key predictors such as the level of antisocial behaviour were controlled for. While both these factors varied significantly across the drinking classes when examined in isolation, their predictive association with alcohol consumption six years later is due to correlations with other 'third variable' factors.

185

One important finding emerging from this study is the different subsets of predictors that were significant across the various comparisons made. When hazardous drinking was compared with limited use a broad range of indicators was associated with the odds of being in the two drinking categories. These indicators comprised both social indicators (such as receipt of special education or maternal smoking) and individual/ behavioural indicators (such as BMI or antisocial behaviour). However, while the gap in the level of consumption decreased between the various pairs of drinking classes included within the model, the number of significant indicators decreased.

When the logistic model comprises of only heavy and hazardous drinkers the only significant predictor is maternal drinking during pregnancy. This confirms the findings of existing case controlled and clinical sample studies that familial drinking is associated with increased risk of later adolescent drinking problems (e.g. Hill & Yuan, 1999; Reich, Earls, Frankel, & Shayka, 1993; Sher, 1991). In one of the few other community based studies examining this issue (the Early Developmental Stages of Psychopathology Study), Lieb et al., (2002) also found that maternal (and paternal) drinking history predicted dependent adolescent transition from occasional use to regular use and hazardous use. In terms of extending current knowledge, this study shows that the temporal association between risk exposure and later outcome can extend over a considerable period of time (from the prenatal period to late adolescence). It also has shown that this risk exposure can also differentiate between drinking patterns, even at the extreme level of adolescent consumption and even after controlling for other known risk factors.

The significance of parental drinking suggests three possible mediating processes. First, the links between maternal and dependent child drinking could be due to a shared genetic liability. What is suggested here is that the genetic vulnerability that contributes to a mother's inability to restrain her consumption of alcohol during pregnancy (when she is most likely to be bombarded by numerous anti-drinking health messages) may also contribute to her child's inability to restrain their drinking at age 16. It is generally accepted that alcohol behaviours are highly heritable (McGue, 1994) .

Another possible mechanism is that early pregnancy drinking results in minor neurological deficits during the early stages of foetal development. These deficits could then interfere with the child's ability to regulate and control their own behaviour resulting in higher levels of antisocial behaviour and alcohol consumption. And finally, it is possible that the findings also represent an indirect social mediated risk. For example, Nash, McQueen and Bray (2005) found that family environment, and in particular parental expectations about adolescent drinking, moderated adolescent alcohol consumption. Unfortunately, however, this study is not of a design that can pick apart the genetic and neurobiological factors that underpin increased liability to adolescent alcohol problems (for a discussion of these factors see Zucker, 2006).

Implications

Early antisocial behaviour is a strong predictor of later drinking problem amongst adolescents. This supports the established Problem Behaviour Theory (Jessor & Jessor, 1977), and more specific deviant proneness models outlined above. This finding has two main implications for the design of alcohol abuse prevention programmes. First, it may be advantageous to address adolescent alcohol problems through the provision of childhood externalising behaviour programmes. Reducing or disrupting the development of antisocial behaviour in children may impact on young peoples' likelihood of developing later alcohol misuse problems. The efficacy of prevention programmes challenging heavy drinking amongst adolescents may be restricted if antisocial behaviour is not addressed or permitted to develop unrestricted. Secondly, children and adolescents in contact with the Criminal Justice System (CJS) can be recognised as young people at increased risk of serious alcohol problems. The developmental association between alcohol and antisocial behaviour compounds the clustering of negative outcomes amongst a small subpopulation of young people. The CJS does, however, provide a valuable opportunity to provide selective prevention interventions for the reduction of alcohol related harm. There is a long history of CJS interventions aimed at reducing alcohol and offending behaviours within the UK (Baldwin, 1990; 1991).

Beyond the deviant proneness pathway, little else appears to be a consistent predictor of drinking status. In particular, social indicators did not appear to be independently associated with later drinking outcomes. However, it must be said that logistic regression models may not be necessarily the best test of complex moderating or mediating roles. It may still be the case that social processes do play an important role in the etiology of adolescent alcohol use, but that once antisocial behaviour and maternal alcohol consumption are accounted for within a logistic model these effects are no longer observed (due to the way in which regression model parameters are estimated). More complex statistical procedures such as structural equation modelling may be required to fully tease apart these complex interrelationships between predictors of adolescent drinking.

Successful adaptation in late childhood is associated with moderate, albeit underage, alcohol consumption in adolescence. It could be argued that alcohol consumption at around age 16 is a normal part of successful adolescent development. Children who do well at school, are popular with their peers and have a good relationship with their parents do go on to engage in moderate underage drinking. To fully understand the role that alcohol consumption plays in successful adolescent development and the transition to adulthood, requires the consideration of the continuity between adolescent and adult drinking patterns. If these patterns do exhibit a high degree of temporal stability, that is, they are linked with moderate and controlled adult drinking it could be argued that even though drinking at age 16 is considered inappropriate, at least in social policy terms, it plays an important function in the development of the behavioural and social skill required to manage exposure to mood altering substances. Later analysis will examine this continuity.

Whilst the difficulties of interpreting the relationship between maternal drinking in pregnancy have been outlined above, the finding still warrants careful consideration. As social policy implications, however, are likely to differ across the potential causal processes, a response to this research is to suggest further work to fully explore this important predictor. Notwithstanding this requirement, it is still possible to consider the implication of this finding. If maternal drinking represents a genetic etiological pathway, the important point to note is that it appears that mother's drinking in addition to fathers drinking is indicative of heightened risk amongst the young person. To date, most research examining the children of alcoholics has focused on the dependant offspring of male problem drinkers (for example Sher, 1991; Tarter et al., 2004). Further recognition is required of the increased risk of having a mother with a drinking problem. Special consideration should be given to the needs of children and young people of mothers in contact with alcohol services in addition to the needs of the mother. If maternal drinking

188

represents a neurological risk process it highlights the importance of health education messages presented to women of childbearing age. It could be possible that the alcohol consumption reported here represents normal, that is, non-pregnant drinking in the very early stages of pregnancy before the mother is aware of her pregnancy. If this is the case then the message to women should be to ensure that care is taken with regards to the level of alcohol consumed, when the possibility of pregnancy is heightened.

SUMMARY

Two etiological models were presented and tested in this chapter; a deviant proneness model and a negative affect model. The deviant proneness pathway emphasised the role of behavioural undercontrol, characterised by impulsivity, sensation seeking, inattention and disinhibition, in the development of adolescent problem alcohol use. Young people with high levels of behavioural disinhibition may fail to develop suitable regulatory competence over their developing alcohol use. This model also recognised the role that socialisation processes (family and peers) can play in moderating the relationship between undercontrol and drinking outcomes.

The negative affect etiological pathway proposes a link between alcohol use and comorbid affective disorders (anxiety and depression). Here, problem drinking may develop as a method for coping with extreme emotional thoughts and feelings as a source of self-medication. In addition to these two models a range of other identified risk factors were reviewed including cognitive ability and functioning parental alcohol and drug use, family capital, and early maturation.

This study provided an analysis of a UK community sample, which addresses a number of known weaknesses within the existing knowledge base, including the over-reliance on US clinical case controlled studies. Multivariate logistic regression analysis (with multiple imputation for missing values) was used to identify early childhood predictors of later adolescent drinking behaviour. In particular, the analysis sought to examine the relative importance of various indicators of behavioural undercontrol and negative affect in identifying adolescent problem drinkers. In addition, the models also included indicators of family socialisation and other risk factors such as executive cognitive functioning.

Adolescent drinking was predicted by a constellation of characteristics that included maternal drinking during pregnancy, antisocial behaviour, extraversion, and gender. Once these indicators were taken into account there was little evidence for a predictive influence of negative affect, cognitive ability, or family capital. When young people who are drinking at the higher levels are compared, (heavy drinkers versus hazardous drinkers), only maternal drinking is significantly associated with increased odds of being in the hazardous category. This, together with the behavioural undercontrol predictors may suggest a genetically mediated etiological risk process. In contrast, children with cognitive difficulties as indexed by receipt of special education, cognitive functioning or difficulties at school reported the highest levels of abstinence.

There is some evidence, albeit in the form of univariate findings, that suggests that moderate drinking at age 16 is not associated with indicators of unsuccessful childhood adaptation. Rather, it seems that those children with indicators of successful childhood development, including success at school, established peer friendships, and good parental relationships do not progress to abstinence in adolescence but rather, moderate drinking outcomes. However, once maternal drinking and behavioural undercontrol (as indicated by the levels of antisocial behaviour and extraversion) were controlled for, no real variation in these indicators of successful adaptation were noted across the drinking categories.

What are of almost equal importance to the positive associations found in this analysis are the negative findings, where hypothesised relationships were not supported by the data. In particular, adolescent problem drinking was not associated with low family capital. No differences in the likelihood of being in the different drinking classes were noted across the different income groups. Neither did parental interest in the child's education predict later drinking.

Certain dimensions of behavioural undercontrol, together with maternal drinking did appear to be the most important predictors of adolescent hazardous drinking. Family socialisation, beyond that captured by maternal drinking behaviour, did not appear to contribute to increased risk above that accounted for by undercontrol. However, the model did not permit the testing of moderating or mediating interaction between undercontrol and socialisation. This would require a more sophisticated structural model. Negative affect did not appear to be predictive of drinking behaviour. However, this does not mean that a negative affect pathway may not be important in explaining the drinking behaviour of subpopulations within the overall cohort or may be influential at a later developmental period. Further models would be required to explore this issue. There is limited evidence of alternative predictors of adolescent drinking behaviour outside of the main undercontrol pathway.

These findings have considerable implications for the design and development of interventions aimed at preventing or reducing the harm associated with adolescent drinking. These finding identify two key opportunities for service development. The first is in relation to early intervention service for children at risk of conduct or antisocial behaviour problems. These young people are exhibiting behavioural undercontrol and are at increased risk of later alcohol problems in addition to any conduct problems they may have. This research would suggest that alcohol education should be considered as an important component in any services provided to this population. The second intervention opportunity is within services provided to mother with drinking problems. In addition to the needs of the mother, the needs of the child should be given serious consideration to reduce the risk of a generational transmission of drinking problems.

8 LIFE COURSE OUTCOMES OF HAZARDOUS DRINKING IN ADOLESCENCE

There is an ever-growing body of research examining the adult sequelae of adolescent drinking. Associations have been noted between adolescent alcohol consumption and adult drinking, educational and employment outcomes, and health problems. This chapter examines the extent to which adolescent drinking patterns as assessed by the latent class model are linked to a range of adult outcomes measured at age 26. The chapter begins by examining the existing research literature. It identifies gaps in the current methodological, conceptual and knowledge base relevant to this body of work, and the contribution that this analysis could make to address these gaps. The chapter then presents the methods, analysis and findings from further empirical investigation of the 16-year-old and 26-year-old sweeps.

CONSEQUENCES OF TEENAGE DRINKING
Alcohol

Short-term longitudinal studies have shown a degree of continuity in young adult alcohol consumption extending over several years (Andersen, Due, Holstein & Iversen, 2003; Ferguson et al., 1995; Grant, Harford, & Grigson, 1988). The stability of alcohol consumption patterns over longer time periods has also been confirmed by several longitudinal studies (Bennett, McCrady, Johnston, & Pandina, 1999; Pape & Hammer, 1996; Wells, Horwood, & Fergusson, 2004). Bonomo, Bowes, Coffey, Carlin and Patton (2004), employing similar consumption indicators to this analysis, examined the continuity of drinking behaviours between ages 15 and 21. Alcohol dependence in young adults was predicted by the frequency of drinking at age 15, binge drinking, alcohol related injuries, intense drinking (blackouts and unable to stop drinking), smoking and antisocial behaviour, but not psychological distress (depression and anxiety). Casswell, Pledger, & Pratap, (2002), used latent class mixture models to examine the continuity of both the volume and quantity of alcohol consumption between the age of 18 and 26.[8.16] While the frequency of drinking was rather stable over time, the volume of alcohol consumed declined in two of the three subgroups of young drinkers identified. In one of the few UK studies of the stability of drinking behaviours, Jefferis, Power and Manor, (2005) utilised data from the 1958 National Child Development Study and found that binge (heavy episodic) drinking in early adulthood (age 23) was associated with binge drinking at age 42.

The work reviewed above stands in contrast to much of the early longitudinal studies on drinking continuities. For example, studies by Plant et al., (1985), Donovan, Jessor & Jessor, (1983) and Temple and Fillmore, (1985-1986) all concluded that there was little continuity between adolescent and adult drinking. A number of issues may contribute to these divergent research findings. These include differing ages of respondents at initial assessment and subsequent follow-up period; differing measures used to assess alcohol consumption, and most importantly, the use of 'absolute' (interval level) versus 'relative' (ordinal level) assessments of consumption (see Pape & Hammer, 1996 for a full discussion of these issues). This final point refers to the fact that a single interval level measure - say units of alcohol consumed in the previous week - is unlikely to be stable over any length of time. It will be subject to random fluctuations in both the behaviour and the accompanying level of measurement error (it is unlikely that measurement error remains constant over time). This would lower any measure of association used with an absolute measure. Ordinal measures, in contrast may be more stable and less susceptible to these fluctuations. However, as with any ordinal measures of any behavioural continuum, there is an associated loss of information. What is if interest, here, is the relative position in drinking behaviour that one occupies relative to other individuals and the continuities in positions over time.

Education and Employment

Alcohol may be linked to poor occupational attainment in a number of ways (for full details see MacDonald & Shields, 2001). First, heavy drinking may create health problems that may affect an individual's attendance record and ability to function

---

[8.16] Latent class mixture models are models that combine both categorical and continuous latent and manifest variables. In this case, the study identifies latent classes (categorical latent variable) amongst changes in the volume of alcohol consumed over time (latent continuous variable).

consistently well within the workplace, Second, excessive levels of drinking may interfere with management perceptions of an employees performance. For example, inappropriate levels of consumption at office social events, being drunk or smelling of alcohol whilst at work may signal a person unfit for promotion or responsibility. Third, drinking patterns may directly interfere with work performances. Heavy drinking in adolescence or early adulthood may also impact on an individual's accumulation of qualifications, work related skills and experiences (human capital), reducing their likelihood of gaining employment in a competitive job market (Bryant, Jayawardhana, Samaranayake, & Wilhite, 1996).

Studies that have examined the relationship between drinking and occupational attainment in cross-section have shown inconsistent findings. French and Zarkin (1995) found an inverse U shaped relationship between alcohol and wages with moderate drinkers earning more than either light drinkers or non-drinkers. This was supported by a recent UK study (Macdonald & Shields, 2001). However, later work by Zarkin failed to confirm this relationship (Zarkin, French, Mroz, & Bray, 1998). While those who drank earned more than non-drinkers, the benefit remained even at the higher levels of consumption. Alcohol use also appears to have little impact on the hours young males work (Zarkin, Mroz, Bray & French, 1998), however, there is some evidence of its effect on general employment status (MacDonald & Shields, 2004) and on sickness absence (Marmott, North, Feeney, & Head, 1993).

While cross-sectional studies have added much to our knowledge regarding the complex relationship between current drinking and employment outcomes, they fail to provide insights into the developmental nature of such associations. To date, there have been few longitudinal studies of alcohol and employment and those completed have also provided somewhat inconsistent results. In a study of German school leavers, Matt, Seus & Schumann (1997) found that while the failure to obtain any vocational qualifications was associated with later alcohol use, heavy drinking itself was not associated with general difficulties in the workplace. However, it may impact on the future number of hours worked even after accounting for the relationship between alcohol use and education (Bryant et al., 1996).

Employment status may also influence drinking behaviour in young adults. McMorris and Uggen (2000) found that during the transition to adulthood, for a limited period of time, first employment was associated with increased alcohol use. They suggested that this was due to the increased independence from parents generated by the increased income earned. In particular, income may influence the frequency of drinking rather than quantity of alcohol usually consumed (Casswell, Pledger, & Hooper, 2003). Quantity, in contrast, was found to be most influenced by educational attainment.

While dropping out of school (reduced human capital for later employment) was associated with poor academic ability and parental educational attainment, it was also predicted by earlier alcohol consumption for young males but not females (Mensch & Kandel, 1998). Using data from the Christchurch Longitudinal study, Wells, et al. (2004) found associations between adolescent drinking and later educational and employment outcomes. Once covariates were introduced into the models, however, these associations disappeared except for unemployment rates during the period 16-21. Therefore, the effects of heavy drinking in adolescence on adult employment appear to be relatively short lived, disappearing by age 21. The authors concluded that while adolescent drinking appeared to be associated with a range of adult outcomes, including education and employment, it did not appear to be causally linked to them.

Health

Alcohol consumption has been linked to a range of health problems including but not limited to cardiac problems, gastrointestinal diseases, psychiatric disorders, and injuries and accidents (Rehm, Ashley, & Dubois. 1997; Room, Babor, & Rehm, 2005; Edwards et al., 1994).

Coronary heart disease (CHD)

In most alcohol-related diseases as drinking increases so too does the risk of the disease. The one possible exception is CHD and other cardiovascular illnesses (Babor et al., 2003). Studies of a middle-aged population have shown that the relationship between alcohol and CHD was a shallow U shaped curve, with light or moderate drinkers having a slightly lower risk of CHD and strokes than non-drinkers or heavy drinkers (Corrao, Rubbiati, Bagnardi, Zambon, & Poikolainen, 2000; Hines & Rimm, 2001; McElduff & Dobson, 1997; Mukamal, et al., 2003; Puddey, Rakic, Dimmitt, & Beilin, 1999;

Reynolds, Lewis, Nolen, Kinney, Sathya, & He, 2003; Romelsjö et al., 2003; Shaper, Wannamethee, & Walker, 1994; Wannamethee & Shaper, 1999).

Much of the early research in this area suffered from a number of methodological limitations, including weak measurement of drinking behaviour, limited control of possible confounding variables (in particular social class) and a failure to account for variations in drinking behaviours during the follow-up period (usually in excess of 10 years or more) (see Andreasson, 1998; Filmore, 2000). More recent studies show considerable methodological development. Poikolainen, Vahtera, Vitanen, Linna, and Kivimäki, (2005) attempted to identify novel cofounders that may explain the relationship between alcohol and CHD; however, of the 16 comparisons made none was a likely candidate for the unknown confounder. Emberson, Shaper, Wannamethee, Morris and Whincup (2005), controlled for variations in alcohol consumption over a 20-year period. Once this additional control was applied the risks for non-drinking were reduced and the risks for moderate and heavy drinking increased. As Filmore (2000) suspected, with increasing methodological sophistication the U-shaped curve becomes more linear.

Studies are now emerging that examine the relationship between alcohol consumption and heart problems in young adults. Gillman, Cook, Evans, Rosner, and Hennekens (1995) found that blood pressure was higher amongst young adults who abstained and those who drank 3 or more drinks per day, even after controlling for a range of covariates. Blood pressure was lowest amongst light drinkers. Drinking has also been shown to be associated with increased risk of coronary calcification (a marker for atherosclerosis) in young adults (Pletcher, Varosy, Kiefe, Lewis, Sidney, & Hulley, 2005). However, in this study there was no additional risk associated with abstinence. All alcohol consumption was found to confer risk in a linear dose-response relationship. Binge drinking in particular (drinking 5 or more drinks at one time) was associated with a greatly increased incidence of coronary disease. The risks of a binge drinking consumption pattern was not confined to young people but can also be observed in older adults as well (Murray et al., 2002).

Examining the relationship between alcohol consumption and early expression of CHD is worthy of further study given the findings from older adults. However, the work in this area faces a number of methodological challenges. First, CHD is rarely observed in young adults. While cardiovascular problems will develop throughout the early adult period it is only in middle age that most of the clinical manifestations and diagnoses occur. As a result the numbers of individuals presenting with indicators of CHD within self-report surveys such as the BCS70 are small, limiting the type of analysis that can be undertaken. Second, it is necessary to take account of pre-existing CHD amongst respondents within any analysis as early heart problems may influence alcohol consumption, that is, teenagers with CHD may be more likely to abstain from alcohol than healthy young people, confounding analysis of alcohol consumption and adult CHD. Finally, as with studies of alcohol and CHD amongst older adults, possible confounding factors need to be controlled for within the analysis. These include, but are not limited to, smoking (although this may in part be an alcohol effect given that young people tend to smoke more when they drink, Krukowski, Solomon, & Naud, in press), diet, body mass, level of exercise, socio-economic class, psychological distress, self-esteem, (see Poikolainen et. al., 2005). This analysis may be able to contribute to the developing knowledge base in this area. While it does have a number of limitations, in particular its reliance on self-reported health status, it does provide an opportunity to examine the impact of drinking problems at age 16 and health problems in early adulthood whilst controlling for a range of important cofounders. In addition, much of the research examining the health consequences of drinking patterns has used cross-sectional methods. This analysis aims to extend these findings by assessing the extent to which the health consequences are a result of drinking patterns in adolescence above the impact of concurrent drinking.

Mental Health

There is a clear association between heavy drinking and higher rates of adult mental health problems (Crawford, Crome, & Clancy, 2003). However, most studies examining comorbidity have been cross-sectional in nature (for example, Caldwell et al., 2002; Kandel, Huang & Davies, 2001; Lynskey, 1998; Rodgers et al., 2000).

There are a number of prospective studies that have examined the impact that early alcohol consumption has on later psychopathology during the transition to adulthood. McGue and Iacono (2005) found that early adolescent problem behaviour including alcohol use before age 15 was associated with the development of general

197

rather than specific adult psychopathology. The range of adult problems linked with early alcohol use included nicotine dependence, alcohol abuse/dependence, drug abuse/dependence, antisocial personality disorder and major depression. It is likely that relationships between alcohol consumption and psychopathology are reciprocal. Kushner et al., (1999) found that alcohol use disorders influenced future anxiety disorders, which in turn impacted on future alcohol use. Wells, Horwood, & Fergusson (2004) also confirmed the association between adolescent drinking patterns and adult psychopathology. Adolescent heavy drinkers reported higher rates of major depression, suicide ideation, and offending behaviour during the transition to adulthood (age 16-21). However, when controls for background factors and possible confounders were introduced into the models only violent offending remained significant.

Other health outcomes

In addition to heart disease and mental health problems, alcohol consumption has been linked with increased risk of diseases of the digestive system including liver disease and cancer (Corrao, Bagnardi, Zambon, & Arico, 1999; Grønbæk et al., 1998; Voigt, 2005). However, few studies have looked at young adult health outcomes relative to teenage drinking patterns.

Social consequences

Alcohol use also has social consequences (Gmel & Rehm, 2003), estimated to be in the region of 1% to 3% of gross domestic product (Klingeman, 2001). Around 70% of the social costs were comprised of lost earnings of individuals who were unable to perform productive tasks or died early due to alcohol consumption. The remainder of the costs were due the material damage resulting from alcohol use and the indirect costs of providing medical, social and legal services to deal with the resultant problems created by alcohol. Rehm and Gmel (1999) found that drinking volume (high volume per session drinking rather than overall volume) was associated with driving suspensions, traffic accidents, social, marital and work problems, but not unemployment or general accidents. Rossow and Hauge (2004) found that it was heavy drinkers who were most likely to suffer the social costs of alcohol consumption. Heavy alcohol consumption not only increased the risk of committing a behaviour that may result in a social cost, but it also placed individuals in the company of other intoxicated individuals who may commit social harms against them. In a recent review of the literature on the social harm of alcohol consumption, Gmel and Rehm (2003) concluded that most of the studies on this topic were methodologically limited. This somewhat weakened the evidence on the social consequences of alcohol consumption, particularly in relation to the differential effect of different drinking patterns. This study was able to undertake a longitudinal analysis of the impact of drinking patterns from age 16 on the social costs of alcohol consumption experienced during the transition to adulthood. It was able to account for a range of confounders that may have accounted for the inconsistencies noted in previous research.

In summary, the overall aim of this analysis was to examine the association between hazardous drinking patterns in adolescence and a wide range of later developmental outcomes and opportunities in adulthood, after controlling for the confounding effects at the individual, social and family level. There are few longitudinal studies that have examined this range of issues, over such a period of time. Much of the work in this area has been limited by the short follow-up durations. It is possible that many of the inconsistencies in the current research base (for example within the employment literature) may be due to heavy drinkers experiencing short-term negative outcomes (in career progression) which are reversed by mid-adulthood. This analysis was able to examine the impact of adolescent drinking on established adult career pathways rather than short-term consequences of excessive drinking. Also, the McGue and Iacono (2005) study, while being one of the most comprehensive studies of the effect of adolescent alcohol consumption on adult psychopathology, was restricted by a 20-year-old upper limit. This study aims to extend this area of work by examining adult outcomes at a later developmental stage (26 years of age).

This analysis was also able to employ a full range of covariates. To an extent, alcohol consumption may mediate the impact of poverty and inequality on health related [and other] outcomes (Marmot, 1997). This analysis is able to test for alcohol effects while controlling for confounding factors such as socioeconomic conditions. This analysis is also able to employ confounding variables assessed in childhood and adolescence.

This study aims to further test this general model of adolescent drinking sequelae by exploiting a multidimensional typology of drinking patterns rather than employing retrospective indicators of drinking onset.

METHODS

Respondents

The core sample used in this analysis is the 6,516 respondents who were allocated to a latent drinking class (see chapter 5). While the response (outcome) variables were not the alcohol classes, as was the case in the previous two chapters, those cases who had completed the 26-year follow-up (providing outcome data) but not the 16 year old alcohol questions were not included in the analysis. In addition to the 26-year sweep, indicator variables were derived from previous sweeps including birth, 5, 10 and 16. As these measures are derived from items contained within earlier sweeps of the BCS70 the actual working sample with complete data may be somewhat smaller than core sample size. Chapter 4 provides a discussion of the representativeness of the sample.

Measures

Educational qualifications: Respondents were asked to record the type and number of any qualifications obtained during or subsequent to compulsory schooling. Technical, vocational and professional qualifications were also included. Qualifications obtained were then collapsed into a five-category list. Respondents were allocated to the category that corresponded with the highest educational or vocationa qualification obtained (no qualification/CSE-NVQ1/O Levels-NVQ2/A Levels-NVQ3/Higher qualification-NVQ4/Degree or higher-NVQ5 or 6). When educational qualification was used as a covariate in the multivariate models it was recoded as a four category dummy variable with no qualifications as the uncoded reference category.

Current net weekly pay: Respondents were asked to give their current "take home pay" after deductions and including overtime and bonuses.

Current employment status: Respondents were grouped into one of five categories depending on their current employment status (works full-time/works part-time/ not in work/at home full-time/other). For the multivariate analysis this was recoded as a binary variable (in employment/not in employment).

Long-term unemployment: Respondents were classified as long-term unemployed at age 26 if they had never had a full-time or part-time job since age 16.

Social class: On the basis of their current employment, respondents were assigned an Office of Population, Census and Surveys (OPCS) 1991 Socio-Economic Group Code. This is a twenty category occupational code. All coding was undertaken by the SSRU, using the Computer-assisted Standard Occupational Coding (CASOC) developed by the Institute of Employment Research University of Warwick. Given the number of separate occupational codes this variable was treated as having a normal underlying distribution, that is, an interval level variable.

Marital status: Respondents were initially asked about their current relationships. Supplementary questions were asked about their current living arrangements, whether they were living with a husband or wife, living with a partner, or living alone or in some other arrangement, and their current legal status (married-first and only; remarried; separated; divorced; widowed). Respondents were reminded that living together as a couple was not to be counted as married. For the multivariate analysis this was recoded as a binary variable (currently married/not married).

Number of children: This was a count of all dependant children within the household whether they were natural or stepchildren.

Malaise: A 24-item version of the Rutter Malaise Inventory was used (Rutter, Tizard & Whitmore 1970). This differs from the 22-item version used in the 16-year-old sweep. First, the three-point response code (not at all/some of the time/most of time) was replaced by a two-point code (yes/no). Here, reports of 'yes' were considered to be evidence of symptom presence rather than 'most of the time'. Second, to compensate for this, additional modifiers were included in 16 of the 22 youth items. For example, the 16-year-follow-up item 'Do you have backaches?' was 'Do you often have backaches?' in the 26-year old questionnaire. Finally, two additional items were included, 'Are you troubled with rheumatism or fibrositis?' and 'Have you ever had a nervous breakdown?'. The full 24-item scale consists of 15 psychological symptoms (for example, Do you often get worried about things?) and 9 somatic symptoms (for example, Do you suffer from indigestion?). The number of experienced symptoms was counted across the various items. Convention would propose that scores over 8 are considered to indicative of high levels of malaise within the BCS70 cohort (Cheung,

201

2002). For the multivariate analysis respondents were coded as above or below this caseness cut-off. In relation to missing items on the malaise scale, if respondents had more than three items missing and had a total malaise score across the completed items of less than 8, the full total score was set to missing. Therefore, respondents with substantial missing items but with a malaise score over the cut-off of 8 were not set as missing.

Medical complaints: Respondents are asked to list all medical complaints since age 16. It was possible to examine the incidence of both alcohol related and non-alcohol related diseases including the following:

- Mental disorders (organic psychotic disorders, other psychosis; neurotic personality and other non-psychotic disorders, ICD codes 290 to 316);
- Diseases of the circulatory system (chronic rheumatic heart disease, hypertensive disease; ischaemic heart disease; diseases of the pulmonary circulation, cerebrovascular disease, other heart diseases; ICD codes 393-438);
- Diseases of the digestive system (diseases of the oesophagus, stomach and duodenum, liver disorders, ICD codes 530 to 537 and 570 to 573);
- Limiting long term illness: in addition to providing details of specific illnesses or disabilities, respondents were asked whether they suffered from any long term health problem, long standing illness, infirmity or disability of any kind.

Accidents: Respondents were asked whether they had suffered any accident, injury, or assault that required medical treatment. A follow-up item determined the location of the accident, whether it was at home, at work, on the road, playing sport or elsewhere.

Smoking: Respondents were asked to rate their current smoking behaviours (never/used to but not now/occasional/daily). For the multivariate analysis this was recoded as a binary indicator (current smoker/non-smoker).

Body mass index at age 26: Respondents were asked to provide their current height and weight. Body mass index was estimated by dividing weight (in pounds) by height squared (in inches), and multiplying the result by a conversion factor of 703.

Adult alcohol consumption: Alcohol consumption at age 26 was assessed via a quantity/frequency measure. Respondents were asked to recall the number of alcoholic drinks they consumed in previous week across six different alcoholic drink categories (beer/cider/wine/spirits/martini/other). The number of drinks were converted to units and summed across the alcohol categories. This required the multiplication of beer and cider reports by a factor of two, as the drinks were pints. They were also asked to rate the usual frequency of drinking (most days/3-4 times a week/once or twice a week/less often/only on special occasions/never). To generate the final consumption measure the quantity and frequency estimates were multiplied. However, as indicators of socioeconomic status have been found to have different relationships with the various dimensions underlying a measure of alcohol volume (frequency and quantity) (Casswell et al., 2003) both of these dimensions will also be considered separately, in addition to the main volume analysis.

A range of covariates was also included within this analysis. This included:

- Adolescent drinking (latent class assignment at age 16).
- Childhood BMI (age10).
- Edinburgh Reading Test score (at age 10).
- Friendly Maths Test score (at age 10).
- Special education provision (at age 10).
- Gender.
- Maternal alcohol consumption in early pregnancy (retrospective report at age 10).
- Child Behaviour Scale scores (antisocial, inattention, anxiety, extraversion, hyperkinesis; at age 10).

- Paternal smoking (at age 10).
- Maternal smoking (at age 10).
- Paternal drinking (at age 16).
- Maternal drinking (at age 16).
- Drug use (at age 16).
- Smoking (at age 16).
- General Heath Questionnaire score (at age 16).
- Conners' score (at age 16).
- Malaise score (at age 16).
- Overt offending (at age 16).
- Covert offending (at age 16).
- Authority avoidance offending (at age 16).

Full details of the operationalisation of these indicators are given in chapters 4, 5 and 6. In addition, two health related variables were constructed to control for pre-existing heart and mental heath problems. When testing the association between adolescent drinking behaviour and later adult health outcomes, it is essential to control for pre-existing health conditions. It is possible that, for example, a childhood heart condition may influence adolescent drinking that could be later observed to co-vary with adult heart problems. This association would be due to the childhood health problems impacting on adolescent drinking and the adult health condition, rather than any direct alcohol pathway. Medical examiners were asked if the young person (at age 16) had any pathological heart condition or whether there was any evidence of psychological or psychiatric problems; including maladjustment or behavioural problems, depression, aggression, appetite problems (anorexia, bulimia etc.), psychosis, neurosis or suicide attempts/threats. A positive score on any of these latter items was taken as indication of a mental health problem.

Ethnicity: Ethnicity codes were collapsed into four ethnic groups, white (comprising 96% of the sample), Black (0.6%), Asian (2.4%) and Mixed race (1%).

Family structure (At age 16): Mothers were asked about the current structure of their family. Cohort members were allocated to one of four groups (1) Two natural parents (2) Single parents (3) Reconstituted family, and (4) Other.

Family income (at age 16): Parents were asked to estimate their combined income, excluding child benefit payments, but including all other earned and unearned income before tax and other deductions. This was originally recorded in 11 income bands. This was further reduced to 5 income bands: a) less than £5,199 per annum, b) £5,200-£10,399, c) £10,400-£15,599, d) £15,600-£20,799, e) more than £20,800.

Analysis

Basic bivariate analysis was conducted in SPSS. No adjustment was made for missing data in the bivariate analysis. Multivariate analysis (logistic and multiple regression) was conducted in Mplus (Muthén & Muthén, 1998-2005a; Muthén & Muthén, 1998-2005b). To overcome the missing data on the outcome variables and covariates, multiple imputation was employed.

RESULTS

Table 8.1 provides the results of the bivariate analysis. Alcohol consumption at age 16 appears to be associated with later drinking outcomes. Those young people who were classified as hazardous drinkers at age 16 reported drinking more alcohol units, and were more likely to drink alcohol most days, ten years later. To further examine this relationship, the adolescent drinking origins of the top 5% of adult drinkers (those drinking over 1,300 units per year) were examined. Only 3% of these heavy adult drinkers were classified as non-drinkers at age 16. In contrast, over 55% of them were heavy or hazardous drinkers during their teenage years. It is also possible to examine adult drinking in terms of safe drinking limits (21 units per week for men and 14 units per week for women). For men within the sample, around 26% of those in the hazardous drinking class at age 16 drank above the weekly recommended drinking limits at age 26. This compares to 10% of those who had a limited drinking pattern at age 16. For women the corresponding percentages were 15% and 7%. Looking backwards, around 57% of male adults and 48% of female adults drinking above the recommended levels had been heavy or hazardous drinking in their teenage years. It could be assumed that the remainder of those drinking above the recommended limits had their onset of heavy drinking after the age of 16.

In relation to economic outcomes, teenage alcohol consumption was associated with weekly income. Limited use drinkers reported the lowest weekly wage at age 26 (£186.1), followed by occasional users (£191.0). Moderate and heavy users reported the highest weekly incomes (£207.5 and £207.7 respectively). Hazardous drinkers were in between these extremes (£197.8). Limited use and occasional use drinking categories at age 16 also had the largest proportion of individuals who failed to gain a qualification (4.2% and 4.5%), never had a job (6.2% and 2.3%), and were currently in full time employment (68.5% and 74.4%). In contrast, amongst the hazardous drinkers at age 16, 3.2% failed to gain a qualification, 1.2% never had a job, and 76.3 % were currently in full time employment at age 26.

In relation to educational outcomes, the limited use teenage drinkers appear to comprise two groups. Whilst as a category they did contain the highest proportion of young people who failed to gain any qualifications by age 26, they also contained the highest proportion who attained degree level qualifications. In general, young people in the moderate and heavy use drinking categories at age 16 went on to have the most positive employment and economic outcomes ten years later.

Table 8.1: Association between adolescent drinking patterns and later adult health and social outcomes (bivariate models)

	Latent Class					
	Limited use	Occasional use	Moderate use	Heavy use	Hazardous use	*p*
Health outcomes						
Mean alcohol use at 26 (units)	212.5	322.7	400.8	551.8	641.0	**<0.001**
Mean units last week (volume)	7.1	7.5	8.7	11.7	13.6	**<0.001**
Mean BMI	22.8	23.5	23.4	23.7	23.7	**0.021**
Mean malaise score	3.5	3.8	3.6	3.8	4.1	0.069
% Drink most days	3.6	4.1	8.8	13.0	14.8	**<0.001**
% Heart disease	1.2	0.4	0.5	0.3	0.5	0.300
% Mental health problems	0.3	0.7	0.9	1.1	1.2	0.602
% Digestive diseases	0.3	0.1	0.1	0.2	0.5	0.490
% Any long term illness	19.9	16.7	16.7	15.4	14.6	0.317
% Daily smokers	11.6	16.8	20.3	28.6	38.8	**<0.001**
Mean no road accidents	0.14	0.15	0.13	0.17	0.14	0.241
Mean no work accidents	0.08	0.13	0.14	0.18	0.21	**<0.001**
Mean no home accidents	0.01	0.01	0.01	0.01	0.01	0.996
Mean no sport accidents	0.13	0.14	0.19	0.25	0.26	**<0.001**
Mean no other accidents	0.06	0.11	0.12	0.15	0.16	**0.001**
Employment outcomes						
Mean weekly income (£)	186.1	191.0	207.5	207.7	197.8	**<0.001**
% Professional group	10.0	7.4	8.7	8.1	5.5	0.027
% Degree educated	31.0	25.1	28.4	27.2	16.9	**<0.001**
% No qualifications	4.2	4.5	2.3	2.1	3.2	-
% Never had FT job	6.2	2.3	1.8	0.8	1.2	**<0.001**
% Currently in FT employment	68.5	74.4	78.0	77.0	76.3	**<0.009**
Relationship outcomes						
% Divorced	0.6	1.3	1.7	2.2	3.3	**<0.001**
% No dependant children	82.0	78.4	80.8	77.6	74.3	0.360

Notes. Differences in mean scores were tested in one-way ANOVAs. Differences in cross tab cell counts were tested in a chi-squared test.

Table 8.2 provides the outcomes of the multivariate models of adult outcomes with adolescent drinking patterns included as one of a range of childhood, adolescent and adult covariates. The table shows either the logistic or multiple regression coefficients for the five adolescent drinking classes depending on the nature of the adult outcome. It also lists the range of additional covariates included within the model and flags those that were found to be significant. Not all covariates were entered into each model. Covariates were selected on their theoretical relevance to the outcome modelled.

Health outcomes

Even after controlling for multiple covariates, adolescent drinking behaviour predicted adult drinking levels. As the level of adolescent drinking increased so too did the level of adult drinking. Increased adult alcohol consumption was also predicted by maternal alcohol consumption, both during pregnancy and at age 16 (but not paternal drinking at age 16), by being male, having committed authority avoidance offences, and by being from a white British cultural background. In contrast, reporting higher scores on the GHQ and the Conners' scale at age 16 predicted lower levels of adult drinking.

Adult alcohol use was also associated with a number of other adult outcomes including smoking, being educated to degree level, and being single. The links between education and drinking are further supported by the positive links between increased maths ability at age 10 and increased adult alcohol use sixteen years later.

Adolescent drinking behaviour also predicted adult smoking behaviour even after controlling for adult drinking (which itself is significantly associated with smoking at age 26). Given the level of continuity between adolescent and adult drinking, it was not surprising that adolescent heavy smoking also predicted adult smoking, as did parental smoking at age 16 (both father and mother). It is also predicted by parental separation. Children who lived in single parent or reconstituted households were more likely to smoke as adults independent of the smoking behaviour of their parents. In contrast, parental alcohol use in adolescence did not predict later smoking behaviour in their offspring.

Where higher scores on the GHQ and Conners' scale predicted lower adult alcohol consumption, they are both positively associated with later smoking behaviour. The relationship between authority avoidance offending and smoking is similar to that for alcohol, that is to say offenders are more likely to smoke in adulthood than non offenders. Adult smoking is also predicted by overt (violent offending) and illicit drug use independent of other offending behaviour.

Table 8.2: Adolescent drinking patterns and later adult health and social outcomes (adjusted for covariates)

	Regression Coefficient					Covariates
	Latent Class					
	Limited use	Occasional use	Moderate use	Heavy use	Hazardous use	
Health outcomes						
Alcohol use at 26[MR]	0.00	23.68	36.55	96.05**	101.56**	1**, 5, 13, 14, 15**, 16, 17, 18, 19**, 20, 21**, 22**, 23, 24, 25, 26, 27, 28, 29, 30**, 31, 32, 33**, 35, 36, 37**, 38**, 39, 40, 41, 42**, 44**.
Smoking at 26[LR]	0.00	0.26*	0.45**	0.67**	0.68**	1**, 5, 13**,14,16**,18-20, 21**, 22, 23, 24**, 25**, 26*, 27, 28**, 29**, 30*, 31*, 32, 33, 35*, 36**, 37**, 38**, 39, 40*~41, 42**,44**, 43**,
Heart problems[LR]	0.00	-1.16	-1.16	-1.77	-1.69	1, 3, 4**, .5**, 7, 8, 13, 15, 16, 17**, 18, 19, 20**,21- 26, 27**, 28- 31**, 32**, 33, 34**, 35, 36**, 37**, 38, 39, 40*, 41**, 42, 43, 44, 45**.
Mental health[LR]	0.00	0.81	0.94	1.11	1.13	1,3, 4, 5, 6, 13**, 15-29, 30**, 31, 32**, 33 - 44, 46.
Malaise[LR]	0.00	0.02	0.11	0.11	0.20	1**, 2*, 3*, 4, 5, 9, 10-12, 14**, 15**, 16, 17**, 18- 20, 21**, 22, 23**, 24**, 25**, 26 - 29, 30**, 31 - 33, 34*, 35 - 37, 38**, 39**, 40**, 41, 42, 43.
Employment outcomes						
Employment status[LR]	0.00	0.06	0.10	0.17	0.19	1**, 2-5, 13, 14, 15**, 16**, 17**, 18, 19**, 20, 21**, 22**, 23-26, 27**, 28 - 39, 40**, 41, 42, 43*.
Weekly pay[MR]	0.00	5.83	11.35**	9.68	5.33	1**, 5, 9, 10, 11**, 12, 13**, 14**, 15**, 16-20, 21**, 22, 23, 24**, 25, 26**, 27 - 33, 34**, 35**, 36**, 37, 38**, 39**, 40, 41, 42, 43, 44.
Marital outcomes						
Marital status[LR]	0.00	-0.24*	-0.24*	-0.05	0.16	1**, 2-5, 13-14, 15**, 16**, 17**, 18, 19*, 20, 21**, 22*, 23-26, 27*, 28-39, 40*, 41, 42, 43**.

Covariates include: 1. Qualifications; 2. Weekly pay; 3. Employment status; 4. Long-term unemployment; 5. Socioeconomic status; 6. Heart problems; 7. Mental health problems, 8. Digestive illness; 9. Road accidents. 10. Accidents at work; 11. Accidents at home; 12. Other accidents; 13. Malaise at 26; 14. Long-term illness; 15. Smoking at 26; 16. Adult BMI; 17. Child BMI; 18. Edinburgh Reading Test 19. Friendly Maths Test; 20. Special education; 21. Gender; 22. Maternal drinking in early pregnancy; 23. CBS - antisocial; 24. CBS - attention; 25. CBS - anxiety; 26. CBS - extraversion. 27. CBS-hyperkinesis; 28. Paternal smoking at 16; 29. Maternal smoking at 16; 30. Ethnicity; 31. Family structure at 16; 32. Paternal drinking at 16; 33. Maternal drinking at 16; 34. Family income at 16; 35. Smoking at 16; 36. Drug use at 16; 37. GHQ at 16; 38. Conners' at 16; 39. Malaise at 16; 40. Overt offending; 41. Covert offending; 42. Authority avoidance at 16; 43. Alcohol use at 26; 44. Marital status, 45. Heart problems at 16; Mental health problems at 16.

Increasing levels of childhood inattention and anxiety (as assessed by the Childhood Behaviour Scale) were associated with a decreased likelihood of smoking in adulthood. However, a higher childhood rating of extraversion was positively associated with an increased risk of adult smoking. While degree level education was associated with adult drinking, in the smoking model it was associated with a reduced likelihood of smoking. Adult smokers were also more likely to be male, white, single, report high levels of malaise, and have a significantly lower BMI (even after controlling for childhood BMI, which was not significant).

Early models examining the relationship between adolescent drinking and heart disease indicated that moderate drinking was associated with a lower risk of developing heart disease. However, once adolescent heart disease was controlled for, this significant association was removed. In addition to a pre-existing heart condition, adult heart problems were associated with a higher BMI in childhood, attending special education as a child, being more hyperactive as a child, living in a single parent/reconstituted family, reporting higher GHQ scores at age 16, not a heavy smoker at age 16, reporting covert and overt offences, living in a moderate wealth family, and having a father who drank when they were aged 16. Adults with heart problems were also more likely to have never worked, and to belong to a lower socioeconomic status group.

Adolescent drinking does not appear to increase the risk of developing a mental health problem in early adulthood measured in terms of either self-reported ICD-1 0 disorders or an elevated malaise score. Only three significant predictors of self-reported clinical psychiatric conditions were identified, malaise score at age 26 (above the recognised clinical cut-off), ethnicity (being white) and paternal alcohol consumption at age 16. In contrast, having a heavy drinking father at age 16 was associated with a decreased likelihood of a psychiatric disorder at age 26.

Experiencing high levels of malaise (8 or more symptoms) was more common amongst young adults who did not possess a degree level qualification, had a lower weekly wage, were not currently employed, were a current smoker, had a long term limiting illness, were female, or from an ethnic minority. In relation to childhood and adolescent predictors those young children who scored higher on the child behaviour subscales of antisocial behaviour, attentional problems and anxiety were also more likely to be classified as having high level of malaise some 16 year later. Similarly, children who had a high body mass index also were more likely to score high on the malaise inventory. Adult malaise scores were also associated with adolescent Conners' scores, malaise scores and overt offending. Covert offending, in contrast, was associated with decreased risk of malaise.

Employment outcomes

Looking at current employment status, there is little support for teenage drinking patterns being a lasting influence on the ability of the cohort members to find and sustain employment at the time of the 26-year-old questionnaire. Rather, it is concurrent human capital factors, such as a lack of qualifications, having a long-term limiting illness, and a high level of adult malaise, that are associated with unemployment. Unemployment is also more likely amongst women, those who have experienced an accident at home, and those who smoke. While alcohol consumption does not appear to predict later employment patterns, some childhood and adolescent characteristics do. Childhood extraversion and attention problems were associated with adult unemployment as were teenage drug use, smoking and malaise. Young people who grew up in poor households were more likely to be unemployed at age 26, while kids who grew up in more wealthy households were more likely to be in employment ten years later.

In contrast to employment, weekly income at age 26 did differ significantly across the adolescent drinking groups. In particular, latent class three (moderate users) reported a significantly higher weekly income than the limited use group. Income was higher amongst those young adults who had a degree level qualification, were male, were from an ethnic minority, had higher maths scores on the FMT at age 10, or who lived in a wealthy home at age 16. Teenage and adult smoking was associated with lower incomes as were adult malaise and maternal smoking.

Marital outcomes

Both alcohol consumption at age 26 and at age 16 were associated with marital status, but in slightly different ways. Compared to the limited use group, young people who were classified as occasional and moderate drinkers were less likely to be married ten years later. Other differences in marital status across the drinking groups did not reach significance. Increasing adult alcohol consumption was associated with significantly reduced likelihood of not being married. It is worth remembering that both the results control for the impact of maternal drinking during pregnancy, which was found to be a significant predictor of marital status (associated with a reduced likelihood of being married). Increased levels of hyperkinesias and overt offending behaviours were also associated with reduced likelihood of being married, as were current smoking and raised childhood BMI. Interestingly however, those who were married tended to have a higher adult BMI. The relationship between marital status and education was complex. At one level scores on the Friendly Maths Tests (completed at age 10) predicted marital status (higher score greater likelihood of being married). However, when education qualifications are compared, young adults with CSEs or 0 Levels were more likely to be married than those with no qualification. Those educated to degree level were significantly less likely to be married. Overall, 26-year-old female cohort members were significantly more likely to be married than their male counterparts.

DISCUSSION

This study examined the linkages between teenage drinking and alcohol consumption and other outcomes in adulthood. The objective of the analysis was to examine the impact of teenage drinking behaviours on subsequent adult behaviours assessed some ten years later. These adult outcomes included alcohol use, employment success, health problems and social relationships.

The first models to be estimated examined the continuities in alcohol consumption over this 10-year transitional period. Those young people who drank more alcohol at age 16 also drank more alcohol than their peers at age 26. This study supports the conclusion that a clear continuity exists between early drinking behaviours and those of later adulthood. Those consumption patterns established in the teenage years persist, to a large degree, into adulthood. While also finding considerable discontinuity in problem alcohol use, Wells Horwood, & Fergusson (2006) confirmed that late adolescent drinking (age 18) was a strong predictor of later alcohol problems at age 21, as was problem drinking at age 21 predictive of problems at age 25.

Rutter, Kim-Cohen and Maughan (2006) suggested that the continuity between childhood and adult behaviour problems may arise from a common set of time invariant risk factors. Genetic liability is one example of such a long lasting continuous risk factor that may mediate both early and later problem behaviour (Grant et al., 2005). Here, maternal drinking in pregnancy predicted adult drinking even after controlling for maternal and adolescent drinking patterns when the young person was aged 16. As mentioned in the previous chapter, maternal drinking in pregnancy could represent either a genetic mediation, a neurological deficit or priming effect or a social learning process. This study failed to find a neurological deficit that accounted for the heightened risk of teenage or adult alcohol consumption indicated by early maternal drinking. The majority of neuropsychological measures incorporated within the BCS70, including measures of auditory memory, fluid and verbal reasoning, expressive language skills, reading and mathematics abilities, hyperactivity, and attention problems, did not predict either adolescent drinking (previous chapter) or adult drinking behaviour (this chapter). In fact, high scores on the Friendly Maths Test were associated with higher levels of adult drinking, as was being educated to degree level. In contrast, maternal drinking at age 16 did predict adult drinking independent of drinking in early pregnancy. This could suggest the possibility of a social learning effect in addition to any genetic susceptibility indicated by early maternal drinking.

There was a lack of predictive association between child and adolescent indicators of behavioural undercontrol and adult alcohol consumption. This runs contrary to existing research. For example, Zucker (2006), in a recent review, concluded that behavioural undercontrol, and aggression in particular, predicted adolescent and early adult drinking. Likewise studies such as Chassin et al. (2002) have shown that indicators of behavioural undercontrol predict drinking behaviour at least until age 20. This study, in contrast, found that behavioural undercontrol (assessed in terms of early antisocial behaviour, attention problems and hyperkinesis and adolescent ADHD and delinquency) while predictive of adolescent drinking patterns, did not predict adult drinking, once adolescent drinking was controlled for. In fact adolescent ADHD scores were negatively associated with adult drinking (higher scores on the Conners' ADHD rating scale predicted lower alcohol consumption at age 26). As this is one of the few studies that examined drinking behaviour beyond early adulthood (that is beyond the age of 23), it is possible that behavioural undercontrol is influential in determining the onset, early consumption patterns and escalations in use before the onset of adult roles and responsibilities, but is not involved in the continuation of problem drinking behaviours into later adulthood, that is, past the age of around.

There is an inherent contradiction in these findings and those presented in the previous chapter. In the previous chapter, behavioural undercontrol (as indexed by antisocial behaviour problems at age 10) was shown to predict teenage drinking patterns. However, the analysis presented in this chapter would indicate that it is those young people with higher levels of self-control or self-regulation (as indexed by Conners' scores at age 16) who drank at higher levels at age 26. This paradox has also been noted in research on broader antisocial behaviour patterns. As Dishon and Patterson (2006) noted it is those children who are less organised and regulated that are most likely to engage in antisocial behaviour in early childhood, but it those young people who are both antisocial and self-regulated that are most likely to continuing their antisocial behaviour into adulthood. The authors indicate that self-regulation is required to learn and refine the skills necessary to undertake more specialist offences (for example, burglary, robbery) that characterise adult crime. A similar process might be at play here. However, it must be remembered that the outcome variable examined within this study is the quantity of alcohol consumed by respondents and not the existence of alcohol abuse or dependency. Therefore, while higher levels of behavioural control predicted higher levels of drinking, much of that drinking may still be considered as 'controlled drinking' or drinking that avoided the development of alcohol related problems, abuse or dependency. Further work is needed to unpick the developmental relationship between behavioural control/self regulation and the development of drinking patterns.

The lack of a significant relationship between adolescent problems behaviour (excluding alcohol use) and adult drinking also has implication for Problem Behaviour Theory (Jessor & Jessor, 1977). This theory proposes that behavioural problems in adolescents are not distinct entities, but rather comprise a single common behaviour cluster representing a general underlying tendency towards deviance. Key elements include smoking, alcohol and drug use, overt and covert offending behaviour. While there is a very clear association between alcohol use and the other dimensions of problem behaviour in adolescence (see chapters 6 and 7), these behaviours did not

213

predict alcohol use at age 26. In particular, teenage smoking and drug use, which share a common set of risk factors (Lynskey, Fergusson & Horwood, 1998), were not associated with adult drinking. The only significant predictor of adult drinking out of this cluster of adolescent behaviours was low-level authority avoidance antisocial behaviour. This lack of association may be explained by the existence of two different patterns of early offending behaviours, adolescent limited and life course persistent offending (Moffit, 2006). As Moffit's review highlights, the majority of young people engage in antisocial behaviour that, in developmental terms, is relatively short-lived. It first emerges in early adolescence, peaks in late teens and declines during the transition to young adulthood. As a result, its association with drinking behaviour may be transient in nature, and for most young people it may only be observed during the adolescent years. While the antisocial behaviour declines with age, for some young people, continued heavy drinking could remain. What maintains this continuity in drinking behaviour is, therefore, not proneness to problem behaviour in general, but specifically the patterns of drinking behaviour established during this adolescent period. This association does not rule out a possible decline in individual drinking behaviour over time (as with other dimensions of problem behaviour) associated with the transition to adulthood. However, those young people who drank more as teenagers drank more as adult, irrespective of their engagement in other problem behaviours. This finding supports the conclusion that factors that predict the continuity of drinking behaviour from adolescence to adulthood can be quite different from those that predict the patterns of alcohol consumption in adolescence.

Wells, et al. (2004), using the Christchurch Longitudinal data, found that adolescent drinking patterns predicted a range of adult drinking outcomes; including frequency of drinking, quantity of consumption, largest amount consumed over a twelve- month period and alcohol dependence. Looking at the quantity of alcohol consumed at age 25, this analysis found that adult drinking was not predicted by conduct disorder (age 8), attentional problems (age 8), smoking, drug use (between age 14-16), violent offending (14-16), mental health problems (14-16), or intelligence.[8.17] To an extent, these findings are supported here. Where the studies diverge is in relation to

---

[8.17] The significant predictors of quantity of alcohol consumed at age 25 were adolescent drinking class, gender, birth SES, property offending and suicide attempts before age 16.

parental alcohol consumption. Within the Christchurch study parental drinking or parental alcohol problems did not predict adult drinking. In contrast, the BCS70 analysis indicated that maternal drinking in pregnancy is a strong predictor of both adolescent and adult drinking. This divergence can be explained in a two ways. First, the two studies included different additional covariates in the models; therefore the models control for different risk factors, which may affect model parameter estimates. Second, and perhaps more importantly, Wells and colleagues generated a *"mother/father"* measure of their combined drinking behaviours. This study analysed the drinking behaviours of both mothers and fathers separately, showing that maternal, but not paternal, drinking was the more significant covariate. It is possible that combining the two reports into a single family-level variable, as was done by Wells, reduces the association with later adult drinking in the dependant child.

While adolescent smoking did not predict adult drinking behaviour, adolescent drinking did predict adult smoking. As the level of adolescent drinking increased so too did the odds of being a smoker at age 26. Alcohol consumption at age 26 also predicted concurrent smoking behaviour even after controlling for early alcohol consumption, as did adult smoking predict adult alcohol use. As discussed above, Lynskey and colleagues (1998) demonstrated the high correlation and common set of risk factors shared by adolescent smoking and alcohol use. However, it would appear that while smoking behaviour is not associated with a continuity of alcohol use the reverse is true for alcohol. This may be due to the way in which alcohol influences attempts to quit smoking. Heavy drinkers are less likely to attempt to quit smoking and their attempts are generally less successful (Dawson, 2000b; Zimmerman, Warheit, Ulbrich & Auth, 1990). The social context in which alcohol is commonly consumed (in a pub where tobacco is also frequently used) may result in alcohol acting as a risk factor for a continuation in smoking behaviour.

As with alcohol, there was a link between parental smoking and adult smoking, although in the case of tobacco use, both father's and mother's behaviour were significant predictors of adult smoking in the dependant child rather than just maternal behaviour. The association between parental smoking and adolescent smoking is well established (Bricker, Peterson, Leroux, Andersen, Rajan & Sarason, 2006). This study suggests that parental smoking is also predictive of adult smoking behaviour.

In contrast to alcohol, adolescent indicators of behavioural control predicted smoking at age 26. Both antisocial behaviour (authority avoidance and overt offending) and ADHD were significantly associated with smoking, as were teenage smoking and teenage drug use. Smoking was also associated with emotional stress. Adults who reported high levels of malaise were more likely to smoke than those who reported low levels. This appears to be a concurrent or short-term relationship, where stress predicts current smoking but not future smoking. Neither adolescent malaise or childhood anxiety problems predicted adult smoking. In fact, childhood anxiety levels were negatively associated with adult smoking, while childhood extraversion was positively associated. Again this suggests that the factors involved in the initial development of adolescent smoking may be quite distinct from those risk factors that promote a continuation in smoking behaviour into adulthood. Teenage smoking appears to be part of a wider set of risk taking deviant behaviour that includes alcohol use, antisocial behaviour and drug use (Jessor & Jessor, 1977; Lynskey & Fergusson, 1995). The association arises from a common set of predictors of vulnerability including having substance using friends, behavioural undercontrol and parental substance use (Lynskey et al., 1998). The onset of both alcohol and tobacco use tends to occur at around the same age in individuals, and slightly before progression onto other drug use (Kandel, 2002), with tobacco use being a slightly better predictor of the onset of alcohol use than vice versa (Wetzels et al., 2003). That is to say, almost all smokers will try alcohol but not all teenagers who try alcohol will also try smoking. However, alcohol use predicts the continued use of tobacco better than tobacco use predicts the continued use of alcohol (Jackson et al., 2002). Studies of smoking cessation provide insights into those factors that mitigate against successful cessations. Amongst adults who try to quit smoking those who drink more alcohol and have less stress coping resources (ability to deal with stressful situations) are more likely to fail and continue smoking (Matheny & Weatherman, 1998). Psychosocial stress and negative emotions are also strong predictors of the urge to smoke (Doherty, Kinnumen, Militello, & Garvey, 1995).

Adolescent alcohol consumption was not associated with an increased risk of adult heart disease or mental health problems. However, care should be taken when examining these models due to the small number of cases that reported health conditions (heart conditions n=20; mental health problems n=39). This will have reduced the power of the estimated models. Notwithstanding this limitation, the cardiovascular disease model showed an increasingly negative regression coefficient with increasing alcohol consumption. However, none of the coefficients reached significance once pre-existing heart problems and other covariates were controlled for. This is unsurprising as any cardiological effects of alcohol consumption, be they positive or negative, are unlikely to be observed in such young adults, given the relatively limited alcohol consumption history. Heart problems observed amongst this population are likely to be pre-existing childhood illnesses. In fact, adolescent heart problems and high General Health Questionnaire scores predicted adult heart problems. This suggests that the observed bivariate relationship between adolescent drinking and heart problems (see table 7.1) is more likely to be the result of childhood illness impacting on the likelihood of adolescent drinking behaviours rather than adolescent drinking precipitating adult illnesses. It may be the case that adolescents with congenital or early-diagnosed heart conditions are more supervised, given less opportunity to drink alcohol or are simply more health conscious, thereby consuming little alcohol in their teenage years. As a result, a lack of heart problems is associated with an increased risk of alcohol consumption. The negative association between adolescent smoking and adult heart disease also supports this reverse causation supposition. Smoking is widely regarded as a major cause of CHD, even in small sustained doses (Ezzati, Henley, Thun, & Lopez, 2005; Law, Morris, & Wald, 1997). There is no suggested positive health benefit of moderate smoking, as there is with alcohol consumption. Therefore, the logical interpretation of the association between adolescent smoking and adult heart disease is that the adult disease observed here is a manifestation of an existing childhood condition (as evidenced by the positive association between adolescent and adult heart disease). Therefore, it is the condition that significantly reduces the likelihood of the young person engaging in health-risk behaviour, even in adolescence. There is no evidence that CHD reduces the risk of the adolescent engaging in other risk taking behaviour. Both overt and covert offending in adolescence is positively associated with adult CHD. At present no established theoretical explanation is exists. An association between adolescent delinquency and increased adult mortality (including heart disease) has been noted elsewhere (Laub & Vaillant, 2000), however the authors recognised that the etiological links remained unclear. One possible explanation is that higher blood

217

pressures, heart rates and cardiovascular responses can be detected in aggressive children (Pine et al., 1996). Schneider, Nicolotti & Delamater (2002) also found that aggression and externalising behaviours were elevated in boys with a family history of hypertension. Within the Schneider study, delinquency scores were positively correlated with obesity and high blood pressure. This study also noted a positive relationship between adolescent delinquency, hyperkinesis, and BMI and later heart problems.

Adolescent problems, including mental health, antisocial behaviour alcohol use or drug use, did not predict mental health problems in adulthood. Only three significant predictors of mental health problems were detected within the logistic model estimated. These were ethnicity (white respondents were more likely to report a mental health diagnosis), paternal alcohol consumption in childhood (associated with decreased likelihood of reporting a disorder) and malaise at age 26 (positively associated with adult mental health problems). While the regression equation examining reported malaise scores confirmed the lack of association between adolescent drinking and emotional stress in adulthood, many of the parameters estimated differed substantively from the basic mental health model. A wide range of childhood and adult factors predicted malaise, including childhood ratings of antisocial behaviour, attention problems, anxiety and BMI. Adolescent ADHD, malaise and overt offending were also significantly associated with an increased risk of scoring high on the malaise score. Those reporting high malaise were also more likely to smoke, have a limiting long-term illness, and to be female. Employment was associated with a decreased risk of emotional stress.

Adolescent drinking also appeared to have little impact on later employment outcomes. When modelling both employment status and actual weekly pay, only one significant alcohol finding was observed. Moderate drinkers had a higher weekly pay than other drinkers even when human capital indicators were controlled for. This reinforces the conclusion that adolescent drinking, in its more controlled forms, appears to be normal or even an important part of adolescent development. Even heavy drinking in adolescence is not associated with any direct impact on the world of work. This is in contrast to other adolescent behaviours. Those who reported heavy smoking, drug use, ADHD symptoms, and high malaise were less likely to be in employment 10 years later. However, only heavy smoking in adolescence carried over into a decreased weekly wage. The study also found that adult alcohol consumption was not related to variations in either employment status or weekly pay once other factors were considered. Differences in employment outcomes were mainly explained by educational qualifications, gender and health problems (both long term and current) and childhood socioeconomic status. This study would suggest then that the relationship between alcohol and work based outcomes is relatively weak, either in terms of adolescent or adult drinking. While there is some evidence of a possible U shaped relationship between adolescent drinking and weekly adult wage, the differences only reach significance for one drinking class (moderate use). No other differences were significant.

Interestingly, delinquent behaviour, like alcohol, was not associated with any variations in employment status or weekly wages once other social factors were taken into consideration. Existing typologies of adolescent crime would suggest that young people on an adolescent–limited crime pathway commit most antisocial behaviour (see Moffitt 2006 for a full discussion). This behaviour pattern onsets in early teens but declines rapidly once the young person begins to adopt adult roles and responsibilities, therefore the impact on later social outcomes can be rather limited. It is suspected that a similar process is at play with alcohol. While there is a strong continuity in drinking behaviour, as the young people approach adulthood it is suspected that there is an overall reduction in alcohol consumption. What is maintained is the general ordering of the drinking classes over time (that is, heavy and hazardous drinkers are still those young people who drink the most in adulthood) rather than an individual's actual volume of consumption. This is evidenced by the fact that the average adult weekly consumption of even the hazardous drinkers was still only around 13 units (equivalent of around seven pints of beer per week). While adolescent hazardous drinkers are still drinking more than their peers 10 years later, for many their consumption would not be at levels sufficient to generate any alcohol related problem or alcohol dependency. As a result the continuity of drinking observed in this study does not appear to create much in the way of negative social impact for the young people.

Implications for public health

In summary, adolescent drinking predicted alcohol consumption ten years later. Those young people who were the most frequent drinkers, and who consumed the highest volumes were most likely to be heavy drinkers in adulthood. However, the young adults drinking behaviours did not seem to be associated with much health or social harm. This may largely be due to age. Many of the health consequences of alcohol consumption are due to prolonged excessive drinking and are not manifest until later adulthood. Therefore this study may be assessing health outcomes at too early a developmental stage to detect noticeable differences across the drinking groups. This is not to say that the adolescent hazardous drinkers are not at increased risk of serious health and social problems, but that this research may have to wait on the provision of later data sweeps to detect them.

Notwithstanding this limitation, the increased levels of alcohol consumption predicted by adolescent drinking warrant serious policy and practice consideration. It appears that adult heavy drinking can be predicted to a large degree by adolescent self-report information. As with any problem developmental pathway, early identification offers opportunities for early intervention designed to modify the developmental trajectory anticipated. As with all probabilistic models, including this one, evidence is provided that developmental pathways are not inevitable and, in this case, not all heavy and hazardous drinkers end up drinking excessively in adulthood. Therefore change is possible, and interventions are required that promote this change in young people.

Early work with young offenders (Baldwin 1990, 1991) provides a useful model for the provision of effective controlled drinking programmes to high-risk adolescent groups. The focus of such interventions is not total abstinence, common in many adult treatment programmes, but rather the development of moderate controlled drinking patterns. As Baldwin demonstrated, the application of cognitive behavioural skills training can be effective in promoting a significant reduction in overall consumption, a reduction in associated risk behaviours, and the development of normalised drinking behaviours amongst hazardous adolescent drinkers. While successful outcomes for young people within the Criminal Justice System can be achieved, Baldwin's work did benefit from operating within a system where legal sanctions could be harnessed to enhance compliance amongst participants. The threat of breach proceedings for serious non-compliance was part of the behavioural contract signed by group members. This stick was balanced by the carrot of an agreed reduction in the length of their probation order on successful completion of the programme. The challenge for policy makers, some 15 years later, is the application of such interventions with hidden populations of young hazardous drinkers who may not be in contact with any existing service. The Health Advisory Service report "The Substance of Young Needs" (Health Advisory Service, 2001) provides a useful tiered organizational structure for the development and provision of adolescent alcohol and drug treatment services. Central to this approach is the identification, assessment and referral of young problem drinkers by front-line generic professionals working with young people such as teachers, educational psychologists and primary care staff. Above this first-tier of services lie more specialist youth services that can provide initial input and intervention with low-risk cases. For those cases that cannot be addressed by tier-two services are specialist alcohol and drug agencies that can assess and provide services to meet the needs of more problematic cases. To date, however, there are few examples of this multi-tiered service structure established within local areas (McArdle & Gilvarry, 2006).

Adolescent drinking is also associated with adult smoking. This is also a major public health concern. Here, it is suspected that both smoking and alcohol use onset arises from a common set of risk factors, but once initiation has occurred alcohol plays an important role in maintaining smoking behaviour, and in particular, increasing the risk of relapse after smoking cessation. While most smoking behaviour is not accompanied by alcohol consumption, the reverse is not the case. For those who smoke and drink, their alcohol consumption will almost certainly be accompanied by smoking, and it is this pairing of the behaviours that creates difficulties for drinkers who wish to quit smoking. The forthcoming ban on smoking in public buildings (including licensed premises) may go some way to break the links between alcohol and smoking. Survey evidence following a similar ban in Ireland has indicated that the smoke free laws have contributed to a reduced smoking in pubs and restaurants and contributed to successful smoking cessation attempts (Fong et al., *in press*).

SUMMARY

This chapter set out to examine the relationship between patterns of alcohol consumption at age 16 and adult outcomes at age 26. These included health outcomes (alcohol use, smoking, mental health problems, heart problems, accidents and malaise), employment outcomes (status, pay, and educational attainment) and relationship issues (divorce rates and proportion with dependant children).

The key finding of this analysis is the strong association between adolescent drinking and adult drinking. Those who drank more at age 16 drank more at age 26. While drinking patterns established in adolescence appears to have a direct link with adult drinking, the association is also strengthened by pre-existing risk factors that mediate both early and later drinking behaviour. Maternal drinking in early pregnancy, in particular, was a significant predictor for both adolescent and adult drinking (even after controlling for adolescent drinking). The lack of evidence for neurological deficits as risk factors for adult drinking would suggest that the influence of maternal drinking might be mediated through genetically determined variations in individual sensitivity to alcohol rather than alcohol induced prenatal neurological impairment.

Adult drinking was not predicted by adolescent behavioural undercontrol or antisocial behaviour, beyond their impact on adolescent drinking patterns. While heavy drinking in adolescence appears to be part of a broad cluster of teenage problem behaviours, by age 26 this association is no longer observed. This may be explained, somewhat, by the transitory nature of most adolescent antisocial behaviour. While antisocial behaviour declines with age, alcohol consumption continues.

While adolescent smoking was associated with adolescent drinking, it did not predict adult drinking. However, both adolescent and adult drinking did predict adult smoking. Smoking appears to be associated with the onset of alcohol consumption, but once the two behaviours are established, it appears that they may have a reciprocal causal relationship, and in addition, alcohol consumption may prevent the successful cessation of tobacco use. As with alcohol use, parental smoking behaviour predicts adult smoking.

In relation to other health issues, adolescent drinking patterns are not associated with increased risk of heart disease, digestive illness, malaise, other mental health problems, or other long-term illnesses. Early analysis suggested a slight positive effect for alcohol consumption on heart disease. However, once controls for childhood heart conditions were introduced, it became apparent that early childhood heart problems predicted adolescent abstinence, creating an association between teenage non-drinking and adult heart problems.

Heavy adolescent drinking also appeared to have little impact on later employment outcomes. In fact, moderate drinking at age 16 predicted higher wages at age 26. Adult drinking also did not appear to restrict human capital. Employment outcomes were mainly predicted by childhood socio-economic status, educational qualifications, gender and pre-existing health problems.

While adolescent and adult drinking seemed to have little impact on adult health or financial outcomes, this may in part be due to the age at which the adult assessment was undertaken. By age 26, young adults may not be old enough for the negative effects of sustained heavy drinking to emerge. The BCS70, in effect, may assess adult outcome too early to detect any noticeable difference. Later data sweeps of the BCS70, when cohort members are older, may provide new opportunities to re-evaluate the associations between early drinking patterns and later adult outcomes.

9 CONCLUSIONS

This final chapter aims to review the key study, to discuss their implications for current policy and practice, to identify questions warranting future attention and finally, to consider the strengths and limitations of the research presented.

Alcohol plays a prominent role in modern UK society. Most of the population, particularly young people, drink alcohol. However, a small proportion of drinkers consume alcohol at levels that cause harm to themselves, their families, and those around them. As has been discussed, these individuals are more likely to develop health problems, face financial difficulties and get into trouble with the police (see chapter 2). Alcohol can lead to increased risk of violence, accidents and other dangerous behaviours. The cost to society in terms of increased health care and criminal justice expenditure is considerable. As a result, the reduction of alcohol-related harm is a major public policy concern. In light of this, each of the four jurisdictions within the UK have recently revised their alcohol reduction strategies, aimed at tackling the harmful aspects of modern drinking culture.

Historical analysis of drinking patterns highlights considerable temporal variations (see chapter 2). Many of these shifts have been associated with periods of social and economic change. Young people growing up today are exposed to an alcohol market place that is dominated by a small number of global alcohol producers/distributors, promoting an expanding range of high-strength brand extensions, ready-to-drink spirit mixers and 'shooters'. Licensing deregulation is moving towards a '24-hour' drinking culture, where extreme drunkenness is largely tolerated, leading to increased opportunities for engaging in "hedonistic consumerism" (Measham & Brain, 2005). This changing alcohol market has been, to some extent, an industry response to broader changes in youth culture associated with the dance (rave) scene and the rise of dance drug use (e.g. ecstasy and amphetamines) that began in the mid-1980s (Brain, 2000; Parker et al., 2000).

The Academy of Medical Science report, "Calling Time", summarised many of the current public concerns regarding the health implications of current drinking patterns (Academy of Medical Science, 2004). The report recommended adjusting public policy (raising alcohol taxation and decreasing availability) to reduce the consumption of alcohol at the population level (pg 9).

Primary prevention is also expected to play an important role in reducing population consumption. The basic premise of developmental prevention science (chapter 3) is that a better understanding of the causal mechanisms underlying the development of problem behaviour in adolescents should aid progress towards more effective prevention programmes. Such programmes should aim to mitigate the effects of exposure to risk processes, whilst prompting the development of protective factors and individual resilience. Minimising risk and maximising resilience should result in the reduced likelihood of young people developing serious problem behaviours.

In response to the recognised need for further research into the development of alcohol problems within the UK, this study set out to:

- Classify adolescent drinkers into a number of distinct categories based on the patterns of their alcohol consumption and to validate this new typology (chapter 5);
- Examine the relationship between these adolescent drinking patterns and other behaviours and characteristics at age 16 (chapter 6);
- Investigate the early childhood (from birth to age 10) antecedents of the different drinking patterns observed during the teenage years (chapter 7);
- Examine the adult sequelae (health, economic and social outcomes) of the different drinking patterns at age 26, some ten years later (chapter 8).

KEY FINDINGS
Classifying adolescent drinking patterns at age 16

Major UK school-based surveys have estimated that over 20% of UK 16-year olds have been drunk ten or more time in the last year (for example, see Hibbell, et al., 2004). However, single indicators such as this, have been shown to under-identify adolescents with alcohol problems (Ellickson, McGuigan, Adams, Bell, & Hays, 1996).

Latent class analysis (LCA) is a valuable categorical data reduction tool that can be used to classify individual on the basis of multiple indicators. LCA is increasingly used in the classification of behavioural and psychiatric disorders, including depression (Sullivan, Kessler, & Kendler, 1998), psychosis (Kendler, Karkowski, & Walsh, 1998) and Attention Deficit and Hyperactivity Disorder (ADHD) (Rasmussen, Neuman, Heath, Levy, Hay, & Todd, 2004). Over 10 years ago, Uebersax (1994) identified its potential within the field of addiction research. In particular, a better understanding of the subtypes of alcohol consumption patterns should improve the targeting of prevention and treatment interventions. LCA has advanced our understanding of adult alcohol disorder typologies, their genetic basis, and their association with co-morbid conditions (Hasin, Hatzenbuehler, Keyes, & Ogburn, 2006; Hesselbrock & Hesselbrock, 2006). To date, however, there have only been a limited number of LCA models of adolescent drinking (Chung & Martin, 2001; Fergusson, et al., 1994; Reboussin, Song, Shrestha, Lohman, & Wolfson, 2006), and none of these have used a European sample.

The LCA model estimated within this study categorised adolescents into five distinct groups on the basis of their alcohol consumption patterns. Within this model, a small minority of young people were identified as having a hazardous or problematic alcohol consumption pattern (around one in ten) reporting frequent drinking, high levels of alcohol consumed, frequent binge drinking and multiple alcohol related problems. A further 24% were classified as heavy drinkers. In the only other LCA analysis of 16-year-old drinking patterns, Fergusson and colleagues (1994) classified 9.3% of participants in the Christchurch Health and Development Study as "hazardous drinkers". While the difference in the size of the hazardous drinking population across the two studies may be due to subtle differences in the measures used or cultural differences in adolescent drinking, it does suggest a degree of robustness in the estimates. There does appear to be a sizeable minority of 16 year olds within the general population, around 10 per cent or so, displaying alcohol consumption patterns worthy of public health concern.

The relationship between adolescent drinking patterns and other behaviours and characteristics at age 16

This study found substantial evidence for the validity of this five-class typology. Hazardous drinkers spent more money on alcohol, drank alcohol on more days in the previous week, and had an earlier age of onset of alcohol use (both supervised and unsupervised) than those young people in other drinking classes. Hazardous drinking was more common amongst boys and tended to be associated with other problem behaviours, such as smoking, illicit drug use, violent offending, and educational under-performance. These findings were consistent with a common vulnerability model of adolescent problem behaviour, where certain types of externalising behaviours cluster within individuals (Fergusson & Horwood, 2000; Jessor & Jessor, 1977; Lynskey et al., 1998). One implication of this is that adolescent counselling services are unlikely to meet 'pure' alcohol only cases. Rather they will be faced with young people with a range of complex, interlinked problems and difficulties. While a major review of the implications of alcohol comorbidity has been undertaken for adult treatment services (Crawford, Crome, & Clancy, 2003) our understanding of the impact on adolescent intervention services is still rather limited (Armstrong & Costello, 2002).

One interesting finding was the lack of association between drinking patterns and mental health problems. While studies have estimated that around 60% to 80% of young people with alcohol problems had at least one other psychiatric problem, most of this is accounted for by conduct disorder/offending behaviour. The lack of a relationship between hyperactivity and alcohol use may reflect the developmental nature of the association. While childhood hyperactivity may predict later adolescent drinking (Dawes, et al., 1997; Wilens, 1998), the age-related decline in hyperactivity symptoms across adolescence (Biederman, Mick, & Faraone, 2000) may result in a reduced association when examined in cross-section at age 16.

Beyond the hazardous drinking class, the majority of teenage drinking was not associated, to any large degree, with adolescent problems. It would appear that the high levels of comorbidity between alcohol consumption and other behavioural problems observed in clinical case control studies do not generalise to community studies containing less severe drinking patterns. Below hazardous drinking, there was little evidence of comorbidity associated with alcohol consumption. Teenage drinking per se did not appear to be a marker of 'problem adolescent development'; rather it was only the extreme high-level tail of the drinking spectrum that was indicative of a broad cluster of problem behaviours.

227

Moderate drinking appeared to be an indicator of teenage adaptation not maladaptation. In relation to some indicators, for example self-esteem and mental health outcomes, even heavy drinking could be considered an indicator of adequate adaptation. While this is a relatively narrow examination of adaptation (cross-sectional at age 16) it does suggest that the distinction between normal and abnormal teenage drinking (based on associated adolescent behaviours) should be placed at a higher level (heavy use – hazardous use) than that drawn in current legislation (no use – use). This has profound implications for the design and development of alcohol prevention intervention aimed at adolescents. To date, most prevention interventions have adopted a zero tolerance approach to consumption (i.e. aim to reduce the overall proportion of young people drinking) (Neighbors, Larimer, Lostutter, & Woods, 2006). The results here would suggest that a more appropriate focus may be the prevention of hazardous drinking, rather than on drinking per se, as it is associated with greater adolescent problems.

Early childhood antecedents of adolescent drinking patterns

In relation to the antecedents of drinking behaviour, two alternative models were proposed. In the first, the deviant proneness model, individual 'behavioural undercontrol' or 'behavioural disinhibition' predominantly determines individual risk of problem alcohol use. Disinhibition is a cluster of behavioural traits including impulsivity, inattention and aggression. When disinhibition is high, the likelihood of problem drinking is increased. To date, the evidence supporting elements of this model has been somewhat conflicting. While conduct disorder has been a consistent predictor of alcohol problems, findings in relation to ADHD, often used as an indicator of disinhibition, have failed to show a consistent predictive influence. It may be the case, however, that these conflicting findings represent the limitations of using a broad clinical diagnosis, often within case control studies, as an indicator of a complex causal process. It is possible that only certain dimensions of ADHD are causally related to adolescent drinking.

The second model proposed was the 'negative affect' model. Here, individuals, particularly females, use the mood-altering effects of alcohol to self-medicate emotional problems. Again, the evidence supporting this model is both inconsistent and non-European. Evidence has been found for higher rates of anxiety and depression amongst

228

both high-level drinkers (Rhodes, et al., 1996) and low-level drinkers (Caldwell, et al., 2002). This may represent a non-linear reciprocal relationship between alcohol and negative affect, where alcohol is initially used to reduce anxiety and depression in the short term, but with continued use actually exacerbates anxiety and depression in the longer term (Kushner et al., 2000).

In addition to the two models reviewed, this study also found supporting evidence within the research literature for additional risk factors. These included cognitive executive functioning, parental substance use, family resources, and early maturation.

Preliminary bivariate analysis supported a behavioural undercontrol model of adolescent alcohol use, rather than a negative affect model. Childhood affective problems (teacher reports) predicted lower rather than higher levels of drinking at age 16. Limited use teenagers also had the highest levels of social services intervention in childhood. Teenage hazardous drinkers had the lowest level of reported childhood anxiety problems. They also, in contrast, had the highest level of childhood behavioural undercontrol, such as anti-social behaviour (reported by mothers and teachers), hyperactivity (mothers only), and poor attention (teachers only). They were also reported to be extraverts and popular with their peers.

Significant differences were detected across all the educational tests undertaken. In general, hazardous and heavy drinkers scored well on the British Ability Test and other reading and maths assessments. Low scores on the educational tests at age 10 identified young people who were more likely to be limited drinkers at age 16. When they were children, limited drinkers were also more likely to have had a lower body mass index, have had an external locus of control, have had a later age of menarche (girls only), have had more motor problems, have received special educational provision, have lived in a household with lower family capital as indexed by father's occupation, family income, free school meals.

It must be remembered that a significant association between an antecedent and outcome may be due to their shared association with some third variable and not to the existence of a causal relationship between them. Therefore, it was necessary to replicate the bivariate analysis within a multivariate model (multinomial logistic regression) to test for the significant of relationships between antecedents and outcome whilst controlling for other variable effects. When the significant bivariate indicators were entered into a multivariate model, surprisingly, very few predicted higher levels of adolescent drinking. Of the indicators of behavioural undercontrol, only antisocial behaviour and extraversion differentiated between hazardous drinkers and other classes. No differences in the level of anxiety across the various classes were noted. Likewise, family income, child disclosure, parental smoking, cognitive functioning or locus of control did not predict higher levels of drinking at age 16. Gender differences were noted in the comparisons between hazardous drinkers and both occasional and moderate drinkers, as were differences in child BMI (hazardous vs. limited and occasional). The only predictor that differentiated between hazardous and heavy drinkers was maternal drinking in early pregnancy.

This study would suggest that amongst the various components of behavioural undercontrol it is early-onset antisocial behaviour, in particular, that is associated with higher levels of later alcohol use. It must be remembered that the conceptualisation of antisocial behaviour used here also included items on impulsive-type behaviours as assessed by teachers (see appendix A). These findings clearly indicate that attention problems and hyperactive behaviour, two of the three dimensions of ADHD, are not associated with increased levels of later alcohol use when antisocial/impulsive behaviour is taken into account. This may go some way to explain the inconsistencies in ADHD-alcohol research base. Impulsivity appears to be the only dimension of childhood ADHD that is associated with later alcohol use. This issue is not only of academic interest, but is of real importance for the identification and provision of interventions to high-risk young people. This research would suggest that using a broad indicator of heightened risk, such as an ADHD diagnosis, might be of little value in the targeting of high-risk young people. It is impulsivity (particularly when found within an sociable, popular, extraverted individual) that is a more valuable pointer for vulnerability.

As with the analysis on the correlates of adolescent drinking at age 16, the analysis of the antecedents of drinking behaviour reinforced the conclusion that drinking per se is not associated with negative characteristics or experiences. Teenage drinking, even at the higher end, does not have its origins in poverty, low IQ, external locus of control, emotional problems, motor difficulties, social isolation, major family difficulties (as indexed by social worker contact), birth abnormalities, selected early behaviour problems, or poor self esteem. In general, teenage drinkers appear to have normal childhoods. If anything, early childhood problems are more indicative of the limited use group. This does not suggest that these characteristics are strong predictors of non- use of alcohol; rather it reflects that this class is comprised, in part, of young people who have established medical, educational or social problems that may limit their exposure to alcohol in their teenage years. Alcohol consumption in adolescence is primarily a social activity; therefore, anything that disrupts the social world may limit drinking at this age. For example, young people with medical problems for example do spend less time outside of the family home (as indexed by the average time they have to be home for at night). Also, as extraversion - an indicator of being gregarious, talkative, assertive and deriving pleasure for social groups - increases so to does teenage alcohol consumption. Extraversion, even when assessed long before drinking behaviour begins, is one of the few characteristics that differentiate moderate drinkers from hazardous drinkers.

Increased levels of anxiety and other emotional problems in childhood were associated with a reduced level of alcohol consumption, even in the multivariate models. Again, this reinforces the conclusion that teenage drinking, in general, is a highly social activity undertaken by gregarious, popular children with few major difficulties. Any existing characteristics that may disrupt this social exchange, such as being anxious, worried or depressed, appeared to reduce children's later alcohol consumption. When the extent of negative characteristics increased amongst children, the level of alcohol consumption changed in one of two ways. If the problems were likely to restrict peer interactions, (i.e. learning difficulties) then alcohol consumption appeared to be reduced. If the problems were likely to increase peer interactions (i.e. high level of extraversion in combination with impulsivity) the alcohol consumption increased to hazardous levels.

The only predictor to differentiate heavy drinkers from hazardous drinkers was maternal alcohol consumption in early pregnancy. Unfortunately, this study was unable to unpick the specific mechanism through which the risk exposure operated. Drinking in pregnancy may indicate a genetic mediation (alcoholic mothers who were unable to modify their drinking when pregnant passing on a genetic susceptibility to the reinforcing effects of alcohol to their offspring), a neurological deficit/priming model (where prenatal alcohol exposure alters the developing brain in a way that increases propensity for later problems drinking) or a social learning mechanism (where the child grows up in a family setting where alcohol plays an prominent role). Notwithstanding

231

the fact that the link may be genetic and therefore non-modifiable, this finding would point towards the identification and provision of drinking reduction programmes for mothers with drinking problems as a way of reducing problem teenage drinking. It also highlights the high-risk status of children of problem drinking mothers for later alcohol problems themselves.

The adult sequelae (at age 26) of different adolescent drinking patterns (at age 16)

Many of the inconsistencies in the research into the longitudinal stability of drinking behaviour could be derived from the differences in the research methods used, the random fluctuations in individual drinking behaviour over the shorter term, and variations in the length of follow-up time (short-term studies may give different findings to those tracking behaviour over the longer term). Similar discrepancies have been detected in the evidence base of other adult sequelae of adolescent drinking, for example, employment and mental health outcomes.

The advantage of this study is that it employs one of the few UK data sets that incorporates high quality multidimensional assessment of adolescent drinking behaviour, examines a wide range of adult outcomes, can control for a wide range of possible covariates (from birth to adulthood), and examines impact over a long period of time (10 years). One of the most comprehensive US studies in this area, by McGue & Iacono (2005), only examined early adult outcomes up to the age of 20. This work extends this area of research to age 26.

The level of adolescent drinking significantly predicted the level of adult drinking. When the 16-year old hazardous drinkers reached age 26, they still drank more alcohol overall, drank more frequently and drank more per session, relative to other drinkers. While hazardous drinkers consumed on average 14 units of alcohol per week (still within government recommended safe drinking limits) around 15% reported daily drinking at age 26. While adolescent drinking also predicted adult smoking, teenage smoking did not predict adult drinking, reaffirming the role alcohol may play in preventing smoking cessation.

Other key predictors of adult drinking included maternal drinking (both during pregnancy and when the child was an adolescent), being male, being white, and having committed offences at age 16. In contrast to the analysis of the antecedents of <u>teenage</u>

drinking, presented above, little evidence was found for a behavioural undercontrol model of adult drinking. In fact, higher scores on the Conners' scale predicted lower levels of drinking, not higher. Likewise, there was no evidence of a negative affective pathway to adult drinking, independent of adolescent drinking.

Preliminary bivariate analysis indicated that moderate level alcohol consumption was associated with a lower risk of adult heart problems. This somewhat supported the hypothesis that alcohol consumption can have a protective effect on later heart disease. However, once the existence of childhood and adolescent heart conditions were factored into the analysis, this protective effect was removed. What was happening here, was that children and adolescents with existing heart conditions were more likely to abstain from alcohol or to use at very low levels during their teenage years. The bivariate association between low levels of drinking and higher incidents of heart conditions found amongst adults was due to pre-existing childhood conditions. A similar effect was found for adolescent smoking. Again, it is childhood conditions influencing adolescent smoking, rather than smoking reducing the risk of adult heart disease.

Heart conditions at age 26 were associated with adult unemployment, low socio-economic status, having a high BMI in childhood, having had special education, being hyperkinetic in childhood, having a father who drank heavily, higher General Health Questionnaire scores and reporting overt and covert offending.

Teenage drinking was not associated with any adult mental health problem. In fact, few of the covariates examined did predict mental health problems (malaise, ethnicity and parental alcohol consumption at age 16). This may be due to the very small number of cases that were identified with psychiatric diagnoses, substantially reducing the statistical power of the model estimated.

Adolescent drinking did not appear to have any real impact on adult economic outcomes. Rather, it was concurrent human capital factors (e.g. poor educational qualifications) that appear to be associated with a lack of success in the labour market. Of the early life predictors examined, childhood poverty, extraversion and hyperactivity predicted adult unemployment.

While the level of alcohol consumption at age 16 predicated, to an extent, the level of alcohol consumed in adulthood, it appeared that drinking alcohol at age 16 had few other long-term implications at age 26. If the young person was able to moderate the alcohol consumption at age 16, it, in fact, was associated with positive young adult outcomes. Again, this supports the conclusion that lower level teenage drinking was not a negative adolescent experience. The majority of teenage drinkers went on to meet approach developmental tasks during the transition to adulthood, including moderating their drinking, successfully completing their education, and entering the labour market.

OVERARCHING POLICY AND PRACTICE IMPLICATIONS

A sizeable proportion of young people drink alcohol at high levels. That drinking was associated with an increased risk of experiencing alcohol-related problems. High-level alcohol consumption amongst teenagers was also associated with certain poor adolescent outcomes including under-performance at school, offending behaviour, smoking and drug use. As such, teenage heavy drinking warrants attention both in terms of its potential as a source of social harm but also as a contributory factor in the emergence of other adolescent problems.

However, the simplest policy message that can be derived from this, that more alcohol prevention activity is need with underage drinkers, may be misleading for a number of reasons. First, a straightforward call for more prevention overlooks the finding that the majority of adolescent drinkers, including those drinking at the higher end, have positive adjustment at age 16 and few long-term negative consequences at age 26. In fact, adolescents classified into the moderate drinking category have the highest levels of educational performance and self-esteem, and the lowest levels of malaise, internalising disorders, hyperactivity, and attention problems. With respect to these outcome measures, limited drinkers have a poor adjustment at age 16. While there are some dose-response type associations between increasing levels of drinking and increased negative outcomes (for example, smoking and drug use) in many cases moderate drinking was an indicator of normative/positive adolescent adjustment.

It could be argued that adolescent exposure to, and experimentation with, alcohol is an important stage in the development of self-regulation over a popular and highly accessible adult behaviour (Percy, 2008) It is during the trial and error phase of unsupervised and illicit drinking that young people may develop the regulatory competency to moderate and control their drinking when the full world of alcohol is open to them in early adulthood. It may be more correct to view certain types of teenage drinking patterns as, at worst, a neutral effect on adolescent development, and at best an important stage in the development of the skills and experience required by adults to balance the competing pressures of work and home demands with hedonistic alcohol-related leisure.

If this conclusion is accepted, then adolescent drinking per se may not be considered as wholly problematic when judged against longer-term adult health and social outcome. It could be argued, therefore, that the focus of public policy should be not be directed at all teenage drinking per se, but towards those drinking patterns that are associated with increased risk of more negative adolescent and adult outcomes. This is particularly important given the increased quantity of alcohol consumed by teenagers observed in recent years (Westlake & Yar, 2006). It may well be the case that if a modern cohort of 16-year-olds were compared with the BCS70 cohort, the proportion of heavy and hazardous drinkers would have increased.

A criticism that can be levelled at previous alcohol policies is that strategies developed on the basis of extreme cases, or extreme effects of alcohol consumption, where applied across the board to all drinking patterns. In contrast, it is argued here that modern prevention programmes should recognise the heterogeneity in teenage drinking and the diverse outcomes of those drinking patterns (some positive and some negative) and should adjust accordingly.

A further complicating factor is the so-called 'prevention paradox' (see Rossow & Romelsjö, 2006) This is the observation that amongst adult drinkers the majority of acute alcohol related problems, as distinct from more chronic conditions such as liver cirrhosis, are experienced not by heavy drinkers but by those who drink at more modest levels. This is due to two contributory factors. Firstly, moderate drinkers greatly outnumber heavy or hazardous drinkers. Therefore, even if their risk of harm is lower than other drinking classes the actual numbers of moderate drinkers experiencing harm may exceed heavier drinkers by virtue of them being the majority. Secondly, the risk of experiencing a problem, such as being in an accident or being the victim of a violent crime, is a factor of the level of concurrent alcohol intoxication, and not the level of frequency or overall volume of alcohol consumption. Basically, it not how much you usually drink that matters, but how drunk you actually are at that time. This suggests that attempts to reduce acute alcohol problems should focus on reducing intoxication within the population as a whole, rather than reducing drinking levels amongst high-risk groups (i.e. heavy drinkers) (Rossow & Romelsjö, 2006). While high-risk groups may face more chronic alcohol problems, it is the moderate drinker who is more likely to suffer acute social and health problems. Skog (2006) suggested that binge drinkers (moderate use individuals who have occasional bouts of heavy intoxication) warranted particular attention.

To date there has been little examination of the prevention paradox amongst adolescent drinkers. In one of the few studies conducted in this area, Stockwell et al., (2004) found that most regular alcohol use (assessed in terms of actual numbers of individuals participating) occurred amongst the low risk groups (i.e. those with fewer identified risk factors). They concluded that both universal and target prevention strategies were required. The findings from the Stockwell study are somewhat supported by this research. Chapter 8 examined the proportion of young people within the various drinking classes who went on to drink above the recommended safe drinking limits at age 26. The proportion of hazardous drinkers who had a weekly intake above the recommended limits was more than double that in the occasional drinking group (males: 26% vs 11%; females: 16% vs 5%). However, when the actual number of young people were considered, nearly as many occasional drinkers (age 16) drank more than the recommended units (21 for males; 14 for females) at age 26 as hazardous drinkers (55 occasional vs 71 hazardous) due to the fact that there were more than three times the numbers of adolescent occasional drinkers than hazardous drinkers (23% of the total sample compared with 7%)[9.18]. However, once heavy drinkers are considered, this paradox is weakened. Heavy drinkers are both numerous (25%) and high risk (21% of males and 18% of females drinking above the safe limits).

To date, much alcohol prevention work has focused on the provision of information on the risks associated with the use of alcohol and other drugs. The assumption here is that a better understanding of the potential long term consequences of engaging in alcohol use during adolescence may persuade young people to delay or forgo initiation into the use of alcohol. In addition, prevention programmes have also

---

[9.18]   These proportions are based on the modal assignment of respondents to latent classes and not the gamma parameters (see Chapter 5). Therefore, they differ slightly from the proportions presented in Table 5.13.

included, to varying degrees, the application of cognitive–behavioural skills training to bolster young people's anti-alcohol attitudes and cognitions, social competence, and resistance to social pressures to consume licit and illicit substances. A recent meta-analysis identified a modest (though sometimes partial) positive effect of adolescent school based alcohol prevention, but little evidence that this effect was maintained within the medium or longer term (Foxcroft, Ireland, Lister-Sharp, Lowe, & Breen, 2003). Most prevention programmes, particularly those with origins in the USA, tend to adopt abstinence as the primary outcome goal. As a consequence, few appear to consider the development of controlled substance use as an appropriate outcome. The down side of abstinence orientated initiatives, therefore, is that if a young person does make the transition from non-use to experiential use, the skills and knowledge gained via participation in the prevention programme may provide little by way of protection in relation to the development of regulated consumption patterns. The failure to promote longer term resilience to the development of hazardous or problematic consumption patterns, once use is initiated, may go some way to explain the failure of current prevention programmes to maintain the modest public heath benefits initially achieved.

If moderate adolescent alcohol use is considered to be of little long-term risk to the young person, but to retain a potential for acute risk of intoxication related accidents and other incidents, the logical extension is to consider the inclusion of regulatory skills training within prevention programmes. Such training would aim to develop individual self-regulation over the consumption of psychoactive substances in an attempt to minimise both acute risks and the numbers of young people who make the transition to hazardous alcohol use. Programmes would, therefore, require both universal prevention elements and more targeted components for those young people identified at higher risk. The universal prevention action could aim to teach basic regulation skills including the minimisation or avoidance of acute harm associated with excessive intoxication. In addition, a reduction in the proportion of young people within all adolescent drinking classes who make the progression to heavy adult drinking would also be an appropriate target. It would not be targeted at promoting abstinence.

Notwithstanding the implications of the 'prevention paradox', the findings from this research do indicate the existence of a sizeable proportion of young people who are

237

drinking at very high levels, even in their teenage years. These young people are also more likely to found at the higher end of the adult drinking spectrum. The identification and provision of targeted secondary prevention intervention should be cost effective (Catalano, Haggerty, Gainey, Hoppe & Brewer, 1998).

Within alcohol and drug treatment fields there is an increasing recognition of harm reduction principles as an appropriate and pragmatic response to individual drug use (Des Jarlais, 1995; Marlatt, 1998; MacCoun, 1998). With harm reduction, the initial treatment priority is the reduction of the risk of future drug-related harm to the individual and others, irrespective of the individual's desire to reduce or discontinue consumption. Harm reduction interventions usually involve the alteration of individual consumption patterns to minimise risk. If applied here, an initial target for all (or nearly all) adolescents would be to minimise the occurrence of excessive intoxication when drinking. While there is a considerable literature on the teaching of controlled consumption skills to adults (Denning, 2004; Marlatt & Witkiewitz, 2002) the extent to which such control drinking skills can be taught to under-controlled young people still remains a largely unanswered question. However, if such adolescents fail to develop appropriate regulatory competency their long-term outcomes may be relatively poor.

Models of harm reduction prevention programmes for adolescent are not well developed. Marlatt & Witkiewitz (2002) documented recent harm reduction approaches to prevention of alcohol-related harm. Most of this work has targeted adult or young adult drinkers. The SHAHRP programme is one attempt at developing a school-based harm reduction programme for alcohol-related harm (McBride, Midford, Farringdon, & Phillips, 2000). Outcome data indicates that, whilst students in the control and intervention arms of the study had similar levels of alcohol knowledge and alcohol related attitudes 17 months after the programme, the intervention group had significantly lower levels of alcohol-related harm, such as, getting into trouble with the police or at school, engaging in risky sexual intercourse, hangovers, getting into fights after drinking (McBride, Farringdon, Midford, Meuleners, & Phillips, 2004).

The reduction of inappropriate levels of drinking during pregnancy would appear to be another appropriate target for preventive intervention. Chang, Wilkins-Haug, Berman and Goetz (1999) found that a comprehensive assessment of prenatal alcohol use resulted in a significant reduction in maternal postpartum drinking. The addition of a brief intervention failed to increase the level of drinking reduction beyond that achieved by assessment alone. Using data form the National Maternal and Infant Heath Survey (US), Terza, Kenkel, Lin, and Sakata (in press) also found that brief prenatal caregiver advice lead to a significant reduction in drinking during pregnancy. Sustained positive outcomes for prenatal alcohol interventions (over two years post intervention) have also been found amongst studies with mothers who have serious alcohol problems (Manwell, Fleming, Mundt, Stauffacher, & Barry, 2000). These findings would support the provision of a wide spread alcohol screening programme for pregnant mothers. Such a screening programme alone may have benefits for many alcohol-using mothers, by triggering a self-imposed reduction in alcohol consumption. It would also permit the identification of mothers with serious alcohol problems, who may require the provision of a more specialist intervention. The debate continues as to the extent to which such treatments should be voluntary (Hankin, McCaul & Heussner, 2000).

STRENGTHS AND LIMITATIONS OF THE STUDY

A major strength of this work is that it adopted a developmental approach to investigating adolescent drinking behaviour. Developmental psychopathology is distinct from traditional psychological models for understanding risk, disorder and adaptation across the life course (see chapter 3 for full discussion). Seeing adolescent problems behaviour within a developmental psychopathology framework has stimulated a range of new research areas. For example, examining the interplay between normal and abnormal adolescent behaviour and how this evolves over time has contributed to advances in research knowledge. It has also promoted the integration of diverse research findings generated by the various disciplines that have examined adolescent life (i.e. psychology, sociology, geography, psychiatry, etc). While much developmental research has examined the onset and nature of adolescent alcohol use, many research questions still remain. The application of a developmental framework within this study has contributed to the uncovering of important research findings. In particular, the study has shed light on the antecedents and consequences of moderate drinking and concluded that the concerns about low-level consumption, originating from within a zero tolerance prevention perspective, may be misplaced. If the moral debate surrounding teenage drinking can be placed to one side, alcohol consumption at age 16 appears to be a relatively neutral activity, suggestive not of pathology, but of normal well-adjusted development. The opposite ends of the drinking spectrum may be more symptomatic of negative early experiences and later adult problems, albeit as the result of quite different developmental processes.

To date, most of the major studies on the development of adolescent drinking patterns and their consequences have originated within the US or New Zealand (see reviews in chapters 6, 7 and 8). As this is one of the first UK and European studies to examine this issue over such an extended time period, the findings are important for the design and provision of local (i.e. European) prevention intervention services. However, the study is not simply a replication of existing research within a new jurisdiction, it has also extended and advanced current knowledge. An example of this is the study's testing of the unique contribution to the development of hazardous drinking patterns made by each of the three components of ADHD. This analysis may go someway to determining why so much research in this area has produced highly inconsistent findings. Again, this has important implications for the targeting and provision of services to high-risk young people.

National birth cohort studies, such as the BCS70, offer a number of important methodological advantages over other research designs, when addressing the types of developmental research questions posed in this study (see chapter 3 for a detailed review of these advantages). In particular, their prospective longitudinal perspective permits the examination of the onset and course of behavioural disorders within individuals (without the bias of retrospective recall) and the early childhood predictors of later adolescent and adult outcomes, which is not possible within alternative cross-sectional designs. The BCS70, and similar cohort studies, allow researchers to begin to tease apart the temporal ordering of complex social processes, a necessary part of determining risk and outcome.

This study has harnessed the methodological power of longitudinal birth cohort data within a theoretical and analytical framework of developmental psychopathology. This analysis is able to draw upon the wealth of individual-linked data collected within the survey. For example, the study was able to examine the influence of maternal behaviour during pregnancy on the subsequent behaviours and choices of their offspring in adulthood. Only studies such as this are able to address these types of research questions.

The study also employed innovative statistical techniques for the development of a typology of adolescent drinking behaviour. This addressed a number of methodological limitations inherent within more traditional classification methods. The resultant typology appeared to be valid and highly discriminating (see chapter 4). In addition to the use of latent class methods, the study also employed state-of-the-art methods for minimising biases due to missing data (multiple imputation), a common problem with longitudinal studies.

However, as with any social research, this study has certain limitations. While previous analysis chapters identified and discussed specific technical restrictions, this section will focus on broader problems and issues that warrant consideration. These limitations, to some extent, reflect general weaknesses of secondary analysis as a social research method. However, certain limitations are specific to this analysis.

Age of the data

The data collected on adolescent drinking is now over two decades old. Information obtained on parental behaviours and early childhood social conditions is considerably older. It is highly likely that there have been noticeable changes in parenting practices, youth sub-culture and adolescent drinking patterns in the intervening years. Therefore, when considering the impact of adolescent drinking on adult outcomes, consideration must be given to the 'historical' period in which the data was collected. This may somewhat weaken the generalisability of the study findings to current adolescent drinkers.

This delay between data collection and presentation of results is a common problem associated with single cohort longitudinal research. Whereas cross-sectional studies can collect data across a range of different age groups, all within a single sweep, single age cohort studies must allow time for the cohort member to grow older. Here, *age effects* (changes in behaviour linked to developmental or maturational processes) are the primary focus of the research design, and cohort studies give a more accurate estimation of such age effects. The implications are, however, that a single age cohort study examining adolescent determinants of adult behaviours must wait until the cohort members reach adulthood, meaning that any adolescent data collected are dated.

Period and cohort effects

While cohort studies, such as the BCS70, are designed to examine age effects, these results can be confounded by related *period* and *cohort* effects that may also impact on the social process observed within this study (Sacker & Wiggins, 2002). Period effects are changes in behaviours associated with the specific period in which the data were collected. Such effects influence all age cohorts during the period in which the effect operates. For example, changes in the tax regime for alcohol may instigate secular changes in drinking behaviour (increases or decreases) that are observed across all age ranges. Cohort effects, in contrast are observed differences between different age cohorts due to specific characteristics of the cohort and their interactions with the unique cultural periods in which the cohort grew up. These are lasting differences between different cohort groups. One of the most widely observed cohort effects is the Easterlin effect (Easterlin, 1987), in which the level of adult economic attainments within a cohort was shown to be a function of the size of the cohort and the resulting availability of financial resources and opportunities. Age, period, and cohort effects have been observed in adolescent alcohol use during the period covered by this study (O'Malley, Bachman & Johnston, 1998). Therefore, the interpretation of the age effects observed within this study must countenance possible period and cohort confounders.

Operational definitions

One of the main limitations of secondary analysis is that the range of topics covered by the survey and the actual questions used (and therefore the variables within the dataset) are predefined, not by the secondary analyst, but by the preceding research team. Therefore, secondary analysis always involves a degree of compromise between what the researcher would like to examine and what variables are available within the dataset.

While the quality of the alcohol data (at age 16) and the time period that the BCS70 covers (birth to age 26) makes the BCS70 a valuable, if under-exploited, resource within this field, the range of covariates included within each data sweep, limit the scope of the research questions that can be considered and the models that can be estimated. The measures included at each data sweep were designed by researchers who had to attempt to anticipate the types of research questions, and statistical techniques, that would be a high priority many years later. The secondary analyst is, therefore, bounded by the decisions taken by other researchers (the originators of the data). As a result, any secondary analysis study may be missing important theoretical constructs or they may be measured with a less than optimal method.

Within this study the impact of this restriction has been limited. The main area affected has been the adult outcomes. The 26-year-old follow-up, as it was only a postal survey, collected considerable less data than in previous sweeps (postal plus other methods). In particular the number and range of alcohol measures was significantly reduced from that included at age 16. This meant that a similar classification technique to that used at age 16 (latent class analysis) could not be replicated at age 26. Likewise, some of the other adult outcomes were not devised specifically for the analysis of alcohol effects. So, while the study does address a number of important issues, other key research questions were not addressed due to the natural limitations of the BCS70 dataset.

Given the considerable expense of longitudinal cohort studies, the data collection strategy usually employed tends to be more "wide and thin" rather than "narrow and deep". As a result, studies such as the BCS70 attempt to capture information on a very wide range of medical, educational and social topics to maximise the potential for secondary exploitation. In many cases, only one or two indicators are used to assess key constructs, thus ensuring a large number of separate constructs can be included within the data sweep. Where multiple item measures are used there is a general pressure to reduce the length of such scales. The downside of this approach is that many social phenomenon are complex multi-dimensional processes, and information can be sacrificed. One implication for this study was a restriction in the range of statistical methods that could be used to examine the data. For example, full structural equation models were not estimated due to the limited number of multi-indicators measures, particularly within the 26-year-old data. This meant that more comprehensive testing of the theoretical models presented could not be undertaken beyond that offered by traditional regression techniques. Likewise, latent class growth models or latent transition models were also not feasible, due to the limited number of time points and the lack of continuity in the alcohol measures over time.

FUTURE WORK

While this study has addressed a number of fundamental weaknesses within the existing empirical knowledge base, it has also raised a number of new questions, issues and possibilities that require consideration. Firstly, in recent months the latest sweeps of the BCS70, conducted in 2000 and 2004, have been made available on general release through the Data Archive. While they were to late for inclusion within this thesis, future analysis should examine the continuation of drinking patterns beyond young adulthood. In terms of the examination of alcohol pathways, this current analysis was restricted by only having two alcohol assessments, at age 16 and age 26. Additional assessments at age 30 and age 34 open up the possibility for statistical modelling of the intraindividual differences in drinking patterns, using latent class growth models (Muthén, 2004). This would permit better classification of individual alcohol pathways and the identification of individuals with similar pathways across time.

Now that the preliminary multivariate analysis of the alcohol data within the BCS70 has been completed, a logical next step would be to develop and estimate more complex structural equation models (SEMs) to further investigate the interrelationships between model covariates. The regression analysis presented here, while providing a lot of valuable information about the predictors and consequences of teenage drinking, does not permit the sophisticated testing of theoretical models that incorporate mediating and moderating relationships between covariates. The work presented here offers a general framework for the development and testing of such models.

This study is one of the first to examine the association between moderate adolescent drinking and other indicators of adaptive child, adolescent and young adult development. Further work is required to fully understand the processes underlying this achieved competency. Percy (2008) has argued that moderate drinking in the teenage years plays an active role in the development of substance use self-regulation. While this study suggested that the majority of moderate teenage drinkers achieved a high degree of regulatory competence (few associated concurrent problems and good long term outcomes), the BCS70 was not designed to specifically test this assumption. This research would have important implications for alcohol prevention. A better understanding of the development of alcohol self-regulation and the environmental factors that promote this, may point towards novel methods for teaching self-control and self-restraint to impulsive antisocial hazardous drinkers.

As the BCS70 is a national study with a relatively large sample size it is able to examine rare experiences and characteristics with satisfactory statistical power. Where sample size and sampling design are insufficient is in the study of how local areas and conditions influence teenage drinking behaviours. To examine neighbourhood effects, studies need a large number of respondents in each small area. The BCS70 sample is too widely spread across the UK mainland for this type of analysis to be undertaken. Neighbourhood effects on individual drinking are still a relatively untapped research area.

In addition to these general areas of future work, a large number of more specific research questions can also be generated from this initial work. Three research areas, in particular, can be considered to be of higher priority. The first of these relates to maternal influence on adult drinking. While this study has demonstrated the important link between maternal and adolescent drinking, further work is needed to unpick the actual process through which this influence is mediated. Without this additional knowledge intervention attempts to mitigate the effects of this risk exposure will be hampered.

Secondly, behavioural undercontrol predicts teenage drinking but not adult drinking. While this would suggest that the long-term influence of undercontrol on adult drinking is not a direct causal link but mediated through teenage consumption, further work would be required to fully test this. The implications the findings of this work would be important in setting prevention objectives for high-risk groups. If teenage drinking behaviour mediates the impact of relatively time invariant non-modifiable risk characteristics, such as impulsivity or extraversion, on adult drinking outcomes, then work to moderate alcohol consumption amongst high-risk groups may be an effective risk reduction strategy. If not, prevention interventions may have to attempt to address the underlying cognitive and personality characteristics.

Thirdly, the study shows that not all teenage hazardous drinkers proceed on to be heavy drinkers in adulthood. In fact, some young adults who were more moderated drinkers in the past replaced them in the drinking hierarchy. This suggests that non-observed processes may influence individual vulnerability toward heavy drinking during the intervening ten years. Work examining the more short-term changes and influences on drinking patterns may elucidate additional risk processes emerging in early adulthood.

Fortunately, a new round of short-term longitudinal studies (tracking young people over shorter periods of time usually 5 to 10 years) have been commissioned in recent years, including the Belfast Youth Development Study, The Edinburgh Study on Youth Transitions and Crime, and the Peterborough Adolescent Development Study. These studies have, in general, been established to address the weaknesses inherit in the existing large-scale birth cohort studies. In particular, they have tended to utilise highly localised clustered samples to examine the neighbourhood effects, frequent follow-up to assess the short-term ebbs and flows in behavioural development, and employ data collection tool specifically designed to facilitate complex, state-off-the-art statistical techniques. Together with continued exploitation of the existing birth cohort studies, further work on this new generation of longitudinal research should lead to major breakthroughs in our understandings of the development of problem behaviours in adolescents and young adults.

SUMMARY

This research set out to replicate and extend the existing - predominantly US based - longitudinal research on the antecedents of adolescent drinking. To date, there has been limited testing of current etiological models of adolescent alcohol problems within UK youth culture. Using the BCS70 also permitted the analysis to address many of the methodological limitations inherent in much of the existing research based, in particular the over-reliance on case-control studies of adolescent children of alcoholic parents. Even though the survey data used in this study is dated, it did demonstrate that latent class analysis is a viable analytical strategy for the identification of subpopulations of drinkers. The five classes did appear to be a functional typology, capable of distinguishing adolescents on a range of other related alcohol measures. Notwithstanding some of the limitations of single cohort designs, the analysis did address some outstanding research questions and generated new knowledge regarding the antecedents and consequences of adolescent drinking within the UK context. As with all research, it also raises a number of further research questions that require attention.

The policy implications arising from this work are not straightforward. They are not a simple call for more prevention activity. However, they do provide empirical support for the development of a more pragmatic, sophisticated and targeted approach to preventing alcohol related harm.

REFERENCES

Academy of Medical Sciences (2004). *Calling time: The nation's drinking as a major health issue*. London: Author.

Achenbach, T.M. (1990). Conceptualisation of developmental psychopathology. In M. Lewis & S.M. Miller (Eds.) *Handbook of Developmental Psychopathology*. New York: Plenum Press.

Adalbjarnardottir, S. & Rafnsson, F.D. (2002). Adolescent antisocial behaviour and substance use: Longitudinal analysis. *Addictive Behaviours, 27*, 227-240.

Agnew, R. (1985). A revised strain theory of delinquency. *Social Forces, 64*, 151-167.

Aitken, P.P. (1985). An observation study of young adult drinking groups – II. Drink purchasing procedures, group pressures and alcohol consumption by companions as predictors of alcohol consumption. *Alcohol and Alcoholism, 20*, 445-457.

Akaike, H. (1987). Factor analysis and AIC. *Psychometrica, 52*, 317-332.

Allen, J.P., Litten, R.Z., Fertig, J.B., & Babor, T. (1997). A review of research on the Alcohol Use Disorders Identification Test (AUDIT). *Alcoholism: Clinical and Experimental Research, 21*, 613-619.

Allen, J.P., Porter, M.R., McFarland, F.C., Marsh, P., McElhanney, K.B., (2005). The two faces of adolescents' success with peers: adolescent popularity, social adaptation and deviant behaviour. *Child Development, 76*, 747-760.

Allen, L., Andrew, C., Southworth, A. & Webb (1998). *Report of the Alcohol and Tobacco Fraud Review*. London: Customs and Excise.

Amato, P. (1993). Children's Adjustment to Divorce: Theories and Hypotheses and Empirical Support. *Journal of Marriage and the Family, 55*, 23-38.

Amato, P.R. & Keith, B. (1991). Parental Divorce and the Well-Being of Children: A Meta-Analysis. *Psychological Bulletin, 110*, 26-46.

American Psychiatric Association (2000). *Diagnostic and Statistical Manual of Mental Health Disorders, Fourth Edition, Text Revision (DSM-IV-TR®)*. Arlington, VA: Author.

Andersen, A., Due, P., Holstein, B.E., & Iversen, L. (2003). Tracking drinking behaviours from age 15-19 years. *Addiction, 98*, 1505-1511.

Andersson, T. & Magnusson, D. (1990). Biological maturation in adolescence and the development of drinking habits and alcohol abuse among young males: A prospective longitudinal study. *Journal of Youth and Adolescence, 19,* 33-41.

Andreasson, S. (1998). Alcohol and J-shaped curves. *Alcoholism: Clinical and Experimental Research, 22,* 359S-364S.

Angold, A. Costello, E.J. & Erkanli, A. (1997). Comorbidity. *Journal of Child Psychology and Psychiatry, 40,* 57-87.

Anthony, J.C. (2002). Death of the 'stepping stone' hypothesis and the 'gateway' model? Comments on Morral *et al. Addiction, 97,* 1505-1510.

Anthony, J.C., Warner, L.A., & Kessler, R.C. (1994). Comparative epidemiology of dependence on tobacco, alcohol, controlled substances and inhalants: basic findings from the National Comorbidity Survey. *Experimental and Clinical Psychopharmacology. 2,* 244- 268.

Armsden, G.C. & Greenberg, M.T. (1987). The inventory of parent and peer attachment: individual differences and their relationship to psychological well-being in adolescence. *Journal of Youth and Adolescence. 16,* 427-454.

Armstrong, T.D. & Costello, E.J. (2002). Community studies on adolescent substance use, abuse or dependence and psychiatric comorbidity. *Journal of Consulting and Clinical Psychology, 70,* 1224-1239.

Aro, H. & Taiple, V. (1987). The impact of timing of puberty on psychosomatic symptoms amongst fourteen to sixteen-year-old Finnish girls. *Child Development, 58,* 261-268.

Asher H.B. (1983) *Causal Modelling.* Sage University Paper Series on Quantitative Applications in Social Sciences, Sage:Beverly Hills and London.

Babor, T.F., Caetano, R., Casswell, S., Edwards, G., Giesbrecht, N., Graham, K., Grude, J., Gruenewald, P., Hill, L., Holder, H., Homel, R., Osterberg, E., Rehm, J., Room, R., & Rossow, I. (2003). *Alcohol: No ordinary commodity – research and public policy.* Oxford and London: Oxford University Press.

Babor, T.F., Higgins-Biddle, J.C., Saunders, J.B., & Monteiro, M.G. (2001). *AUDIT the Alcohol Use Disorders Identification Test: Guidelines for use in Primary Care.* Geneva:World Health Organisation.

Bagnall, G. (1988). Use of alcohol, tobacco and illicit drugs amongst 13 year olds in three areas of Britain. *Drug and Alcohol Dependence, 22,* 241-251.

Bailey, S.L. & Rachal, J.V. (1993). Dimensions of adolescent problem drinking.

Journal of Studies on Alcohol. 54, 555-565.

Baldwin, S. (Ed.). (1990). *Alcohol education and offenders.* London: B.T. Batsford Ltd.

Baldwin, S. (1991). *Alcohol Education and Young Offenders: Medium term and short terms effectiveness of education programmes.* Heidelberg: Springer Verlag.

Barman, S.K., Pulkkinen, L., Kaprio J., & Rose, R.J. (2004). Inattentiveness, parental smoking and adolescent smoking initiation. *Addiction, 99*, 1049-1061.

Bartholomew, D.J. & Knott, M. (1999). *Latent variable models and factor analysis.* Kendall's Library of Statistics Volume 7 (Second Edition). Arnold: London.

Bates, P.B., Resse, H.W. & Nesselroade, J.R. (1977). *Life-span Developmental Psychology: Introduction to Research methods.* Monterrey, CA: Brooks Cole.

Bell, N.J., Forthun, L.F. & Sun, S. (2000). Attachment, adolescent competencies and substance use: developmental considerations in the study of risk behaviours. *Substance Use and Misuse, 35*, 1177-1206.

Bennett, M.E., McCrady, B.S., Johnston, V., & Pandina, R.J. (1999). Problem drinking from young adulthood to adulthood: patterns, predictors and outcomes. *Journal of Studies on Alcohol, 60*, 605-614.

Bentler, P.M., Newcomb, M.D., & Zimmerman, M.A. (2002). Cigarette use and drug use progressions: Growth trajectories and lagged effect hypotheses. In D.B. Kandel, (Ed.) (2002). *Stages and Pathways of Drug Involvement: Examining the Gateway Hypothesis* (pp. 223-253).Cambridge: Cambridge University Press.

Berridge, V. (2005) *Temperance: Its history and impact on current and future alcohol policy.* Joseph Rowntree Foundation: York.

Best, D., Rawaf, S., Rowley, J., Floyd, K., Manning, V., & Strang, J. (2001). *Ethnicity and Health, 6*, 51-57.

Biederman, J. & Faraone, S. (2005). Attention-deficit hyperactivity disorder. *The Lancet, 366*, 237-248.

Biederman, J., Wilens, T.E., Mick, E., Faraone, S.V. & Spencer, T. (1998). Does attention- deficit hyperactivity disorder impact on the developmental course of drug and alcohol abuse and dependence? *Biological Psychiatry, 44*, 269-743.

Biederman, J., Wilens, T., Mick, E., Faraone, S.V., Weber, W., Curtis, S., Thornell, A., Pfister, K., Garcia jetton, J., & Soriano, J. (2003). Is ADHD a risk factor for

353

psychoactive substance use disorders? Findings from a four-year prospective follow-up study. *Focus, 1*, 196-204.

Blackman, S.J. (2004). *Chilling out: The cultural politics of substance consumption, youth and drug policy.* Maidenhead, UK: Open University Press.

Bollen, K.A. (2002). Latent variables in psychology and the social sciences. *Annual Review of Psychology, 53*, 605-34.

Bonomo, Y. A., Bowes, G., Coffey, C., Carlin, J.B., & Patton, G.C. (2004). *Addiction. 99*, 1520-1528.

Booth, A., & Crouter, A.C. (2001). *Does it take a village? Community effects of children, adolescents and families.* Mahwah, NJ: Lawrence Erlbaum Associates.

Boreham, R., Fuller, E., Hills, A., & Pudney, S. (2006). *The arrestee survey annual report Oct 2003- Sept 2004.* London: Home Office.

Borsari, B. & Carey, K.B. (2001). Peer influence on college drinking: a review of the research. *Journal of Substance Abuse, 13*, 391-424.

Boyce, W.T., Frank, E., Jensen, P.S., Kessler, R.C., Nelson, C.C., Steinberg, L. & The MacArthur Foundation Research Network on Psychopathology and Development, (1998). Social context in developmental psychopathology: recommendations for future research from the MacArthur Foundation Research Network on Psychopathology and Development. *Development and Psychopathology, 10*, 143-164.

Boyle, M.H., & Willms, J.D. (2001). Multilevel modelling of hierarchical data in developmental studies. *Journal of Child and Adolescent Psychiatry, 42*, 141-162.

Boys, A., Farrell, M., Taylor, C. Masden, J., Goodman, R., Brugha, T., Bebbington, P., Jenkins, R., & Meltzer, H. (2003). Psychiatric morbidity and substance use in young people aged 13-15: results of the child and adolescent survey of mental health. *British Journal of Psychiatry, 182*, 509-517.

Bradley, R.H., & Corwyn R.F. (2002). Socioeconomic status and child development. *Annual Review of Psychology, 53*, 371-399.

Brain, K. (2000). *Youth, alcohol and the emergence of the post-modern alcohol order.* Occasional Paper No. 1. London: Institute of Alcohol Studies.

Brandt, J., Butters, N., Ryan, C., & Byog, R. (1983). Cognitive loss and recovery in long term alcohol abuse. *Archives of General Psychiatry, 40*, 435-442.

Bray, J.H., Adams, G.J., Getz, J.G., & McQueen, A. (2003). Individualisation, peers and adolescent alcohol use: a latent growth analysis. *Journal of Consulting and Clinical Psychology, 71*, 553-564.

Brewers and Licensed Retailers Association (2000). *Statistical Handbook: A Compilation of Drinks Industry Statistics*. London: Brewing Publications Limited.

Bricker, J.B., Peterson, A.V., Leroux, B.G., Andersen, M.R., Rajan, K.B., & Sarason, I.G. (2006). Prospective prediction of children's smoking transitions: role of parents' and older siblings' smoking. *Addiction, 101*, 128 – 136.

Britton, A., Singh-Manoux, A., & Marmot, M. (2004). Alcohol consumption and cognitive functioning in the Whitehall II Study. *American Journal of Epidemiology, 160*, 240-247.

Bronfenbrenner, U. (1979). *The Ecology of Human Development*. Cambridge MA: Harvard University Press.

Brook, D.W., Brook, J.S., Zhang, C., Cohen, P., & Whiteman, M. (2002). Drug use and the risk of major depressive disorder, alcohol dependence and substance use disorder. *Archives of General Psychiatry, 59*, 1039-1044.

Brown, D., & Ellis, T. (1994). *Policing Low Level Disorder: Police use of Section % of the Public Order Act 1986*. Home Office Research Study 135. London: Home Office.

Brown, S.A., Tapert, S.F., Granholm, E., & Delis, D.C. (2000). Neurocognitive functioning of adolescents: Effects of protracted alcohol use. *Alcoholism: Clinical and Experimental Research, 24*, 164-171.

Bryant, R.R., Jayawardhana, A., Samaranayake, V.A., & Wilhite, A. (1996). *The impact of alcohol and drug use on employment: A labour market study using the National Longitudinal Study of Youth*. Discussion Paper 1092-96. Madison: Institute for Research on Poverty, University of Wisconsin-Madison.

Budd, T., (2003) *Alcohol related assault: Findings from the British Crime Survey*. Home Office Research Study 35/03. London: Home Office.

Bukoski, W.J., & Evans, R.I. (Eds.) (1998). *Cost-benefit/cost-effectiveness research on drug abuse prevention: Implications for programming and policy*. NIDA Research Monograph 176, Rockville, MD: National Institute of Drug Abuse.

Burke, J.D., Loeber, R., & Lahey, B.B. (2001). Which aspects of ADHD are associated with tobacco use in early adolescence? *Journal of Child Psychology and Psychiatry. 42*, 493-502.

Butler, N., Despotidou, S., & Shepard, P. (not dated) *1970 British Cohort Study Ten-Year Follow-up; Guide top data available at the ESRC Data Archive*. London: Social Statistics Research Unit, City University.

Butler, N., Haslum, M.N., Barker, W. & Morris, A.C. (1982). *Child Health and Education Study: First Report to the Department Of Education and Science on the 10-Year Follow-up*. Bristol: Department of Child Health, University of Bristol.

Caldwell, T.M., Rodgers, B., Jorm, A.F., Christensen, H., Jacomb, P.A., Korten, A.E., & Lynskey, M.T. (2002). Patterns of associations between alcohol consumption and symptoms of depression and anxiety in young adults. *Addiction, 97*, 583-594.

Carroll, K.M. (1995). Methodological issues and problems in the assessment of substance use. *Psychological Assessment, 7*, 349-358.

Casswell, S., Pledger, M., & Hooper, R. (2003). Socioeconomic status and drinking patterns in young adults. *Addiction, 98*, 601-610.

Casswell, S., Pledger, M., & Pratap, S. (2002). Trajectories of drinking from 18 to 26 years. *Addiction, 97*, 1427-1437.

Catalano, R.F., Haggerty, K.P., Gainey, R.R., Hoppe, M.J., & Brewer, D.D. (1998). Effectiveness of prevention interventions with youth at high risk of drug abuse. In W.J. Bukowski & R.I. Evans (Eds.) *Cost-benefit/Cost-effectiveness research of drug abuse prevention: Implications for programming and policy*. NIDA Research Monograph176. Rockville, MD: National Institute on Drug Abuse.

Centre for Longitudinal Studies (2007). *Following the lives from birth and through the adult years*. CLS Briefing February 2007. London: Institute of Education.

Chang, G., Wilkins-Haug, L., Berman, S., & Goetz M.A. (1999). Brief intervention fro alcohol use in pregnancy: A randomised trial. *Addiction, 94*, 1499-1508

Chassin, L., Pitts, S.C. & Prost, J. (2002). Binge drinking trajectories from adolescence to emerging adulthood in a high-risk sample: predictors and substance abuse outcomes. *Journal of Consulting and Clinical Psychology, 70*, 67-78.

Chen, K., & Kandel, D. (1995). The natural history of drug use from adolescence to the mid-thirties in a general population sample. *American Journal of Public Health, 85*, 41-47.

Cheung, Y.B. (2002). Early origins and adult correlates of psychosomatic distress. *Social Science and Medicine. 55*, 937-948.

Chung, T., & Martin, C.S. (2001). Classification and course of alcohol problems among adolescents in addiction treatment programs. *Alcohol: Clinical & Experimental Research, 25*, 1734-1742.

Cicchetti, D. (1984). The emergence of developmental psychopathology. *Child Development, 55*, 1-7.

Cicchetti, D. (1989). *The emergence of a discipline: Rochester symposium on developmental psychopathology, Volume 1*. Hove and London: Lawrence Erlbaum Associates.

Cicchetti, D. (2006). Development and psychopathology. In D. Cicchetti & D. Cohen (Eds.) *Developmental Psychopathology. Volume 1: Theory and method* (2nd Edit.). Hoboken, NJ: John Wiley & Sons, (pp 1-23).

Cicchetti, D. & Aber, J.L. (1998). Contextualism and developmental psychopathology. *Development and Psychopathology, 10*, 137-141.

Cichetti, D., & Rogosh, F.A. (1996). Equifinality and mulitfinality in developmental psychopathology. *Development and Psychopathology, 9*, 799-817.

Cicchetti, D., & Rogosch, F.A. (2002). A developmental perspective on adolescence. *Journal of Consulting and Clinical Psychology, 70*, 6-20.

Cicchetti, D., & Sroufe, L.A. (2000). Editorial: The past as a prologue to the future: The times, they've been a-changing. *Development and Psychopathology, 12*, 255-264.

Clark, D.B., (2004). The natural history of adolescent alcohol use disorders. *Addiction, 99 (Supplement 2)*, 5-22.

Clark, D.B., & Bukstein, O.G. (1998). Psychopathology in adolescent alcohol abuse and dependence. *Alcohol Health and Research World, 22*, 17-121.

Clark, D.B., Pollock, N., Bukstein, O.G., Mezzich, A. Bromberger, J.T., & Donovan, J.E. (1997). Gender and comorbid psychopathology in adolescents with alcohol dependence. *Journal of the American Academy of Child and Adolescent Psychiatry, 36*, 1195-1203.

Clark, D.B., Vanyukov, M., & Cornelius, J. (2002). Childhood antisocial behaviour and adolescent alcohol use disorders. *Alcohol Research and Health, 26*, 109-115.

Cleveland, H.H., & Wiebe, R.P. (2003). The moderation of adolescent-to-peer similarity in tobacco and alcohol use by school levels of substance use. *Child Development, 74*, 279-291.

Clogg, C.C. (1995). Latent class models. In G. Arminger, C.C. Clogg & M.E. Sobel (Eds). *Handbook of statistical modelling for the social and behavioural sciences.* New York and London: Plenum Press.

Coggans, N. & McKellar, S. (1994). Drug use amongst peers: peer pressure or peer preference. *Drugs: Education, Prevention and Policy, 1*, 15-26.

Coie, J.D., Watt, N.F., West, S.G., Hawkins, D., Asaranow, J.R., Markman, H.J., Ramey, S.L., Shure, M.B., & Long, B. (1993). The science of prevention: a conceptual framework and some directions for a national research program. *American Psychologist, 48*, 1013-1022.

Colder, C.R., & Chassin, L. (1993). The stress negative affect model of adolescent alcohol use and the moderating effects of behavioural undercontrol. *Journal of Studies on Alcohol, 54*, 326-333.

Coleman, J.S. (1990). *Foundation of Social Theory.* Cambridge, MA: Harvard University Press.

Collins, L.M., Fidler, P.L., Wugalter, S.E., & Long, J.D. (1993). Goodness of fit statistics for latent class models. *Multivariate Behavioural Research, 28*, 375-389.

Collins, L.M., Flaherty, B.P., Hyatt, S.L., & Schafer, J.L. (1999). *WinLTA User's Guide, Version 2.0.* University Park: Pennsylvania State University, The Methodology Centre.

Collins, L.M., Lanza, S.T., Schafer, J.L. & Flaherty, B.P. (2002a). *WinLTA user Guide Version 3.0.* University Park: Pennsylvania State University, The Methodology Centre.

Collins, L.M., Lanza, S.T., Schafer, J.L. & Flaherty, B.P. (2002b). *WinLTA Version 3.0* [Computer Software]. University Park: Pennsylvania State University, The Methodology Centre.

Compas, B.E., Hinden, B.R. & Gerhart, C.A. (1995). Adolescent development: Pathways and processes of risk and resilience. *Annual Review of Psychology. 46*, 265-293.

Conners, C. K. (1970). Symptom patterns in hyperkinetic, neurotic and normal children. *Child Development, 41,* 667-682.

Cook, T.D. (2003). The case for studying multiple contexts simultaneously. *Addiction, 98 (Suppl. 1),* 151-155.

Corrao, G., Bagnardi, V., Zambon, A., & Arico, S. (1999). Exploring the dose-response relationship between alcohol consumption and the risk of several alcohol-related conditions: A meta analysis. *Addiction, 94,* 1551-1573.

Corrao, G., Rubbiati, L., Bagnardi, V., Zambon, A., & Poikolainen, K. (2000). Alcohol and coronary heart disease: a meta analysis. *Addiction, 95,* 1505-1523

Costello, E.J., & Angold, A. (2006). Developmental epidemiology. In D. Cicchetti & D. Cohen (Eds.) *Developmental Psychopathology. Volume 1: Theory and method* (2nd Edit.) (pp 41-75). Hoboken, NJ: John Wiley & Sons.

Costello, E.J., Erkanli, A., Federman, E., & Angold, A. (1999). Development of psychiatric comorbidity with substance abuse in adolescents: effects of timing and sex. *Journal of Clinical Child Psychology, 28,* 298-311.

Cox, M.J., & Paley, B. (1997). Families as systems. *Annual Review of Psychology, 48,* 243-267.

Cox, W.M., & Klinger, E. (1988). A motivational model of alcohol use. *Journal of Abnormal Psychology, 97,* 168-180.

Crawford, V., Crome, I.B., & Clancy, C. (2003). Co-existing problems of mental heath and substance misuse (dual diagnosis): A literature review. *Drugs: Education, Prevention and Policy, 10 (Suppl.),* S1-S74.

Croon, M. (1990). Latent class analysis with ordered latent classes. *British Journal of Mathematical and Statistical Psychology, 43,* 171-192.

Cummings, E.M. & Davies P.T. (2002). Effects of marital conflict on children: recent advances and emerging themes in process-orientated research. *Journal of Child Psychology and Psychiatry, 43,* 31-63.

Curran, P.J., & Willoughby, M.T. (2003). Implications of latent trajectory models for the study of developmental psychopathology. *Development and Psychopathology, 15,* 581-617.

Davidson, R.J. (1987). Assessment of the alcohol dependency syndrome: a review of self-report screening questionnaires. *British Journal of Clinical Psychology, 26,* 243-255.

Davidson, R.J. & Raistrick, D. (1986). The validity of the Short Alcohol Dependency Data (SADD) Questionnaire. *British Journal of Addiction, 81*, 217-222.

Dawes, M.A., Antelman, S.M., Vanyukov, M.M., Giancola, P., Tarter, R.E., Susman, E.J., Mezzich, A., & Clark, D.B. (2000). Developmental sources of variation in liability to adolescent substance use disorders. *Drug and Alcohol Dependence, 61*, 3-14.

Dawes, M.A., Tarter, R.E., & Kirisci, L. (1997). Behavioural self-regulation: Correlates and 2 year follow-up for boys at risk of substance abuse. *Drug and Alcohol Dependence, 45*, 165-176.

Dawson, D.A. (2000a). Alternative measures and models of hazardous consumption. *Journal of Substance Abuse, 12*, 79-91.

Dawson, D.A. (2000b). Drinking as a risk factor for sustained smoking. *Drug and Alcohol Dependence, 59*, 235-249.

Dawson, D.A. (2003). Methodological issues in measuring alcohol use. *Alcohol Research & Health, 27*, 18 – 29.

Dawson, D.A., & Room, R. (2000). Towards agreement on ways to measure and report drinking patterns and alcohol-related problems in adult general population surveys: the Skarpö Conference overview. *Journal of Substance Abuse, 12*, 1-21.

Deal, J.E., Hagan, M.S., Bass, B. Heatherington, E.M., & Clingempeel, G. (1999). Marital Interaction in Dyadic and Triadic Contexts: Continuities and Discontinuities. *Family Process, 38*, 105-115.

Deas, D., & Thomas, S.T. (2002). Comorbid psychiatric factors contributing to adolescent alcohol and other drug use. *Alcohol Research & Health, 26*, 116-12.

Dehgenhardt, L., Hall, W., & Lynskey, M. (2001). Alcohol, cannabis, and tobacco use amongst Australians. A comparison with their associations with other drugs use, and use disorders, affective and anxiety disorders and psychosis. *Addiction, 96*, 1603-1614.

Del Boca, F.K., & Darkes, J. (2003). The validity of self-reports of alcohol consumption: state of the science and challenges for research. Addiction, *98 (Suppl. 2)*, 1-12.

Dempster, A.P., Laird, N.M., & Rubin, D.B. (1977). Maximum likelihood estimation with incomplete data via the E-M algorithm. *Journal of the Royal Statistical Society*

Series B, 39, 1-22.

Denning, P. (2004). *Practicing harm reduction psychotherapy: An alternative approach to the addictions.* New York: Guildford Press.

Department of Health (1999). *Statistics on Alcohol: 1976 onwards.* Statistical Bulletin 99/24. London: Author.

Department of Health (2000). *Health Survey for England Trends 1993-1999.* London: Author.

Department of Health (2004). *Statistics on Alcohol: England, 2004.* London: Author.

Department of Health, Social Service and Public Safety (2006). *New Strategic Direction fro alcohol and Drugs 2006-2011.* Belfast, Author.

Des Jarlais, D.C. (1995). Harm reduction – a framework for incorporating science into policy. *American Journal of Public Heath, 85,* 10-12.

Despotidou. S., & Shepard, P. (not dated). *BCS70- The British Cohort Study: The twenty Six –Year Follow-up. A Guide to Data Available at the Economic and Social Research Council Data Archive.* London: Social Statistics Research Unit.

DeWit, D.J., Adlaf, E.M., Offord, D.R., & Ogborne, A.C. (2000). Age of first alcohol use: A risk factor for the development of alcohol disorders. *American Journal of Psychiatry* 157, 745-750.

Dick, D.M., Rose, R.J., Viken, R.J., & Kaprio, J., (2000). Pubertal timing and substance use: association between and within families across late adolescence. *Developmental Psychology, 36,* 180-189.

Dishon, J.T., & McMahon, R.J. (1998). Parental monitoring and the prevention of problem behaviour: A conceptual and empirical reformulation. In R.S. Ashery, E.B. Robertson, & K.L. Kumpfer (Eds.). *Drug Prevention Through Family Interventions.* NIDA Research Monograph 177. Rockville, MD: NIDA .

Dishon, T.J., & Owen, L.D. (2002). A longitudinal analysis of friendships and substance use: Bi-directional influences from adolescence to adulthood. *Developmental Psychology, 38,* 480-491.

Dishon, T.J., & Patterson, G.R. (2006). The development and ecology of antisocial behaviour in children and adolescents. In D. Cicchetti & D. Cohen (Eds.) *Developmental Psychopathology. Volume 3: Risk Disorder, and Adaptation* (2nd Edit.). Hoboken, NJ: John Wiley & Sons, (pp 503-541).

Disney, E.R., Elkins, I.J., McGue, M., & Iacono, W.G., (1999). Effects of ADHD, conduct disorder, and gender on substance use and abuse in adolescents. *American Journal of Psychiatry, 156*, 1515-1521.

Doherty, K., Kinnumen, T., Militello, F.S., & Garvey, A.J. (1995). Urges to smoke during the first month of abstinence: relationship to relapse and predictors. *Psychopharmacology, 119*, 171-178.

Donovan, J.E., Jessor, R., & Jessor, L. (1983). Problem drinking in adolescence and young adulthood: A follow-up study. *Journal of Studies on Alcohol, 44*, 109-137.

Dorn, N., & Murji, K. (1992). Drug prevention: a review of the English language literature. ISDD Research Monograph 5. London: ISDD.

Drummond, C.D. (2004). An alcohol strategy for England: The good, the bad and the ugly. *Alcohol and Alcoholism, 39*, 377-379.

Duncan, G.J., & Brookes-Gunn, J. (1997). *Consequence of growing up poor*. New York: Russell Sage Foundation.

Duncan, S.C., Duncan, T.E., Biglan, A., & Ary, D. (1998). Contributions of the social context to the development of adolescent substance use: A multivariate latent growth modelling approach. *Drug and Alcohol Dependence, 50*, 57-71.

Duncan, S.C., Duncan T.E., & Strycker, L.A. (2002) A multilevel analysis of neighbourhood context and youth alcohol and drug problems. *Prevention Science, 3*, 125 – 133.

Dunn, J. (2004). Annotation: Children's relationships with their nonresident fathers. *Journal of Child Psychology and Psychiatry, 45*, 659-671.

Dunn, J., Cheng, H., O'Connor, T.G., & Bridges, L. (2004). Children's perspectives on their relationships with their non-resident fathers: influences, outcomes and implications. *Journal of Child Psychology and Psychiatry, 45*, 553-566.

Durlak, J.A., & Wells, A. (1997). Primary prevention mental health programs for children and adolescents: a meta-analytic review. *American Journal of Community Psychology, .25*, 115-152.

Easterlin, R.A. (1987). *Birth and Fortune*. Chicago: University of Chicago Press.

Ebata, A.T., Petersen, A.C., & Conger, J.J. (1990). The development of psychopathology in adolescence. In J. Rolf, A.S. Masten, D. Cicchetti, K.H. Nuechterlein, & S. Weintraub, (eds.), *Risk and protective factors in the development of psychopathology.* Cambridge, UK: Cambridge University Press.

Edwards, G. (1986). The alcohol dependence syndrome: a concept as stimulus to enquiry. *British Journal of Addiction, 81,* 171-183.

Edwards. G., Anderson, P., Bador, T.T., Casswell, S., Ferrence, R., Giesbrecht, N., Godfrey, C., Holder, H.D., Lemmens, P., Mäkelä, K., Midanik, L.T. Norstrom, T., Osterberg, E. Romelsjö, A., Room, R., Simpura, J. & Skog, O. (1994). *Alcohol policy and the Public Good.* Oxford: Oxford University Press.

Edwards, G., & Holder, H.D. (2000). The alcohol supply: its importance to public health and safety, and essential research questions. *Addiction, 95 (Suppl. 4),* S621-S627.

Ellickson, P.L., McGuigan, K.A., Adams, V., Bell, R.M., & Hay R. (1996). Teenagers and alcohol misuse in the United States: by any definition a big problem. *Addiction,* 91, 1489-1504.

Elliot, C.D., Smith, P., & McCulloch, K. (1997). *BAS British Abilities Scales II Technical Manual.* Windsor: NFER-Nelson.

Emberson, J.R., Shaper, A.G., Wannamethee, S.G., Morris, R.W., & Whincup, P.H. (2005). Alcohol intake in middle age and the risk of cardiovascular disease and mortality: Accounting for intake variations over time. *American Journal of Epidemiology, 161,* 856-863.

Erens, B., & Hedges, B. (1998). Alcohol consumption. In P. Prescott-Clake & P. Primatesta (Eds.). *The Health of Young People 1995-1997. Volume 1: Findings.* London: The Stationary Office.

Ezzati, M., Henley, S.J., Thun, M.J. & Lopez, A.D. (2005). Role of smoking in global and regional cardiovascular mortality. *Epidemiology, 112,* 489-497.

Ezzati, M., Lopez, A.D., Rodger, A., Vander Hoorn, S., & Murray, C.J.L., & The Comparative Risk Assessment Collaborating Group (2002). Selected major risk factors and the global and regional burden of disease. *The Lancet, 360,* 1347-1360.

Farrington, D.P. (1988). Studying changes within individuals: The causes of offending. In M. Rutter (Ed.). *Studies of Psychosocial Risk: The power of Longitudinal Data.* Cambridge: Cambridge University Press.

Federman, E. B., Costello, E.J., Angold, A., Farmer, M.Z., & Erkanli, A. (1997). Development of substance use and psychiatric comorbidity in an epidemiological study of white and American Indian young adolescents the Great Smoky Mountain Study. *Drug and Alcohol Dependence, 44,* 69-78.

Felner, R.D., Brand, S., DuBois, D.L., Adan, A.M., Mulhall, P.F., & Evans, E.G. (1995). Socioeconomic disadvantage, proximal environmental experiences, and socioemotional and academic adjustment in early adolescence: investigation of a mediated effects model. *Child Development, 66,* 774-92.

Fergusson, D.M., & Horwood L.J. (2000). Alcohol abuse and crime: a fixed-effects regression analysis. *Addiction, 95,* 1525–1536.

Fergusson, D.M., Horwod, L.J., & Lynskey, M.T. (1994). The childhood of multiple problem adolescents: A 15-year longitudinal study. *Journal of Child Psychology and Psychiatry, 35,* 1123-1140.

Fergusson, D.M., Horwood, L.J., & Lynskey, M.T. (1995). The prevalence and risk factors associated with abusive or hazardous alcohol consumption in 16-year-olds. *Addiction, 90,* 935-946.

Fergusson, D.M., Horwood, L.J., & Ridder, E.M. (2005). Show me a child at seven II: childhood intelligence and later outcomes in adolescence and young adulthood. *Journal of Child Psychology and Psychiatry, 46,* 850-858.

Fergusson, D.M., Lynskey, M.T., & Horwood, L.J. (1996). Alcohol misuse and juvenile offending in adolescents. *Addiction, 91,* 483-494.

Fergusson, D.M., Poulton, R., Horwood, J., Milne, B., & Swain-Campbell, N. (2003). *Comorbidity and coincidence in the Christchurch and Dunedin longitudinal studies.* A report for the New Zealand Ministry of Social Development, Department of Labour and Treasury. (http://www.chmeds.ac.nz/research/chds/publications/2003/comor.pdf)

Fergusson, D.M., Swain-Campbell, N.R., & Horwood, L.J. (2002). Deviant peer affiliations, crime and substance use: a fixed effects regression analysis. *Journal of Abnormal Child Psychology, 30,* 419-430.

Fillmore, K.M. (2000). Is alcohol *really* good for the heart? *Addiction, 95,* 173-174.

Finn, P.R., & Hall, J., (2004). Cognitive ability and risk for alcoholism: Short-term memory capacity and intelligence moderate personality risk for alcohol problems. *Journal of Abnormal Psychology, 113,* 569-581.

Foley, K.L., Altman, D., Durant, R.H., & Wolfson, M. (2004). Adults approval and adolescent alcohol use. *Journal of Adolescent Health, 35,* 17-26.

Fong, G.T., Hyland, A., Borland, R., Hammond, D., Hastings, G., McNeill, A., Anderson, S., Cummings, K.M., Allwright, S., Mulcahy, M., Howell, F., Clancy, L., Thompson, M.E., Connolly, G., & Driezen, P. (*in press*). Reductions in tobacco smoke pollution and increases in support for smoke-free public places following the implementation of comprehensive smoke-free workplace legislation in the republic of Ireland: Findings form the ITC Ireland/UK survey. Tobacco Control,

Foxcroft, D.R., Ireland, D., Lister-Sharp, D.J., Lowe, G., & Breen, R. (2003). Longer term primary prevention for alcohol misuse in young people: a systematic review. *Addiction, 98,* 397-411.

Foxcroft, D.R., & Lowe, G. (1997). Adolescent's alcohol use and misuse: The socialising influence of perceived family life. *Drugs: Education Prevention and Policy. 4,* 215 - 230

French, M.T., & Zarkin, G.A. (1995). Is moderate alcohol use related to wages? Evidence from four worksites. *Journal of Health Economics, 14,* 319-344.

Fuller, E. (Ed) (2005). *Smoking, drinking and drug use amongst young people in England 2004.* London: Health and Social Care Information Centre.

Galambos, N.L., Barker, E.T., & Almeida, D.M. (2003). Parents do matter: trajectories of change in externalising and internalising problems in early adolescence. *Child Development, 74,* 578-594.

Galambos, N.L., & Ehrenberg (1997). The family as heath risk and opportunity: A focua on divorce and working families. In J. Schulenberg, J.L. Maggs, & K. Hurrelmann (Eds.). *Health Risks and Developmental Transitions During Adolescence.* Cambridge: Cambridge University Press.

Gammage, P. (1975). Socialisation, schooling and locus of control. Bristol University: PhD. Thesis.

Giesbrecht, N. (2000). Roles of commercial interests in alcohol policies: recent developments in North America. *Addiction, 95, (Suppl. 4),* S581-S596.

Gill, J.S. (2002). Reported level of alcohol consumption and binge drinking within the UK undergraduate student population over the last 25 years. *Alcohol & Alcoholism, 37,* 109-120.

Gillman, M.W., Cook, N.R., Evans, D.A., Rosner, B., & Hennekens C.H. (1995). Relationship of alcohol intake with blood pressure in young adults. *Hypertension, 25,* 1106-1110.

Gilvarry, E. (2000). Substance abuse and young people, *Journal of Child Psychology and Psychiatry, 41,* 55-80.

Ginther, D. K., & Pollack, R. A. (2001). *Does family structure affect children's educational outcomes?* Paper presented at Society of Labour Economists' Annual Conference.

Glantz, M.D., & Leshner, A.I. (2000). Drug abuse and developmental psychopathology. *Development and Psychopathology, 12,* 795-814.

Gmel, G., & Rehm, J. (2003). Harmful alcohol use. *Alcohol, Research & Health, 27,* 52-62.

Goldberg, D. (1978). *Manual for the General Health Questionnaire.* Windsor: National Foundation for Education Research.

Goldblatt, P., Nutall, C.P., & Lewis, C. (1998) *Reducing offending: an assessment of research evidence on the ways of dealing with offending behaviour.* Home Office Research Study 187. London: Home Office.

Golding, J. (not dated). *The 1970 British Cohort Study 5-year follow-up: Data deposited with the ESRC Data Archive.* Bristol: Institute of Child Health University of Bristol.

Goodman, A., & Butler, N.R. (not dated). *BCS70- The British Cohort Study: The Sixteen –Year Follow-up. A Guide to the BCS70 16 Year Data Available at the Economic and Social Research Council Data Archive.* London: Social Statistics Research Unit.

Goodman, E., & Huang, B. (2002). Socioeconomic status, depressive symptoms, and adolescent substance use. *Archives of Paediatrics & Adolescent Medicine, 156,* 448-453.

Gottfredson, M.R., & Hirschi, T. (1990). *A General Theory of Crime.* Stanford, C.A.: Stanford University Press.

Goyette, C.H., Conners, C.K., & Ulrich, R.F. (1978). Normative data on the Revised Conners Parent and Teachers Rating Scale. *Journal of Abnormal Psychology, 6,* 221-236.

Grant, B.F., Harford, T.C., & Grigson, M.B. (1988). Stability in alcohol consumption amongst youth: a national longitudinal survey. *Journal of Studies on Alcohol, 49,* 253-260.

Grant, B.F., Stinson, F.S., & Harford, T.C. (2001). Age of onset of alcohol use and DSM-IV alcohol abuse and dependency. *Journal of Substance Abuse, 13,* 493-504

Grant, J.D., Scherrer, J.F., Lynskey, M.T., Lyons, M.J., Eisen, S.A., Tsaung, M.T., True, W.R., & Bucholz, K.K. (2005). Adolescent alcohol use is a risk factor for adult alcohol and drug dependence: Evidence from a twin design. *Psychological Medicine, 35,* 1-10.

Greenblatt, J.C. (2000). *Patterns of Alcohol Use Among Adolescents and Associations with Emotional and Behavioural Problems.* OAS Working Paper. Rockville MD: Substance Abuse and Mental Health Services Administration, Office of Applied Studies.

Greenway, J.R. (1998). The "improved" public house, 1870-1950: the key to civilised drinking or the primrose path to drunkenness. *Addiction, 93,* 173-181.

Grieshaber-Otto, J., Sinclair, S., & Schacter, N. (2000). Impacts of international trade, services and investment treaties on alcohol regulation. *Addiction, 95, (Suppl. 4),* S491-S504.

Grønbæk, M., Becker, U., Johansen, D., Tønnesen, H., Jensen, G., & Sørensen, T.I.A. (1998). Population based cohort study of the association between alcohol intake and cancer of the upper digestive tract. *British Medical Journal, 317,* 844-848.

Gruber, E., DiClemente, R.J., Anderson, M.M., & Lodico, M. (1996). Early drinking onset and its association with alcohol use and problem behaviour in late adolescence. *Preventive Medicine, 25,* 293-300.

Gruenewald, P.J., Ponicki, W.R., & Holder, H.D. (1993). The relationship of outlet density to alcohol consumption: A time series cross-sectional analysis. *Alcoholism: Clinical and Experimental Research, 17,* 38-47.

Gual, A., & Colom, J. (1997). Why has alcohol consumption declined in countries of southern Europe? *Addiction, 92,* (Suppl. 1). S21-S31.

Hagenaars, J.A. (1990). Categorical Longitudinal Data; Loglinear panel, trend, and cohort analysis. Newbury Park: Sage.

Hagenaars, J.A. (1993). *Loglinear models with latent variables.* Sages University

Paper Series on Quantitative Applications in Social Science, 07-094. Newbury Park, CA: Sage.

Hagenaars, J.A., & McCutcheon, A.L. (Eds.) (2002). *Applied latent class analysis.* Cambridge: Cambridge University Press.

Hankin, J., McCaul, M.E., & Heussner, J. (2000). Pregnancy, alcohol-abusing women. *Alcoholism: Clinical and Experimental Research, 24,* 1276-1286.

Harkin, A., Anderson, P., & Goos, C. (1997). *Smoking, drinking and drug-taking in Europe.* Copenhagen: World Health Organisation Regional Office for Europe.

Harris, J.R. (1995). Where is the child environment? A group socialisation theory of development. *Psychological Review, 102,* 458-489.

Harris, J.R. (1998). *The Nurture Assumption: Why Kids Turn Out the Way They Do.* New York: Simon Schuster.

Hasin, D., Hatzenbuehler, M.L, Keyes, K., & Ogburn, E. (2006). Substance use disorders: Diagnostic and Statistical Manual of Mental Disorders, fourth edition (DSM-IV) and International Classification of Diseases, 10th edition (ICD-10). *Addiction, 101, (Suppl. 1),* 59-75.

Hawker, A. (1978). *Adolescence and Alcohol.* London: Edsall.

Hawkins, J.D., & Catalano, R.F. (1992). *Communities that care: Action for drug abuse prevention.* San Francisco: Jossey-Bass.

Hawkins, J.D., Catalano, R.F., & Arthur, M.W. (2002). Promoting science based prevention in communities. *Addictive Behaviours, 27,* 951-976.

Hawkins, D., Catalano, R.F., & Miller, J.Y. (1992) Risk and protective factors for alcohol and other drug problems in adolescence and early adulthood: implications for substance abuse prevention. *Psychological Bulletin, 112,* 64-105.

Hay D.F., & Angold, A. (1993) Introduction: Precursors and causes in development and pathogenesis. In Hay D.F. & Angold, A. (Eds.) *Precursors and causes in development and psychopathology* (pp. 1 – 23). Wiley: Chichester.

Hay, D.F., & Angold, A. (Eds.). (1993). *Precursors and Causes in Development and Psychopathology.* London: John Wiley & Sons.

Health Advisory Service (2001). *The Substance of Young Needs: Review 2001.* Brighton: Pavilion Publishing.

Heather, N., & Robertson, I. (1997). *Problem Drinking.* (3rd Edition). Oxford: Oxford

Medical Publications.

Henrich, C.C. (2006). Context in action: Implications for the study of children and adolescents. *Journal of Clinical Psychology, 62,* 1083-1096.

Hesselbrock, V.M., & Hesselbrock, M.N. (2006). Are there empirically supported and clinically useful subtypes of alcohol dependence? *Addiction, 101 (Suppl. 1),* 97-103.

Hetherington, E. M., Bridges, M., & Insabella, G. M. (1998). What matters? What does not? Five perspectives on the association between marital transitions and children's adjustment. *American Psychologist, 53,* 167-184.

Hibell, B., Andersson, B., Bjarnson, T., Ahlstrom, S., Balakireva, O., Kokkevi, A., & Morgan, M. (2004). *The ESPAD Report 2003: Alcohol and other drug use amongst students in 35 European countries.* Stockholm Sweden: The Swedish Council for Information on Alcohol and Other Drugs (CAN).

Hill, S.Y., & Yuan, H. (1999). Familial density of alcoholism and the onset of adolescent drinking. *Journal of Studies on Alcohol, 60,* 7-17.

Hines, L.M., & Rimm, E.B. (2001). Moderate Alcohol consumption and coronary heart disease. *Postgraduate Medical Journal, 77,* 747-752.

Hinshaw. S.P. (2002). Process, mechanism and explanation related to externalising behaviour in developmental psychopathology. *Journal of Abnormal Child Psychology, 30,* 431-446.

Hirschi, T. (1969) *Causes of Delinquency.* Berkley: University of California Press.

Hoffman, J.P. (2002). The community context of family structure and adolescent drug use. *Journal of Marriage and Family, 64,* 314-330.

Home Office (1994). *Criminal Statistics England and Wales 1994* London: HMSO.

Home Office (2005). *Criminal Statistics England and Wales 2004.* London: Author.

Horwitz, A. (2003). *Creating mental illness.* Chicago: The University of Chicago Press.

Hughes, K., Mackintosh, A.M., Hastings, G., Wheeler, C., Watson, J. & Inglis, J. (1997). Young people and designer drinks: quantitative and qualitative study. *British Medical Journal. 314,* 414-424.

Hupkens, C.L.H., Knibbe, R.A. & Drop, M.J. (1993). Alcohol consumption in the European Community: Uniformity and diversity in drinking patterns. *Addiction, 88,*

1391-1404.

Husson, A.M., & Chassin, L. (1994). The stress-negative affect model of adolescent alcohol use: disaggregating negative affect. *Journal of Studies on Alcohol, 55,* 707-718.

Hyatt, S.L., Collins, L.M., & Schafer, J.L. (1999). *Using data augmentation to conduct hypothesis testing in LTA.* Technical Report 99-34. University Park: Pennsylvania State University, The Methodology Centre.

Iacono, E.G., Carlson, S.R., Taylor, J., Elkins, I.J. & McGue, M. (1999). Behavioural disinhibition and the development of substance-use disorders: findings from the Minnesota Twin Family Study. *Development and Psychopathology, 11,* 869-900.

Ialongo, N.S., Rogosh, F.A., Cicchetti, D., Toth, S.L., Buckley, J., Petras, H., & Neiderhiser, J. (2006). A developmental psychopathology approach to the prevention of mental health disorders. In D. Cicchetti & D. Cohen (Eds.) *Developmental Psychopathology. Volume 3: Risk Disorder, and Adaptation* (2nd Edit.). Hoboken, NJ: John Wiley & Sons (pp 968-1018).

Information Service Directorate (2006). *Alcohol Statistics Scotland 2007.* Edinburgh: The Author.

Institute of Child Health (not dated) The 1970 Birth Cohort: Data deposited with the ESRC. Bristol: Institute of Child Health, University of Bristol.

Ito, T., Miller, N., & Pollock, V.E. (1996). Alcohol and aggression: A meta-analysis on the moderating effects of inhibitory cues, triggering events and self-focused attention. *Psychological Bulletin, 120,* 60-82.

Jackson, K.M., Sher, K.J., Cooper, M.L., & Wood, P.K. (2002). Adolescent alcohol and tobacco use: onset, persistence and trajectories of use across two samples. *Addiction, 97,* 517-531.

Jackson, K.M., Sher, K.J., & Wood, P.K. (2000). Trajectories of concurrent substance use disorders: A developmental, typology approach to comorbidity. *Alcoholism: Clinical and Experimental Research, 24,* 902-913.

Jackson, M.C., Hastings, G., Wheeler, C., Eadie, D., & Mackintosh, A.M. (2000). Marketing alcohol to young people: implications for industry regulation and research policy. *Addiction, 95,* (Suppl. 4), S597-S608.

Jacob, T., & Johnson, S. (1997). Parenting influences on the development of alcohol abuse and dependence. *Alcohol, Health & Research World. 21*, 204-209.

Jacob, T., & Leonard, K. (1994). Family and peer influences in the development of adolescent alcohol abuse. In R., Zucker, G., Boyd & J. Howard (Eds.). *The Development of Alcohol Problems: Exploring the Bio-psychosocial Matrix of Risk.* Rockville M.D.: National Institute on Alcohol Abuse and Alcoholism.

Jaffee, S.R., Moffitt, T.E., Caspi, A., & Taylor, A. (2003). Life with (or without) father: The benefits of living with two biological parents depend on the father's antisocial behaviour. *Child Development, 74*, 109-126.

Jefferis, B.J. Power, C., & Manor, O. (2005). Adolescent drinking level and adult binge drinking in a national birth cohort. *Addiction, 100*, 543-549.

Jensen, P.S., Hoagwood, K., & Zitner, L. (2006). What's in a name: Problems versus prospects in current diagnostic approaches. In D. Cicchetti & D. Cohen (Eds.) *Developmental Psychopathology. Volume 1: Theory and method* (2nd Edit.). Hoboken, NJ: John Wiley & Sons, (pp 24-40).

Jernigan, D.H. (2000). Applying commodity chain analysis to changing modes of alcohol supply in a developing country. *Addiction, 95, (Suppl. 4)*, S465-S476.

Jessor, R., & Jessor, S.L. (1977). *Problem Behaviour and Psychosocial Development: A Longitudinal Study of Youth.* New York: Academic Press.

Johnson, J.L., & Leff, M. (1999). Children of substance abusers: Overview of research findings, *Paediatrics, 103*, 1085-1099.

Johnstone, B.M. (1994). Sociodemographic, environmental and cultural influences on adolescent drinking behaviour. In R., Zucker, G., Boyd & J. Howard (Eds.). *The Development of Alcohol Problems: Exploring the Bio-psychosocial Matrix of Risk.* Rockville M.D.: National Institute on Alcohol Abuse and Alcoholism.

Kandel, D.B. (Ed.) (2002). *Stages and Pathways of Drug Involvement: Examining the Gateway Hypothesis.* Cambridge: Cambridge University Press.

Kandel, D.B., Huang, F., & Davies, M. (2001). Comorbidity between patterns of substance use of dependence and psychiatric syndromes. *Drug and Alcohol Dependence, 64*, 233-241.

Kandel, D.B., & Logan, J.A. (1984). Patterns of drug use from adolescence to young adulthood: 1. Periods of risk for initiation, continued use and discontinuation. *American Journal of Public Health, 74*, 660-666.

Kandel, D.B., & Yamaguchi, K. (1993). From beer to crack: developmental patterns of involvement in drugs. *American Journal of Public Health*, *83*, 851-855.

Kandel, D.B., & Yamaguchi, K. (2002). Stage of drug involvement in the US population. In D.B. Kandel (Ed.). *Stages and Pathways of Drug Involvement: Examining the Gateway Hypothesis*. Cambridge: Cambridge University Press.

Kandel, D.B., Yamaguchi, K., & Chen, K. (1992). Stages in the progressions of drug involvement from adolescence to adulthood: Further evidence for the gateway theory. *Journal of Studies on Alcohol*, *53*, 447-457.

Kaplan, H.B. (1995). Drugs crime and other deviant adaptations. In H.B. Kaplan (ed*)* *Drugs, Crime and Other Deviant Adaptations*: Longitudinal Studies. New York: Plenum Press.

Kaplow, J.B., Curran, P.J., Angold, A., & Costello, E.J. (2001). The prospective relationship between dimensions of anxiety and the initiation into adolescent alcohol use. *Journal of Clinical Child Psychology*, *30*, 316-326.

Kariouz, S., & Adlaf, E.M. (2003). Schools, students and heavy drinking: a multilevel analysis. *Addiction Research and Theory*, *11*, 427-439.

Kazdin, A.E., Kraemer, H.C., Kessler, R.C., Kupfer, D.J. and Offord, D.R. (1997) Contributions of risk factor research to developmental psychopathology. *Clinical Psychology Review, 17*, 375-406.

Kelley, B.T., Loeber, R., Keenan, K., & DeLamatre, M. (1997). *Developmental Pathways in Boys Disruptive and Delinquent Behaviour*. Juvenile Justice Bulletin Washington DC: Office of Juvenile Justice and Delinquency Prevention.

Kendler, K.S., Karowski, L.M., & Walsh, D. (1998). The structure of psychosis: latent class analysis of the Roscommon Family Study. *Archives of General Psychiatry*, *55*, 492-499.

Kerr, M., & Stattin, H. (2000). What parents know, how they know it, and several forms of adolescent adjustment: Further support for a reinterpretation of monitoring. *Developmental Psychology*, *36*, 366-380.

Kilty, K.M. (1990). Drinking styles of adolescent and young adults. *Journal of Studies on Alcohol*, *51*, 556-564.

King, S.M., Iacono, W.G., & McGue, M. (2004). Childhood externalizing and internalizing psychopathology in the prediction of early substance use. *Addiction*,

99, 1548-1559.

Kline, R.B. (2004). *Principles and practice of structural equation modeling.* Guildford Press: New York.

Klingeman, H. (2001). Alcohol and its Social Consequences – the Forgotten Dimension. Copenhagen: World Health Organisation Regional Office for Europe.

Kortteinen, T. (1984). Wine production in the European Community sine 1975. *British Journal of Addiction, 79*, 319-325.

Krueger, R.F., Caspi, A. & Moffitt, T.E. (2000). Epidemiological personology: The unifying role of personality in population-based research on problem behaviors. *Journal of Personality, 68*, 967-98.

Krukowski, R.A., Solomon, L.J., & Naud, S. (2005). Triggers of heavier and lighter cigarette smoking in college students. *Journal of Behavioural Medicine, 28*, 335-345.

Kumar, R., O'Malley, P.M., Johnston, L.D., Schulenberg, J.E., & Bachman, J.G. (2002). Effects of school-level norms on student substance use. *Prevention Science, 3*, 105-124.

Kumpfer K.L. & Turner C.W. (1991) The social ecology model of adolescent drug use: implications for prevention. *The International Journal of the Addictions. 25*, 435-463.

Kumpfer, K.L., Olds, D.L., Alexander, J.F. Zucker, R.A., & Gary, L.E. (1998). The family etiology of youth problems. In R.S., Ashery, E.B., Robertson & K.L. Kumpfer (Eds.). *Drug Abuse Prevention Through Family Interventions.* NIDA Research Monograph 177. Rockville, MD: NIDA .

Kumpulainen, K. (2000). Psychiatric symptoms and deviance in early adolescence predict heavy alcohol use three years later. *Addiction, 95*, 1847-1857.

Kushner, M.G., Abrams, K., & Borchardt, C. (2000). The relationship between anxiety and alcohol use disorders: A review of major perspectives and findings. *Clinical Psychology Review, 20*, 149-171.

Kushner, M.G., Sher, K.J., & Erickson, D.J. (1999). Prospective analysis of the relationship between DSM-III anxiety disorders and alcohol use disorders. American Journal of Psychiatry, *156*, 723-732.

Labouvie, E., & White, H.R. (2002). Drug sequences, age of onset, and use trajectories as predictors of drug abuse/dependence in young adults. . In D.B. Kandel, (Ed.) (2002). *Stages and Pathways of Drug Involvement: Examining the Gateway Hypothesis* (pp. 19-41).Cambridge: Cambridge University Press.

Lahey, B.B., Waldman, I.D., & McBurnett, K. (1999). Annotation: The development of antisocial behaviour: An integrative causal model. *Journal of Child Psychology and Psychiatry, 40,* 669-682.

Laird, R.D., Pettit, G.S., Bates, J.E., & Dodge, K.A. (2003). Parents' monitoring relevant knowledge and adolescents' delinquent behaviour: Evidence of correlated developmental changes and reciprocal influences. *Child Development, 74,* 752-768.

Laub, J.H., & Vaillant, G.E. (2000). Delinquency and mortality: A 50-year follow-up study of 1,000 delinquent and non-delinquent boys. *American Journal of Psychiatry, 157,* 96-102.

Law, M.R., Morris, J.K. & Wald, N.J. (1997). Environmental tobacco smoke exposure and ischaemic heart disease: an evaluation of the evidence. *British Medical Journal, 315,* 973-980.

Lawrence, D. (1981). The development of a self-esteem questionnaire. *British Journal of Educational Psychology. 51,* 245-251.

Lazarsfeld, P.F., & Henry, N.W. (1968). *Latent Structure Analysis.* Boston: Houghton Mifflin Company.

Le Blanc, M., & Loeber, R. (1993). Precursors, Causes and the Development of Criminal Offending. In D.F., Hay & A. Angold (Eds.). *Precursors and Causes in Development and Psychopathology.* London: John Wiley & Sons.

Ledoux, S., Miller, P., Choquet, M., & Plant, M. (2002). Family structure, parent-child relationships, and alcohol and other drug use among teenagers in France and the United Kingdom. *Alcohol and Alcoholism, 37,* 52-60.

Lerner, R.M., Ostrom, C.W., Freel, M.A. (1997). Preventing health-compromising behaviours amongst youth and promoting their positive development: A developmental contextual perspective. In J. Schulenberg, J.L. Maggs & K. Hurrelmann (Eds.). *Health Risks and Developmental Transitions During Adolescence.* Cambridge: Cambridge University Press.

Lerner, R.M., Walsh, M.E., & Howard, K.A. (1998). Developmental-contextual considerations: Person-context relations as the bases for risk and resilience in child and adolescent development. In Ollendick, T. (Ed.). *Comprehensive Clinical Psychology: Volume 5, Children and Adolescents: Clinical Formulations and Treatments.* Amsterdam: Elsevier Science.

Leventhal, T., & Brooks-Gunn, J. (2000). The neighborhoods they live in: the effects of neighborhood residence on child and adolescent outcomes. *Psychological Bulletin, 126,* 309-37.

Lieb, R., Merikangas, K.R., Hofler, M., Pfister, H., Isensee, B., & Wittchen, H.U. (2002). Parental alcohol use disorders and alcohol use and disorders in offspring: a community sample. *Psychological Medicine, 32,* 63-78.

Linver, M.R., Brooks-Gunn, J., & Kohen, D.E. (2002). Family processes as pathways from income to young children's development. *Development Psychology, 38,* 719-734.

Little, R.A.J., & Rubins, D.B. (1987). *Statistical analysis with missing data.* New York: J. Wiley and Sons.

Loeber, R., & Farrington, D.P. (1994). Problems and solutions in longitudinal and experimental treatment studies of child psychopathology and delinquency. *Journal of Consulting and Clinical Psychology, 62,* 887-900.

Loehlin, J.C. (2004). Latent variable modeling: An introduction to factor, path and structural analysis. Lawrence Erlbaum Associates. New Jersey.

Lynskey, M.T. (1998). The comorbidity of alcohol dependence and affective disorders: Treatment implications. *Drug and Alcohol Dependence, 52,* 201-209.

Lynskey, M.T., & Fergusson, D.M. (1995). Childhood conduct problems, attention deficit behaviors, and adolescent alcohol, tobacco and illicit drug use. *Journal of Abnormal Child Psychology, 23,* 281-302.

Lynskey, M.T., Fergusson, D.M., & Horwood, L.J. (1998). The origins of the correlation between tobacco, alcohol and cannabis use during adolescence. *Journal of Child Psychology and Psychiatry, 39,* 995-1005.

Lynskey, M.T., Heath, A.C., Nelson, E.C., Bucholz, K.K., Madden, P.A.F., Slutske, W.S., Statham, D.J., & Martin, N.G. (2002). Genetic and environmental contributions to cannabis dependence in a national young adult twin sample. *Psychological Medicine, 32,* 195-207.

MacCallum, F., & Golombok, S. (2004). Children raised in fatherless families from infancy: a follow-up of children of lesbian and single heterosexual mothers at early adolescence. *Journal of Child Psychology and Psychiatry, 45*, 1407-1419.

MacCoun, R.J. (1998). Toward a psychology of harm reduction. *The American Psychologist, 53*, 1199-1208.

MacDonald, Z. & Shields, M.A. (2001). The impact of alcohol consumption on occupational attainment in England. *Economica, 68*, 427-453

MacDonald, Z. & Shields, M.A. (2004). Does problem drinking effect employment? Evidence from England. *Health Economics, 13*, 139-155.

Macready, G.B. & Dayton, C.M. (1994). Latent class model for longitudinal assessment of trait acquisition. In A. Von Eye & C.C. Clogg. (Eds.). *Latent variable analysis: Applications for developmental research.* Thousand Oaks: Sage Publications.

Magidson, J., & Vermunt, J.K. (2003). Latent class models. In D. Kaplan (Ed.). *Handbook for quantitative analysis.* Newbury Park: Sage.

Magnuson, K.A., & Duncan, G. (2002). Parents in Poverty. In M. Bornstein (Ed.). *Handbook of Parenting* (pp. 95–121). Mahwah, N.J.: Lawrence Erlbaum Associates.

Magnusson, D. (1993). Human ontogeny: A longitudinal perspective. In D. Magnusson, & P. Casear, (Eds.). (1993). *Longitudinal research on individual development: Present status and future perspectives.* Cambridge: Cambridge University Press.

Magnusson, D., & Casear, P. (Eds.). (1993). *Longitudinal research on individual development: Present status and future perspectives.* Cambridge: Cambridge University Press.

Manwell, L.B., Fleming, M.F., Mundt, M.P., Stauffacher, E.A., & Barry, K.L. (2000). Treatment of problems alcohol use in women of childbearing age: results of a brief intervention trail. *Alcoholism: Clinical and Experimental Research, 24*, 1517-1524.

Marlatt, G.A. (Ed) (1998). *Harm reduction: Pragmatic strategies for managing high risk behaviours.* New York: Guildford Press.

Marlatt, G.A., & Witkiewitz, K. (2002). Harm reduction approaches to alcohol use: Health promotion, prevention, and treatment. *Addictive Behaviors, 27*, 867-886.

Marmot, M. (1997). Inequalities, deprivation and alcohol use. *Addiction, 92 (Suppl. 1)*,

S13- S20.

Marmott, M.G., North, F. Feeney, A., & Head, J. (1993). Alcohol consumption and sickness absence: From the Whitehall II Study. *Addiction, 88,* 369-382.

Marsh, A., Dodds, J., & White, A. (1986). *Adolescent Drinking.* London: HMSO.

Masten, A.S. (2006). Developmental psychopathology: Pathways to the future. *International Journal of Behavioural Development, 30,* 47-54.

Masten, A.S., & Coatsworth, J.D. (1998). The development of competence in favourable and unfavourable environments. *American Psychologist, 53,* 205-220.

Masten, A.S., Coatsworth, J.D., Neeman, J., Gest, S.D., Tellegen, A., Gramezy, N. (1995) The structure and coherence of competency from childhood through adolescence. *Child Development, 66,* 1635-1659.

Matheny, K.B., & Weatherman, K.E. (1998). Predictors of smoking cessation and maintenance. *Journal of Clinical Psychology, 54,* 223-235.

Matt, E., Seus, L., & Schumann, K.F. (1997). Health risk and deviancy in the transition from school to work. In J. Schulenberg, J.L. Maggs, & K. Hurrelmann, (eds.), *Health risks and developmental transitions during adolescence.* Cambridge: Cambridge University Press.

Maxwell, C., Kinver, A., & Phelps, A. (2006). *Scottish School Adolescent Lifestyle and Substance Use Survey (SALSUS) national report: Smoking, drinking and drug use among 13 and 15 year olds in Scotland in 2006.* Edinburgh; Scottish Executive.

Mayhew, P., Aye Maung, N., & Mirrlees-Black, C. (1993). *The 1992 British Crime Survey.* Home Office Research Study 132. : London: Home Office.

McArdle, P., & Glivarry, E. (2006). The principles and service organisations in England. In H, A. Liddle & C. L. Rowe (Eds.) *Adolescent Substance Abuse: Research and Clinical Advances.* Cambridge University Press: Cambridge, pp 189-203.

McBride, N., Farringdon, F., Midford, R., Meuleners, L., & Phillips, M. (2004). Harm minimisation in school drug education: final results of the School Health and Alcohol Harm Reduction Programme (SHAHRP). *Addiction, 99,* 278-291.

McBride, N., Midford, R., Farringdon, F., & Phillips, M. (2000). Early results from a school alcohol harm minimization study: the School Health and Alcohol Harm Reduction Project. *Addiction, 95,* 1021-1042.

McElduff, P., & Dobson, A.J. (1997). How much alcohol and how often? Population case control study of alcohol consumption and risk of a major coronary event. *British Medical Journal, 314*, 1159-1164.

McGue, M. (1994). Genes, environment, and the etiology of alcoholism. In R., Zucker, G., Boyd & J. Howard (Eds.). *The Development of Alcohol Problems: Exploring the Bio-psychosocial Matrix of Risk.* Rockville M.D.: National Institute on Alcohol Abuse and Alcoholism (pp 1-40).

McGue, M., & Iacono, W.G. (2005). The association of early adolescent problem behavior with adult psychopathology. *American Journal of Psychiatry, 162*,1118-1124,

McHale, J.P., & Rasmussen, J. (1998). Co-parenting and family group-level dynamics during infancy: Early family predictors of child and family functioning during preschool. *Development and Psychopathology, 10*, 39–59.

McKeganey, N. Forsyth, A., Barnard, M., & Hay, G. (1996). Designer drinks. *British Medical Journal, 313*, 401.

McLanahan, S. (1999). Father absence and the welfare of children. In E. M. Hetherington (Ed.), *Coping With Divorce, Single Parenting, and Remarriage*, pp. 117-146. Mahwah, NJ: Lawrence Erlbaum Associates.

McLanahan, S.S. (1997). Parent absence or poverty: Which matters more? In G.J. Duncan, & J. Brooks-Gunn (Eds.). *Consequences of growing up poor.* New York: Russell Sage Foundation.

McLanahan, S., & Sandefur, G. (1994). *Growing up with a Single Parent: What Hurts, What Helps.* Harvard University Press, Cambridge, Mass.

McMorris, B.J., & Uggen, C. (2000). Alcohol and employment in the transition to adulthood. *Journal of Health and Social Behaviour, 41*, 276-294.

Measham, F., & Brain, K. (2005). 'Binge' drinking, British alcohol policy and the new culture of intoxication. *Crime Media and Culture, 1*, 262-283.

Menard, S. (1991). *Longitudinal Research.* Sage University Paper Series on Quantitative Applications in the Social Sciences, 07-076, Newbury Park, CA: Sage.

Menard, S., & Huizinga, D. (1989). Age, period, and cohort effects on self-reported alcohol, marijuana, and polydrug use: Results from the National Youth Survey. *Social Science Review 18*, 174-194.

Mensch, B.S., & Kandel, D.B. (1998). Dropping out of high school and drug involvement. *Sociology of Education, 61*, 95-113.

Meyers, K., Hagan, T.A., Zanis, D., Webb, A., Frantz, J., Ring-Kurtz, S., Rutherford, M. & McLellan, A.T. (1999). Critical issues in adolescent substance use assessment. *Drug and Alcohol Dependence, 55*, 235-246.

Miller, P., & Plant, M. (1996). Drinking, smoking and illicit drug use among 15 and 16 year olds in the United Kingdom. *British Medical Journal, 313*, 394-397.

Miller, P., & Plant, M. (2001). Drinking smoking and illicit drug use amongst 15 and 16 year old school students in Northern Ireland. Belfast: DHSS&PS.

Miller, R., Devine, P., & Schubotz, D. (2003). Secondary analysis of the 1997 and 2001 Northern Ireland Health and Well-being Surveys. Belfast: DHSS&PS.

Mirrlees-Black, C., Mayhew, P., & Percy, A. (1996). *The 1996 British Crime Survey: England and Wales.* Home Office Statistical Bulletin, Issue 19/96. London: Home Office.

Mitchell, J. (1992). Self-regulation and "addictive behaviour": Some theoretical remarks. *The International Journal of the Addictions, 27*, 743-748.

Moffitt, T.E. (2006). Life course-persistent versus adolescent limited antisocial behaviour. In D. Cicchetti & D. Cohen (Eds.) *Developmental Psychopathology. Volume 3: Risk Disorder, and Adaptation* (2nd Edit.). 570-598.

Moffitt, T.E., Caspi, A., Rutter, M., & Silva, P.A. (2001). *Sex differences in antisocial behaviour: Conduct disorder, delinquency and violence in the Dunedin Longitudinal Study.* Cambridge: Cambridge University Press.

Molina, B.S.G., Smith, B.H., Pelham, W.E. (1999). Interactive effects of attention deficit disorder and conduct disorder on early adolescent substance use. *Psychology of Addictive Behaviours, 13*, 348-358.

Morral, A.R., McCaffrey, D.F., & Paddock, S.M. (2002). Reassessing the marijuana gateway effect. *Addiction, 97*, 1493-1504.

Moskowitz, D.S., & Hershberger, S.L. (2001). *Modeling intraindividual variability with repeated measures data.* Mahwah, NJ: Lawrence Erlbaum Associates.

Moskowitz, J.M. (1989) The primary prevention of alcohol problems: a critical review of the research literature. *Journal of Studies on Alcohol, 50*, 54-88.

Moss, H.B., Kirischi, L., Gordon, H.W., & Tarter, R.E. (1994). A neuropsychological profile of adolescent alcoholics. *Alcoholism: Clinical and Experimental Research*, *18*, 159-163.

Moss, H.B., & Lynch, K.C. (2001). Comorbid disruptive behaviour disorder symptoms and their relationship to adolescent drug use disorders. *Drug and Alcohol Dependence, 64*, 75-83.

Mukamal, K.J., Conlgrave, K.M., Mittleman, M.A., Camargo, C.A., Stampher, M.J., Willet, W.C., & Rimm, W.C. (2003). Roles of drinking pattern and type of alcohol consumed in coronary heart disease in men. *The New England Journal of Medicine*, *348*, 109-118.

Murray, R.P., Connett, J.E., Tyas, S.L., Bond, R., Ekuma, O., Silversides, C.K., & Barnes, G.E. 2002). Alcohol Volume, Drinking Pattern, and Cardiovascular Disease Morbidity and Mortality: Is There a U-shaped Function? *American Journal of Epidemiology, 155*, 242-248.

Muthén, B.O. (2004). Latent variable analysis: Growth Mixture modeling and related techniques for longitudinal data. In D. Kaplan (Ed.) *Handbook of quantitative methodology for the social sciences*. Newbury Park, CA: Sage publications.

Muthén, B.O., & Muthén, L.K. (1998-2005a). Mplus version 3. [Computer Programme]. Los Angeles, CA: Muthén & Muthén.

Muthén, L.K., & Muthén, B.O. (1998-2005b). Mplus user's guide. (3th edn.). [User Manual]. Los Angeles, CA: Muthén & Muthén.

Nash, S.G., McQueen, A., & Bray, J.C. (2005). Pathways to adolescent alcohol use: Family environment, peer influence, and parental expectations. *Journal of Adolescent Health, 37*, 19-28.

NatCen (2003). *Health Survey for England 2003: Summary of key findings*. Office of National Statistics: London.

NatCen/NFER (2007). *Smoking Drinking and Drug use amongst young people in England in 2006: Headline Figures*. Leeds: The Information Centre.

Neighbors, C., Larimer, M.E., Lostutter, T.W., Woods, B.A. (2006). Harm reduction and individually focused alcohol prevention. *International Journal of Drug Policy*, *17*, 304-309.

Nesselroade, J.R., & Schmidt McCollam, K.M. (2000). Putting the process in developmental processes. *International Journal of Behavioural Development. 24*,

295-300.

Newman, D.L., Moffitt, T.E., Caspi, A., & Silva, P.A. (1998). Comorbid mental disorders: implications for treatment and sample selection. *Journal of Abnormal Psychology, 107*, 305-311.

Niemelä, S., Sourander, A., Poikolainen, K., Helenius, H., Sillanmaki, L., Parkkola, K., Piha, J., Kumpulainen, K., Almquist, F., & Moilanen, I. (2006). Childhood predictors of drunkenness in late adolescence amongst males: A 10-year population-based follow-up study. *Addiction, 101*, 512-521.

Nigg, J.T. (2006). Temperament and developmental psychopathology. *Journal of Child Psychology and Psychiatry. 47*, 395-422.

Noland, J.S., Singer, L.T., Arendt, R.E., Minnes, S., Short, E.J., & Beaver, C.F. (2003). Executive functioning in preschool-age children prenatally exposed to alcohol, cocaine and marijuana. *Journal of Computer Assisted Tomography, 27*, 647-656.

Norstrom, T. (2002). (Ed.) *Alcohol in post war Europe: Consumption, drinking patterns, consequences, and policy responses in 15 European Countries.* Stockholm: National Institute of Public Health (Sweden).

O'Connor, J. (1970). *The young drinkers: A cross-cultural study of social and cultural influences.* London: Tavistock Publications.

O'Connor, T.G. (2002). Annotation: the 'effects' of parenting reconsidered: Findings, challenges, and applications. *Journal of Child Psychology and Psychiatry, 43*, 555-572.

O'Connor, T.G., Dunn, J. & Jenkins, J.M. (2001). Family settings and children's adjustment: differential adjustment within and across families. *British Journal of Psychiatry, 179*, 110-115.

O'Connor, T.G., Hetherington, E.M., & Reiss, D. (1998) Family systems and adolescent development: Shared and non-shared risk and protective factors in non-divorced and remarried families. *Development and Psychopathology, 10*, 353-375.

O'Malley, P.M., Bachman J.G., & Johnston, L.D. (1998). Period, age and cohort effects on substance use amongst young Americans: A decade of change, 1976-1986. *American Journal of Public Health, 78*, 1315-1321.

Oetting, E.R., (1999). Primary socialisation theory. Developmental stages, spirituality, government institutions, sensation seeking and theoretical implications. V.

Substance Use and Misuse. 34, 947-982.

Oetting, E.R., Deffenbacher, J.L., & Donnermeyer, J.F. (1998). Primary socialisation theory. The role played by personality traits in the etiology of drug use and deviance. II. *Substance Use and Misuse. 33*, 1337-1366.

Oetting, E.R., & Donnermeyer, J.F. (1998). Primary socialisation theory. The etiology of drug use and deviance. I. *Substance Use and Misuse. 33*, 1629-1665.

Oetting, E.R., Donnermeyer, J.F., & Deffenbacher, J.L. (1998). Primary socialisation theory. The influence of the community on drug use and deviance. III. *Substance Use and Misuse. 33*, 1629-1665.

Oetting, E.R., Donnermeyer, J.F., Trimble, J.E., & Beauvis, F. (1998). Primary socialisation theory: Culture, ethnicity and cultural identification. The links between culture and substance use. IV. *Substance Use and Misuse. 33*, 2075-2107.

Office of National Statistics (2006). *Alcohol related death rate almost doubles since 1991.* News Release 18th July 2006. [Downloaded on 20th July 2006 from http://www.statistics.gov.uk/pdfdir/aldeaths0706.pdf]

Orford, J. (1984). *Excessive Appetites: A psychological view of addictions.* London: John Wiley & Sons.

Orford, J. (2001). Conceptualising addiction: addiction as an excessive appetite. *Addiction, 96,* 15-31.

Oscar-Bergman, M., & Marinkovic, K. (2001). Alcoholism and the brain. *Alcohol, Research & Health, 27,* 125-133.

Pape, H., & Hammer, T. (1996). How does young people's alcohol consumption change during the transition to early adulthood? A Longitudinal study of change at aggregate and individual levels. *Addiction, 91,* 1345-1357.

Parcel, T.L., & Menaghan, E.G. (1993). Family social capital and children's behaviour problems. *Social Psychology Quarterly. 56,* 120-135.

Parke, R.D. (2004). Development in the family. *Annual Review of Psychology, 55,* 365-399.

Parker, H., Aldridge, J., & Measham, F. (1998). *Illegal leisure: The normalisation of adolescent recreational drug use.* London: Routledge.

Patterson, G.R., DeGarmo, D.S., & Knutson, N. (2000). Hyperactivity and antisocial behaviours: Comorbid or two time points in the same process? *Development and*

Psychopathology, 12, 91-106.

Patton, G.C., McMorris, B.J., Toumbourou, J.W., Hemphill, S.A., Donath, S., & Catalano, R.F. (2004). Puberty and the onset of substance use and abuse. *Paediatrics, 114*, 300-306.

Pearl, J. (2000). *Causality: Models, Reasoning and Inferences*. New York: Cambridge University Press.

Percy, A. (2008). Adolescent substance use: A developmental disorder of self-regulation? *International Journal of Behavioural Development, 32*, 5, 451-458

Percy, A. & Iwaniec, D. (2007). The validity of a latent class typology of adolescent drinking patterns. *Irish Journal of Psychological Medicine. 24*, 13-18.

Percy, A., Carr-Hill, R., Dixon, P., & Jamison, J. (2000). Assessing the local need for family and child care service: a small area utilization approach. *Child Welfare, LXXIX*, 535-554.

Percy, A., McAlister, S., Higgins, K., McCrystal, P., & Thornton, M. (2005). Response consistency in young adolescents' drug use self-reports: A recanting rate analysis. *Addiction, 100*, 189-196.

Peterson, JB., Rothfleisch, J., Zelazo P.D., & Pihl, R.O. (1990). Acute alcohol intoxication and cognitive functioning. *Journal of Studies on Alcohol, 51*, 114-122.

Petraitis, J., Flay, B.R., Miller, T.Q., Torpy, E.J., & Greiner, B. (1998). Illicit substance use among adolescents: A matrix of prospective predictors. *Substance use and Misuse, 33*, 2561-2604.

Pickles, A. (1993). Stages, precursors and cause in development. In D.F., Hay & A. Angold (Eds.). *Precursors and Causes in Development and Psychopathology*. London: John Wiley & Sons.

Pickles, A. & Angold, A. (2003). Natural categories or fundamental dimensions: On the carving nature at the joints and the rearticulation of psychopathology. *Development and Psychopathology, 15*, 529-551.

Pine, D.S., Wasserman, G., Coplan, J., Staghezza-Jaramillo, B., Davies, M., Fried, J.E., Greenhill, L., & Shaffer, D. (1996). Cardiac profile and disruptive behaviour in boys at risk for delinquency. *Psychosomatic Medicine, 58*, 342-353.

Plant, M., Bagnall, G., Foster, J. & Sales, J. (1990). Young people and drinking: results of an English National Survey. *Alcohol and Alcoholism, 25*, 685-690.

Plant, M., Peck, D., & Samuel, E. (1985). *Alcohol, Drugs and School Leavers*. London: Tavistock.

Plant, M., & Plant, M. (1992). *Risk-takers: Alcohol, drugs, sex and youth*. London: Tavistock/Routledge.

Pletcher, M.J., Varosy, P., Kiefe, C.I., Lewis, C.E., Sidney, S. & Hulley, S.B. (2005). Alcohol consumption, binge drinking and early coronary calcification: findings from the Coronary Artery Risk Development in Young Adults (CARDIA) Study. *American Journal of Epidemiology, 161*, 423-433.

Pogorny, A., Miller, B.A., & Kaplan, H.B. (1972). The brief MAST: a shortened version of the Michigan Alcoholism Screening Test. *American Journal of Psychiatry, 129*, 342-345.

Poikolainen, K., Vahtera, J., Virtanen, M., Linna, A., & Kivimaki, M. (2005).Alcohol and coronary heart disease risk-is there an unknown confounder? *Addiction, 100*, 1150-1157.

Pollock, N.K. & Martin, C.S. (1999). Diagnostic orphans: adolescents with alcohol symptoms who do not qualify for DSM-IV abuse of dependency diagnosis. *American Journal of Psychiatry, 156,* 879-901.

Poulin, C., Hand, D., Boudreau, B., & Santor, D. (2005). Gender differences in the association between substance use and elevated depressive symptoms in a general adolescent population. *Addiction, 100*, 525-535.

Puddey, I.B., Rakic, V., Dimmitt, S.B., & Beilin, L.J. (1999). Influence of pattern of drinking on cardiovascular disease and cardiovascular risk factors – a review. *Addiction, 94*, 649-663.

Pulkkinen, L., & Pitkanen, T. (1994). A prospective study of the precursors to problem drinking in young adulthood. *Journal of Studies on Alcohol, 55*, 578-87.

Ragin, A., Rasinski, K.A., Cerbone, F.G., & Johnston, R.A. (1999*). The Relationship between Mental Health and Substance Abuse Amongst Adolescents*. Rockville MD: Substance Abuse and Mental Health Services Administration, Office of Applied Studies.

Raistick, D., Hodgson, R., & Ritson, B. (1999). *Tackling alcohol together: The evidence base for UK alcohol policy*. Free Association Books: London.

Ramsay, M., & Percy, A. (1996). *Drug Misuse Declared: Results from the 1994 British*

Crime Survey. Home Office Research Study, 151. Home Office: London.

Rasmussen, E.R., Neuman, R.J., Heath, A.C., Levy, F., Hay, D.A., & Todd, R.D. (2004). Familial clustering of latent class and DSM-IV defined attention deficit/hyperactivity disorder (ADHD) subtypes. *Journal of Child Psychology and Psychiatry, 45,* 589-598

Reboussin, B.A., Song, E.Y., Shrestha, A., Lohman, K.K., & Wolfson, M. (2006). A latent class analysis of underage problem drinking: Evidence from a community sample of 16-20 year olds. *Drug and Alcohol Dependence, 83,* 199-209.

Registrar General (2006). *Registrar General Northern Ireland Annual Report 2005.* Belfast: Northern Ireland Statistics and Research Agency.

Rehm, J., & Gmel, G. (1999). Patterns of alcohol consumption and social consequences. Results form and 8-year follow-up study in Switzerland. *Addiction, 94,* 899-912.

Rehm, J., & Gmel, G. (2000). Aggregating dimensions of alcohol consumption to predict medical and social harm. *Journal of Substance Abuse, 12,* 155-168.

Rehm, J., Ashley, M.J., & Dubois, G. (1997). Alcohol and health: Individual and population perspectives. *Addiction, 92 (Suppl. 1),* S109 – S115.

Rehn, N., Room, R., & Edwards, G., (2001). *Alcohol in the European region – consumption, harm and policies.* World Health Organisation Regional Office for Europe: Copenhagen.

Reich. W., Earls, F., Frankel, O., & Shayka, J.J. (1993). Psychopathology in children of alcoholics. *Journal of the American Academy of Child and Adolescent Psychiatry, 32,* 995-1002.

Reynolds, K., Lewis, B., Nolen, J.D.L., Kinney, G.L., Sathya, B., & He, J. (2003). Alcohol consumption and risk of stroke. Journal of the American Medical Association, *289,* 579-588

Rhodes J.E., & Turner, L.A. (1990). A social stress model of substance abuse. *Journal of Consulting and Clinical Psychology, 58,* 395-401.

Robe, L.B., Robe, R.S., & Wilson, P.A. (1980). Maternal heavy drinking related to delayed onset of daughters' menstruation. *Current Studies on Alcohol, 7,* 515-520.

Robins, L. N., & Przybeck, T.R. (1985). Age of onset of drug use as a factor in drug use and other disorders. In C.L. Jones, & R.J. Battjes (Eds.). *Etiology of drug abuse: implications for prevention* (pp187-192). Washington, D.C: National Institute of Drug Abuse.

Rodgers, B., Korten, A.E., Jorm, A.F., Jacomb, P.A., Christensen, H., & Henderson, A.S. (2000). Non-linear relationships in associations of depression and anxiety with alcohol use. *Psychological Medicine, 30*, 421-432.

Rodgers, B., Windsor, T.D., Anstey, K.J., Dear, K.B.G., Form, A., & Christensen, H., (2005). Non-linear relationships between cognitive function and alcohol consumption in young, middle-aged and older adults: The PATH Through Life Project. *Addiction, 100*, 1280-1290.

Roeder, K., Lynch, K.G., & Nagin, D.S. (1999). Modelling uncertainty in latent class membership: a case study in criminology. *Journal of the American Statistical Association, 94*, 766-776.

Rohde, P., Lewinsohn, P.M. & Seeley, J.R. (1996). Psychiatric comorbidity with problematic alcohol use in high school students. *Journal of the American Academy of Child and Adolescent Psychiatry, 35*, 101-109.

Romanus, G. (2000). Alcopops in Sweden – a supply side initiative. *Addiction, 95, (Suppl. 4)*, S609-S620.

Romelsjö, A., Branting, M., Hallqvist, J., Alfredsson, L., Hammar, N., Leifman, & Ahlbom, A. (2003). Abstention, alcohol use and risk of myocardial infarction in men and women taking account of social support and working conditions: The SHEEP case–control study. *Addiction, 98*, 1453-1462.

Room, R. (2000). Measuring drinking patterns: the experience of the last half-century. *Journal of Substance Abuse, 12*, 23-31.

Room, R. (2004). Disabling the public interest: Alcohol strategies and polices for England. *Addiction, 99*, 1083-1089.

Room, R., Babor, T., & Rehm, J. (2005). Alcohol and the public health. *Lancet, 365*, 519-530.

Rose, A developmental behavioural-genetic perspective on alcoholism risk. *Alcohol Health and Research World, 22*, 131-143.

Rossow, I., & Hauge, R. (2004). Who pays for the drinking? Characteristics of the extent and distribution of social harm from others' drinking. *Addiction, 99*, 1094-1102.

Rossow, I., & Romelsjö, A. (2006). The extent of the "prevention paradox" in alcohol problems as a function of population drinking patterns. *Addiction, 101*, 84-90.

Rubin, D.B. (1987). *Multiple imputation for non-response in surveys*. J. Wiley and Sons: New York.

Rutter, M. (Ed.). (1988). *Studies of psychosocial risk: The power of longitudinal data.* Cambridge: Cambridge University Press.

Rutter, M. (1990). Psychosocial resilience and protective mechanisms. In J. Rolf, A.S. Masten, D. Cicchetti, K.H. Neuchterlein, and S. Weitraub. *Risk and Protective Factors in the Development of Psychopathology*. Cambridge: Cambridge University Press.

Rutter, M. (1993). Developmental psychopathology as a research perspective. In D. Magnusson, & P. Casear, (Eds.). (1993). *Longitudinal research on individual development: Present status and future perspectives*. Cambridge: Cambridge University Press.

Rutter, M. (1994a). Beyond longitudinal data: Causes consequences, changes and continuity. *Journal of Consulting and Clinical Psychology, 62*, 927-940.

Rutter, M. (1994b). Family discord and conduct disorder: Cause, consequence, or correlate. *Journal of Family Psychology, 8*, 170-186.

Rutter, M. (ed.) (1995*) Psychosocial Disturbances in Young People: Challenges for Prevention*. Cambridge: Cambridge University Press.

Rutter, M. (1999a). Psychosocial adversity and child psychopathology. *British Journal of Psychiatry, 174*, 480-493.

Rutter, M. (1999b). Resilience reconsidered; conceptual considerations and empirical findings. In J.P. Shonkoff & S.J. Meisels (Eds). *Handbook of Early Childhood Intervention*. New York: Cambridge University Press.

Rutter, M. (2000). Psychosocial influences: critiques, findings and research tools. *Development and Psychopathology, 9*, 193-229.

Rutter, M. (2001). Conduct disorder: future directions. An Afterword. In J. Hill & B. Maughan (Eds). *Conduct disorders in childhood and adolescence*. Cambridge: Cambridge University Press.

Rutter, M., & Smith, D.J. (1995*) Psychosocial Disturbances in Young People: Time Trends and their Causes*. Chichester: John Wiley and Sons.

Rutter, M., & Sroufe, L.A. (2000). Developmental psychopathology: concepts and challenges. *Development and Psychopathology*, *12*, 265-296.

Rutter, M., Giller, H., & Hagel, A. (1998). *Antisocial behaviour by young people*. New York: Cambridge University Press.

Rutter, M., Kim-Cohen, J. & Maughan, B. (2006). Continuities and discontinuities in psychopathology between childhood and adult life. *Journal of Child and Psychology and Psychiatry*, *47*, 276-295.

Rutter, M., Maughan, B., Meyer, J., Pickles, A., Silberg, J., Simonoff, E., & Taylor, E. (1997). Heterogenity of Antisocial behaviour: Causes, continuities and consequences. In R. Dienstbier & D.W. Osgood (Eds.), *Motivation and Delinquency*. Nebraska Symposium on Motivation, vol. 44, Lincoln: University of Nebraska.

Rutter, M., Tizard, J., & Whitmore, K. (1970). *Education Health and Behaviour*. London: Longmans.

Sacker, A. (2002). Personal Communication.

Sacker, A. & Wiggins, R.D., (2002). Age-period-cohort effects on inequalities in psychological distress, 1981-2000. *Psychological Medicine*, *32*, 977-990

Sacker, A., Wiggins, R.D., Clarke, P., & Bartley, M. (2003). Making sense of symptom checklists: a latent class approach to the first 9 years of the British Household Panel Survey. *Journal of Public Health Medicine*, *25*, 215-222.

Sameroff, A. J. (1983). Developmental systems: Contexts and evolution. In W. Kessen (Ed.)., Handbook of child psychology: Vol. 1, History, theory, and methods. New York: Wiley, pp. 237-294.

Sanchez-Craig, M. (1986). Is it useful to think of Alcohol Dependence as a continuum? *British Journal of Addiction*, *81*, 187-190.

Schafer, J.L. (1997) *The analysis of incomplete multivariate data*. London, UK: Chapman and Hall:

Schafer, J.L. (2000). NORM version 2.03. [Computer programme]. University Park: The Methodology Centre, Pennsylvania State University.

Schafer, J.L., & Graham, J.W. (2002). Missing data: our view of the state of the art. *Psychological Methods*, *7*, 147-177.

Schafer, J.L., & Olsen, M.K. (1998). Multiple imputation for multivariate missing-data problems: a data analyst's perspective. *Multivariate Behavioral Research*, *33*, 545-571.

Schneider, K.M., Nicolotti, L., & Delamater, A (2002). Aggression and cardiovascular response in children. *Journal of Paediatric Psychology*, *27*, 565-573.

Schoon, I., Bynner, J, Joshi, H., Parsons, S., Wiggins, R.D., & Sacker, A. (2002). The influence of context, timing, and duration of risk experiences for the passage from childhood to midadulthood. *Child Development*, *73*, 1468-1504.

Schulenberg, J., Maggs, J.L., Dielman, T.E., Leech, S.L., Kloska, D.D., Shope, J.T., & Laetz, V.B. (1999). On peer influences to get drunk: a panel study of young adolescents. *Merrill-Palmer Quarterly*, *45*, 108-142.

Scottish Executive (2002a). *Plan for action on alcohol problems*. Edinburgh: Author.

Scottish Executive (2002b). *Statistics on alcohol in Scotland*. Edinburgh: Author.

Sewel, K. (2002). *International Alcohol Policies: A selected literature review*. Health and Community Care Research Programme Research Findings No. 15. Edinburgh: Scottish Executive Central Research Unit.

Shaper, A.G., Wannamethee, G., & Walker, M. (1994). Alcohol and coronary heart disease: A perspective from the British Regional Heart Study. *International Journal of Epidemiology*, *23*, 482-494.

Shaw, M., Dorling, D., & Brimblecombe, N. (1998). Changing the map: Health in Britain 1951-91. *Sociology of Health and Illness*, *20*, 694-709.

Sher, K.J. (1991). *Children of Alcoholics: A critical appraisal of theory and research*. Chicago: University of Chicago Press.

Sher, K.J. (1994). Individual-level risk factors. In R., Zucker, G., Boyd & J. Howard (Eds.). *The Development of Alcohol Problems: Exploring the Bio-psychosocial Matrix of Risk*. Rockville M.D.: National Institute on Alcohol Abuse and Alcoholism (pp 77-108).

Sher, K.J., & Gotham, H.J. (1999). Pathological alcohol involvement: A developmental disorder of young adulthood. *Development and Psychopathology*, *11*, 933-956.

Sher, K.J., Gotham, H.J., Erickson, D., & Wood, P.K. (1996). A prospective, high-risk study of relationship between tobacco dependence and alcohol use disorders. *Alcoholism: Clinical and Experimental Research*, *20*, 485-492.

Sher, K., Grekin, K., & Williams, N.A. (2005). The development of alcohol use disorders. *Annual Review of Clinical Psychology, 1*, 493-523.

Shiner, R., & Caspi, A. (2003). Personality differences in childhood and adolescence: measurement, development and consequences. *Journal of Child Psychology and Psychiatry, 44*, 2-23.

Sieving, R.E., Perry, C.L., & Williams, C.L (2000). Do friends change behaviour, or do behaviours change friendships? Examining paths of influence in young adolescents' alcohol use. *Journal of Adolescent Health, 26*, 27-35.

Silbereisen, R.K., Robins, L., & Rutter, M. (1995). Secular trends in substance use: Concepts and data on the impact of social change on alcohol and drug use. In M. Rutter, & D. Smith (Eds.). *Psychosocial Disorders in Young People: Time Trends and their Causes.* Chichester: John Wiley.

Simpura, J., & Karlsson, T. (2001). Trends in drinking patterns in fifteen European countries, 1950 to 2000: A collection of country reports. Helsinki: Stakes.

Simpura, J., Karlsson, T., & Leppanen, K. (2002). European trends in drinking patterns and their socio-economic background. In T. Norstrom (Ed.) Alcohol in post war Europe: Consumption, drinking patterns, consequences, and policy responses in 15 European Countries. Stockholm: National Institute of Public Health (Sweden).

Single, E., Ashley, M.J., Bonby, S., Rankin, J., & Rehm, J. (1999*). Evidence Regarding the Level of Alcohol Consumption Considered to be Low-Risk for Men and Women.* Canberra ACT: Australian Commonwealth Department of Health and Aged Care.

Singleton, R.A., Straits, B.C. & Straits, M.M. (1993). *Approaches to Social Research.* Oxford: Oxford University Press.

Smith, B.H., Molina, B.S.G., & Pelham, W.E. (2002). The clinically meaningful link between alcohol use and attention deficit hyperactivity disorder. *Alcohol Research World, 26*, 122-129.

Sobel, M. (1994) Causal inferences in latent variable models. In A. von Eye and C.C. Clogg (Eds.) *Latent Variable Analysis.* Thousand Oaks: Sage.

Spring, J.A., & Buss, D.H. (1977). Three centuries of alcohol in the British diet. *Nature 272*, 567-572.

Spencer, M.B., Harpalani, V., Cassidy, E., Jacobs, C.Y., Donde, S., Goss., T.N., Munoz-Miller, M., Charles, N., & Wilson, S. (2006). Understanding vulnerability and resilience from a normative developmental perspective: Implications for Racially and ethnically diverse youth. In D. Cicchetti & D. Cohen (Eds.) *Developmental Psychopathology. Volume1: Theory and Method* (2nd Edit.). Hoboken, NJ: John Wiley & Sons (pp 627672).

Sroufe, L.A. (1989) Pathways to adaptation and maladaptation: pathology as developmental deviation. In D. Cicchetti, (ed) *The emergence of a discipline: Rochester symposium on developmental psycholpathology, Volume* 1. Hove and London: Lawrence Erlbraum Associates.

Stattin, H., & Kerr, M. (2000). Parental monitoring: A reinterpretation. *Child Development, 71*,1072-1085

Stattin, H., & Magnusson, D. (1990). *Pubertal maturation in female development.* Hillside, NJ: Erlbaum.

Steinhausen, H., & Winkler Metzke, C. (2003). The validity of adolescent types of alcohol use. *Journal of Child and Adolescent Psychology, 44*, 677-686

Stockwell, T., Murphy, D., & Hodgson, R. (1983). The severity of alcohol dependence questionnaire: its use reliability and validity. *British Journal of Addiction, 78*, 145-155.

Stockwell, T., Toumbourou., J.W., Letcher, P., Smart, D., Sanson, A., & Bond, L. (2004). Risk and protective factors for different intensities of adolescent substance use: When does the Prevention Paradox apply? *Drug and Alcohol Review, 23*, 67-77.

Strategy Unit (2004). *Alcohol related harm reduction strategy for England.* London: The Cabinet Office.

Sullivan, P.F., Kessler, R.C., Kendler, K.S. (1998). Latent class analysis of lifetime depressive symptoms in the National Comorbidity Survey. *American Journal of Psychiatry, 155*, 1398-1406.

Sutherland, I, & Shepherd, J.P. (2001a). The prevalence of alcohol, cigarette and illicit drug use in a stratified sample of English adolescents, *Addiction, 96*, 637-640.

Sutherland, I. & Shepherd, J.P. (2001b). Social dimensions of adolescent substance use. *Addiction, 96*, 445 – 458.

Sutherland, I., & Willner, P. (1998). Patterns of alcohol, cigarette and illicit drug use in English adolescents, *Addiction, 93*, 1199-1208.

Swadi, H. (1988). Drug use and substance use among 3,333 London adolescents. *British Journal of Addiction, 83*, 935-942.

Swadi, H. (1999). Individual risk factors for adolescent substance use. *Drug and Alcohol Dependence, 55*, 209-224.

Swanson, J.M., Sergeant, J.A., Taylor, E., Sonuga-Barke, E.J.S., Jensen, P.S., & Cantwell, D.P. (1998). Attention-deficit hyperactivity disorder and hyperkinetic disorder. *Lancet, 351*, 429-433.

Tapert, S.F., & Brown, S.A. (2000). Substance dependence, family history of alcohol dependence and neuropsychological functioning in adolescence. *Addiction, 95*, 1043-1053.

Tapert, S.F., & Schweinsberg, A.D. (2005). The human adolescent brain and alcohol use disorders. In M. Galanter (Ed.). *Recent developments in alcoholism*, Vol. *17*, pp177-197. New York: Springer.

Tarter, R.E., Kirisci, L., Habeych, M. Reynolds, M., & Vanyukov, M. (2004). Neurobehavioral disinhibition in childhood predisposes boys to substance use disorders by young adulthood: direct and mediated etiological pathways. *Drug and Alcohol Dependence, 73*, 121-132.

Tarter, R.E., Kirisci, L., & Mezzich A. (1997). Multivariate typology of adolescents with alcohol use disorders. *American Journal of Addiction, 6*, 150-158.

Tarter, R.E., & Vanyukov, M. (1994). Alcoholism: A developmental disorder. *Journal of Consulting and Clinical Psychology, 62*, 1096-1107.

Tarter, R., Vanyukov, M., Giancola, P.R., Dawes, M., Blackson, T., Mezzich, A., & Clark, D.B. (1999). Etiology of early onset substance use disorder: a maturational perspective. *Development and Psychopathology, 11,* 657-683.

Temple, M.T., & Fillmore, (1985-1986). The variability of drinking patterns and problems among young men, age 16-31: A longitudinal study. *International Journal of the Addictions, 20*, 1595-1620.

Terza, J.V., Kenkel, D.S., Lin, T., & Sakata, S. (in press). Care-giver advice as a preventative measure fro drinking during pregnancy: Zeros, categorical outcomes responses and endogeneity. *Health Economics*.

Tobler, N. (1986). Meta-analysis of 143 adolescent drug prevention programs: quantitative outcome results from program participants compared to a control or comparison group. *Journal of Drug Issues, 16*, 537-567.

Tobler, N. (1992). Drug prevention can work: Research findings. *Journal of Addictive Behaviours, 11*, 1-28.

Tonry, M., Ohlin, L.E. & Farrington, D.P. (1991). *Human Development and Human Behaviour: new Ways of Advancing Knowledge*. New York: Springer-Verlag.

Uebersax, J. (2000a). *A practical guide to local dependence in latent class models.* (http://ourworld.compserve.com/homepages/jsuebersax/condep.htm)

Uebersax, J. (2000b). *A brief study of local maximum solutions in latent class analysis.* (http://ourworld.compserve.com/homepages/jsuebersax/local.htm)

Uebersax, J. (2001). *Latent class analysis: frequently asked questions.* (http://ourworld.compserve.com/homepages/jsuebersax/faq.htm)

Urberg, K.A., Degirmencioglu, S., & Pilgrim, C. (1997). Close friends and group influence on adolescent cigarette smoking and alcohol use. *Developmental Psychology, 33*, 834-844.

Urberg, K.A., Luo, Q., Pilgrim, C., & Degirmencioglu, S. (2003). A two-stage model of peer influence in adolescent substance use: individual and relationship-specific differences in susceptibility to influence. *Addictive Behaviours, 28*, 1243-1256.

Vanyukov, M.M., Tarter, R.E., Kirisci, L., Kirillova, G.P., Maher, B.S., & Clark, D.B. (2003.). Liability to substance use disorders: 1. Common mechanisms and manifestations. *Neuroscience and Behavioural Reviews, 27*, 507-515.

Vermunt, J.K. (1997a). *LEM: a general program for the analysis of categorical data* [Computer programme]. Tilberg NL: Tilberg University.

Vermunt, J.K. (1997b). *LEM: a general program for the analysis of categorical data* [User manual]. Tilberg NL: Tilberg University.

Vermunt, J.K. (1997c). *Log-linear models for event histories*. Thousand Oaks: Sage Publications.

Voigt, M.D. (2005). Alcohol and hepatocellular cancer. *Clinical Liver Diseases. 9*, 151-169.

Walsh, B. (1997). Trends in alcohol production, trade and consumption. *Addiction, 92*, (Supplement 1), S61-S66.

Walton, S. (2001). *Out of it: A cultural history of intoxication*. London, UK: Hamish Hamilton.

Wannamethee, S.G., & Shaper, A.G. (1999). Regular alcohol intake and decreased risk of coronary disease events but not total mortality in men. *American Journal of Public Health, 89*, 685-690.

Weinberg, N.Z., Rahbert, E., Colliver, J.D., & Glantz, M.D. (1998). Adolescent substance abuse: A review of the past 10 years. *Journal of the American Academy of Child and Adolescent Psychiatry, 37*, 252-261.

Weinhert, F.E., & Schneider, W. (1993). Cognitive, emotional and social development. In D. Magnusson & P. Casear (Eds.), *Longitudinal research on individual development: Present status and future perspectives.* Cambridge: Cambridge University Press.

Weissenborn, R. & Duka, T. (2003). Acute effects on cognitive function in social drinkers: their relationship to drinking habits. *Psychopharmacology, 165*, 306-312.

Wells E.L., & Rankin J.H. (1991). Families and delinquency: a meta-analysis of the impact of broken homes. *Social Problems, 38*, 71-93.

Wells, J. E., Horwood, L.J., & Fergusson, D.M. (2004). Drinking patterns in mid-adolescence and psychosocial outcomes in late adolescence. *Addiction, 99*, 1529-1541.

Wells, J. E., Horwood, L.J., & Fergusson, D.M. (2006). Stability and instability in alcohol diagnosis from ages 18 to 21 and ages 21 to 25. *Drug and Alcohol Dependence. 81*, 157-165.

Westlake, S. & Yar, M. (2006). Smoking, drinking and drug use. In M. Bajekai, V. Osborne, M. Yar, & H. Meltzer, (Eds.) *Focus on health: 2006 edition* (pp. 33-46). London: Office For National Statistics

Wetzels, J.J.L., Kremers, S.P.L., Vitoria, P.D., & de Vries, H. (2003). The alcohol-tobacco relationship: a prospective study among adolescents in six European countries. *Addiction, 98*,1755-1763.

White, H.R., Loeber, R., Stouthamer-Loeber, M., & Farrington, D.P. (1999). Developmental associations between substance use and violence. *Development and Psychopathology, 11*, 785-803.

Wichstrom, L. (2001). The impact of pubertal timing on adolescents' alcohol use. *Journal of Research on Adolescence, 11*, 131-150.

Wilcox, P. (2003). An ecological approach to understanding youth smoking trajectories: problems and prospects. *Addiction, 98 (Suppl. 1)*, 57-77.

Wilens, T.E. (1998). AOD use and attention deficit/hyperactivity disorder. *Alcohol Health and Research World, 22*, 127-130.

Willet, J.B. Singer, J.D., & Martin, N. (1998). The design and analysis of longitudinal studies of development and psychopathology in context: Statistical models and recommendations. *Development and Psychopathology, 10*, 395-426

Wills, T.A., & Cleary, S.D. (1999). Peer and adolescent substance use amongst 6th – 9th graders: latent growth analysis of influence versus selection mechanisms. *Health Psychology, 18*, 453-463.

Wilson, G.B. (1940). *Alcohol and the Nation*. London: Nicholson and Watson.

Windham, G.C., Bottomley, C., Birner, C. & Fenster, L. (2004). Age at menarche in relation to maternal use of tobacco, alcohol coffee, and tea during pregnancy. *American Journal of Epidemiology, 159*, 862-871.

Windle, M. (1996). An alcohol involvement typology for adolescents: Convergent validity and longitudinal stability. *Journal of Studies on Alcohol, 57*,627-637.

Woodward, L.J., & Fergusson, D.M. (2001). Life Course Outcomes of Young People With Anxiety Disorders in Adolescence. *Journal of the American Academy of Child & Adolescent Psychiatry, 40*, 1086-1093.

World Health Organisation (2002). *The world heath report 2002: Reducing risks, promoting health*. Geneva: Author.

Wright, J.P., Cullen, F.T., & Miller, J.T., (2001). Family social capital and delinquency involvement. *Journal of Criminal Justice, 29*, 1-9.

Wright, L. (1999). *Young People and Alcohol. What 11- to 24-year olds know, think and do*. London: Health Education Authority.

Yamaguchi, K., & Kandel, D.B. (2002). Loglinear sequence analysis: gender and racial/ethnic differences in drug use progressions. In D.B. Kandel, (Ed.) (2002). *Stages and Pathways of Drug Involvement: Examining the Gateway Hypothesis* (pp. 187-222).Cambridge: Cambridge University Press.

Yeung, W.J., Linver, M.R., & Brooks-Gunn, J. (2002). How money matters for young childrens' development: parental investment and family processes. *Child Development, 73*, 1861-1879.

Zarkin, G.A., French, M.T., Mroz, T., & Bray, J.W. (1998). Alcohol use and wages:

New results form the National Household Survey on Drug Abuse. *Journal of Health Economics, 17*, 53-68.

Zarkin, G.A., Mroz, T., Bray, J.W., & French, M.T. (1998). The relationship between drug use and labor supply. *Labour Economics, 5*, 385-409.

Zimmerman, P., Wittchen, H.U., Hofler, M., Pfister, H., Kessler, R., & Lieb, R. (2003). Primary anxiety disorders and the development of subsequent alcohol use disorders: a 4-year community study of adolescent and young adults. *Psychological Medicine, 33*, 1211-1222.

Zimmerman, R.S., Warheit, G.J., Ulbrich, P.M., & Auth, J.B. (1990). The relationship between alcohol use and attempts and success at smoking cessation. *Addictive Behaviour, 15*, 197-207.

Zucker, R.A. (1994). Pathways to alcohol problems and alcoholism: A developmental account of the evidence for multiple alcoholisms and for contextual contributions to risk. In R., Zucker, G., Boyd & J. Howard (Eds.). *The Development of Alcohol Problems: Exploring the Bio-psychosocial Matrix of Risk.* Rockville M.D.: National Institute on Alcohol Abuse and Alcoholism.

Zucker, R.A. (2006). Alcohol use and alcohol use disorders: A developmental-biopsychosocial systems formulation covering the life course. In D. Cicchetti & D.J. Cohen (eds.). *Developmental Psychopathology,* Volume 3: Risk, Disorder and Adaptation (2nd edition), Hoboken, New Jersey: Wiley and Sons, Inc.

Zucker, R.A., & Harford, T.C. (1983). A national study of adolescent drinking practices in 1980: Demography. *Journal of Studies on Alcohol, 44*, 974-985

APPENDIX: SUPPLEMENTARY ANALYSIS

EXPLORATORY FACTOR ANALYSIS OF THE MODIFIED RUTTER A SCALE (MATERNAL COMPLETION – 16 YEAR OLD SWEEP).

A 19-item shortened form of the Rutter A Scale was included in the Parental Interview Schedule. Butler et al. (1982) provides full details of the rational for the item selection. Exploratory factor analysis was undertaken to identify the latent factor structure of the scale. The results revealed five factors with eigenvalues over 1. Examination of the scree plot, and the fact that some factors had a limited number of items loading on them, a three-factor solution was selected, with each factor showing an eigenvalue over 1.3. The two factors excluded had eigenvalues of 1.062 and 1.035 respectively. These three factors account for 29% of the variance within the data.

The results of a varimax rotation are presented in Table A.1. The three factors were labelled Externalising Problems (alpha = 0.745) (example item: takes things that belong to others), Internalising Problems (alpha = 0.6684) (example item: is often worried) and Hyperactivity (alpha = 0.6704) (example item: is squirmy/fidgety).

EXPLORATORY FACTOR ANALYSIS OF THE MODIFIED CONNERS RATING SCALE (MATERNAL COMPLETION– 16 YEAR OLD SWEEP)

A 19-item shortened form of the Conners' Rating Scale was included in the Parental Interview Schedule. Butler et al. (1982) provides full details of the rational for the item selection. Exploratory factor analysis was undertaken to examine the latent factor structure of the various items used. Five factors were extracted (see Table A.2 for factor loadings). These factors account for 47% of the variance. The five factors were labelled; Oppositional behaviour (alpha = 0.812) (example item: is sullen or sulky), Impulsivity (alpha = 0.7194) (example item: is impulsive, excitable), Gross motor problems (alpha = 0.7508) (example items: is noticeably clumsy), Inattention (alpha = 0.7848) (example item: inattentive, easily distracted), Fine motor problems (example item: has difficulty using scissors).

Table A.1 Rutter A Scale Rotated Factor Matrix: age 16

	Factor		
	1	2	3
	Externalising problems	Internalising problems	Hyperactivity
Very restless			.607
Squirmy/fidgety			.727
Destroys others and own things	.492		
Frequently fights with others	.526		
Not much liked by other	.287		
Often worried		.664	
Tends to do things on own		.366	
Irritable, flies off handle	.360	.435	
Miserable, unhappy tearful or distressed	.322	.498	
Takes things belonging to others	.614		
Has twitches mannerisms or tics			
Frequently sucks thumb			
Frequently bites nails or fingers			
Often disobedient	.584		
Cannot settle to anything	.309		.426
Fearful or afraid of new things		.528	
Fussy or over-particular		.387	
Often tells lies	.656		
Bullies others.	.522		

Notes

Extraction Method: Maximum Likelihood.

Rotation Method: Varimax with Kaiser Normalisation.

Factor loadings below 0.25 are suppressed. Major factor loading highlighted in bold. Substantive cross-loadings underlined.

Table A.2 Conners Rating Scale Rotated Factor Matrix: age 16

	Factor				
	1	2	3	4	5
	Oppositional Behaviour	Impulsivity	Gross motor problems	Inattention	Fine motor problems
Noticeably clumsy			.715		
Trips or falls easily			.726		
Inattentive	.229	.346		.573	
Makes odd noises		.459			
Difficulty picking up small objects					.665
Drops things			.561		.326
Obsessional about unimportant things	.407	.340			
Easily frustrated	.552	.411			
Restless/over active	.286	.617			
Impulsive	.377	.490			
Interferes with activity of others	.357	.426			
Sullen/sulky	.598				
Short attention span	.217	.239		.737	
Rhythmic tapping or kicking		.381			
Cries for little cause	.416				.223
Quick mood changes	.794				
Outburst of temper	.712	.244			
Difficulty using scissors					.599
Difficulty concentration		.253		.611	

Notes

Extraction Method: Maximum Likelihood.

Rotation Method: Varimax with Kaiser Normalisation.

Factor loadings below 0.25 are suppressed.

Major factor loading highlighted in bold. Substantive cross-loadings underlined.

EXPLORATORY FACTOR ANALYSIS OF THE CHILD BEHAVIOUR SCALE (TEACHER COMPLETION– 10 YEAR OLD SWEEP)

The Child Behaviour Scale was a 53 item scale comprised of selected elements of the Rutter B Scale for Teachers (Rutter et al., 1970) and the Conners' Teachers Rating Scale (Conners, 1970). Butler et al. (1982) provides details of the rational for the selecting the various items from each of the originating scales. In addition to these items, a number of specific questions were included to address behavioural issues that were not covered by the two scales. These included anxiety and fine and gross motor control. Fourteen of the 53 items related specifically to hyperactivity. As with the previous scales outlined above, exploratory factor analysis was undertaken on the survey items. This revealed eight latent factors (eigenvalues ranging from 16.53 to 1.160). These eight scales accounted for 63.4% of the variance in the selected items. Table A.3 gives the varimax rotated factor matrix. The main factor loadings are highlighted in bold and substantive cross loading are underlined. Only one item was dropped from the subsequent scale summation ("Drops things being carried?") as this loaded highly on both fine motor control and gross motor control (.407 and .405 respectfully).

The items in the first scale, labelled 'antisocial behaviour', relate to disruptive, aggressive and impulsive behaviours. These included temper tantrums, mood swings, destroying things and being over active. A distinction was drawn between this and the second factor, inattention, and the eighth factor - hyperactivity. Inattention was comprised of behaviours such as daydreaming, failing to complete class work, or being easily distracted, while hyperactivity was defined by repetitive and intrusive behaviours including tapping or humming.

The third factor was comprised of items relating to internalising problems, such as being anxious, nervous and worried. A number of the items that comprised this scale also have modest cross loading on factor 1- antisocial behaviour.

Factors 4 and 5 were comprised of items on clumsiness and poor hand-eye coordination. The distinction is made between fine motor skills (manipulates small objects) and gross motor skills (difficulty kicking a ball). There were a number of cross loading between these two scales. The final two scales (scales six and seven) were labelled 'introversion', and 'toileting problems'.

Table A.3 Child Behaviour Scale Rotated Factor Matrix

	1 ASB	2 INA	3 ANX	4 FMC	5 GMP	6 EXTRA	7 TOIL	8 HYP
Displays outbursts of temper	**.792**							
Quarrels with other kids	**.791**							
Teases other children	**.769**							
Bullies other children	**.753**							
Changes mood quickly	**.734**		.266					
Interferes with others	**.708**	.361						
Sullen or sulky	**.668**					.258		
Complains about things	**.642**							
Destroys belongings	**.616**							.291
Shows restless or over-active behaviour	**.616**	.275				-.309		.328
Excitable impulsive	**.609**					-.434		
Is easily frustrated	**.595**							
Squirmy and fidgety	**.511**	.505						.333
Accident prone	.321			.254	.285			
Easily distracted	.385	**.769**						
Shows perseverance	-.271	**-.725**						
Pays attention in class	-.279	**-.719**						
Fails to finish tasks		**.699**						
Completes tasks		**-.685**		-.280				
Forgetful on complex task		**.681**	.271					
Becomes bored during class	.382	**.671**						
Child is daydreaming		**.622**						
Confused or hesitant		**.599**	.426					
Cannot concentrate on particular task		**.582**						
Shows lethargic/listless behaviour		**.489**				.352		
Worried and anxious			**.836**					
Anxious-unworried			**.775**					
Behaves 'nervously'			**.725**					
Afraid of new things/situations		.314	**.616**					
Fussy or over-particular	.296		**.500**		.256			
Relations with others	.378		**.445**			.290		

Appendix A

	1 ASB	2 INA	3 ANX	4 FMC	5 GMP	6 EXTRA	7 TOIL	8 HYP
unhappy/tearful								
Obsessional about unimportant tasks	.384		**.396**		.257			
Cries for little cause	.343		**.380**					
Can use manipulative equipment				**-.703**				
Manipulates small objects with hands				**-.629**				
Holds instruments appropriately				**-.554**				
Difficulty picking up small objects				**.525**	.424			
Inadequate control of pencil/paint brush				**.498**				
Works deftly with hands		-.321		**-.493**				
Drops things being carried				**.407**	.405			
Dresses/undresses competently				**-.373**				
Clumsy at Games				.365	**.628**			
Difficulty Kicking Ball				.297	**.571**			
Fearful in Movements			.321		**.487**	.269		
Trips Falls Bumps	.283			.325	**.465**			
Extrovert-Introvert			-.434			**-.601**		
Rather Solitary			.362			**.484**		
Soils pants during class							**.782**	
Wetting pants during class							**.671**	
Truants from school							**.352**	
Rhythmic Tapping in Class	.436							**.579**
Hums or Makes Odd Vocals	.448							**.564**
Has twitches, mannerisms/tics								**.351**

Notes

Extraction Method: Maximum Likelihood. Rotation Method: Varimax with Kaiser Normalization.

ASB = Antisocial behaviour; INA - Inattention; ANX = Anxiety; FMc = fine motor control; GMp = gross motor problems; EXTRA = extraversion (items in this subscale were reverse coded to from the parameters shown here to ensure that high values reflected high extraversion rather than high introversion; TOIL = toileting; HYP = hyperactivity. Factor loadings below 0.25 are suppressed. Major factor loading highlighted in bold. Substantive cross-loadings underlined.

Breinigsville, PA USA
13 January 2011
253257BV00001B/148/P